W9-DBP-830

Unless Recalled Earlier
Date Due

ILL 11/13/90			

BRODART, INC.   Cat. No. 23 233   Printed in U.S.A.

The Kondratieff
Waves

THE KONDRATIEFF WAVES

Nathan H. Mager

PRAEGER

New York
Westport, Connecticut
London

Library of Congress Cataloging-in-Publication Data

Mager, N. H. (Nathan H.), 1913-
  The Kondratieff waves.

  Includes index.
  1. Long waves (Economics) 2. Kondrat'ev,
N. D. (Nikolai Dmitrievich), 1892-
I. Title.
HB3729.M34 1986   338.9'00724   86-9319
ISBN 0-275-92149-2 (alk. paper)

Library of Congress Catalog Card Number 86-9319
ISBN: 0-275-92149-2

First published in 1987

Praeger Publishers, 521 Fifth Avenue, New York, NY 10175
A division of Greenwood Press, Inc.

Printed in the United States of America

The paper used in this book complies with the Permanent Paper Standard issued by the National Information Standards Organization (Z39.48-1984).

10 9 8 7 6 5 4 3 2 1

Contents

List of Tables and Figures

TABLES

FIGURES

About Economics, Cycles, And Economic Cycles

ANCIENT CONCEPTS

There is a general reluctance to accept the fact that economic forces run in preordained, mechanistic cycles, particularly those forces involving the actions of intelligent humanity. The doctrine of free will and the human capacity for self-determination is as deeply ingrained in us as a religious belief. However, as Shakespeare noted some 300 years ago, "There is a tide in the affairs of men. . . ." It was not the first observation of the phenomenon.

Economic forecasting by means of magical numbers, the movement of the planets, and other cyclical phenomena has been a human talent, pastime, and profession for at least 5,000 years, and perhaps even before history, when people first discovered rhythms in nature. Nostradamus, a sixteenth century doctor, made something of a name for himself with the kind of ambiguous prophecies that everyone could point to as having foretold just what was happening "now." The French Revolution made his reputation in 1793 when the French recalled his forecast about Nantes: "The city's leaders in revolt will, in the name of liberty, slaughter the inhabitants without regard to age or sex."

The medieval Cabala as early as year 1200 used acrostics and the 24 letters of the Hebrew alphabet to solve problems and interpret the signs of their day. That tradition evolved to predict Armageddon and/or the end of the world, which failed to occur on various predicted occasions. But it is, after all, probably really only an error in numbers that the world did not come to an end on December 31, 999, or on other dates computed from various data.

Natural forces do, of course, act in a series of cycles. Some of these cycles—the diurnal cycle, biological rhythms, seasonal cycles—are such common occurrences that they are accepted and integrated into the pattern of our lives. The long-term cycles of temperature changes are also part of history.

The Foundation for the Study of Cycles has cataloged 1,380 economic cycles ranging in length from 20 hours to 700 years. Among these are 75 cycles ranging from 16 to 60 years that record general business activity, and 23 cycles that record crises, depressions, and recessions ranging from 3.5 to 108 years. Many traders and speculators find and act on such cyclical behavior.

THE NATURAL CYCLES

The cyclical fluctuations of agricultural production—which for the longest period in history was the principal economic element—provide some clues but no complete answers. One early economist made quite a name for himself by predicting the seven-year cycle that was later given Biblical authentication. The long-wave cycle, too, has an early heritage. In pre-Biblical times the Israelites recognized, or created for their own agronomic purposes, a 50-year cycle. For six years, a parcel of land was planted, but during the seventh it lay fallow. And after seven such cycles, in the fiftieth year, the land was to remain fallow for a second year. Moreover, in this "Sabbatical Year of Jubilee," all debts were canceled, indentured servants and slaves were set free, and foreclosed land reverted to its original owners.

This had a salubrious effect on long-term debtors, but obviously loans were hard to come by and interest rates were inclined to rise as the fiftieth year approached. So, in an economic sense, the value of land followed a 50-year cycle. A property that was to be reclaimed in six years was worth much less than land purchased in year 20 of the cycle. In this sense, the 50-year cycle was ordained by the Bible, or by the word of God if you accept it in those terms. At least one symptom of the end of each modern long-term cycle persists. Long-term loans tend to be difficult to get, and interest rates increase as an economic cycle reaches its peak, and loans tend to be made for shorter terms.

Until the end of the nineteenth century, agriculture was the dominant sector in the economy. The traditional cycles of production, and thus of prices, were greatly affected by weather. Bad weather meant poor crops, thus higher prices. This logically led to a study of cycles in other natural phenomena.

In 1947, Edward R. Dewey and Edwin F. Dakin published an exhaustive text called "Cycles: The Science of Prediction" as a "new approach to economics and the problems of forecasting."[1] It showed how "rhythm and periodicity" exist in the natural world, and that economics, when analyzed with similar statistical tools, displays curvilinear forms and distinct rhythms. They found 57 natural cycles that repeated on an average of 9.6 to 9.7 years. Barometric pressure shows an 8-year cycle; magnetic activity runs in 11.4-year cycles. Sunspots increase and decrease in periodic waves ranging from 7 to 17 years, with an average of 11.11 years.

Long-term measurement of weather was possible by computing the varying widths of tree rings. Growth is soft and porous in summers, hard and compact in winters. For good weather years, the growth is thick, for poor years the layers are thin. One such study of trees in Arizona goes back to the ninth century. It shows a definite 54-year cycle. Some analysts have found a correlation with the 11-year sunspot cycle. A similar, lesser cycle of 16.67 years has been found in Java.

We recite these principally for academic interest. In spite of much speculation, no one has yet established a natural cycle as being related to modern economic cycles, even insofar as it should logically affect agricultural products. But, like natural cycles, economic cycles do exist.

ECONOMIC CYCLES

A cycle is a regular, self-repeating fluctuation of relatively fixed length and amplitude, often existing around some other trend. Economic cycles are not precise. They are self-repeating, but they vary in amplitude, and to some degree in length. For a definition of the business cycle, we borrow in part from Burns and Mitchell.

A cycle consists of expansion occurring at about the same time in many economic activities, followed by a similarly general recession, contractions and revivals which merge into the expansion phase of the next cycle.[2]

This sequence of changes is recurrent but not periodic. Business cycles vary in duration from more than one year to ten or twelve years; they are not divisible into "shorter cycles of similar character with amplitudes approximating their own."

Although the economic cycle has been widely recognized, and extensively discussed, it is viewed differently, and referred to in different terms in various places. The English (and most traders) recognize a trade cycle; the continental Europeans (including the Soviets) call it a *conjuncture* (an interplay of economic forces that run in a specific direction). "Cyclists" see a pattern of events, each stimulating the next, leading to expansion and contraction of the economy in a pattern that, at least until recently, has defied effective manipulation and avoidance. Until 1936 the fluctuations of the "business cycle" were generally accepted as a basic force in "modern economic life," moving around a secular growth trend.

Under the classic concept, the dynamics of the business cycle are created by the forces of supply and demand. Excess demand creates shortages, causing prices to rise, then creating an excess of supply, causing prices to fall, to bring supply and demand into equilibrium. Such rises and falls create the interacting fluctuations in production, prices, employment, income, money supply, interest rates, bankruptcies, and so on. The temporary imbalances create the crises. Movements always go to excess, causing oscillations that move toward equilibrium.

Economic cycles involve changes in every aspect of national income and extend into social and political areas. Since the 1930s there has evolved a vast literature on microeconomics and macroeconomics, on how and why people act the way they do—specifically, the way they respond to supply and demand and changing prices.

Macroeconomics considers the ways that decisions by one group or sector interact with other decisions to produce an overall composition of national income. Microeconomics evaluates the same factors in individual reactions. It is these interactions that create economic trends, which accumulate the pressures that create cycles. These cycles weave around each other and around a secular growth that sometimes disguises them. During the first eight decades of the twentieth century, real gross national product increased 1200 percent, a per capita annual gain of 1.8 percent. But this gain was accompanied by periods of depression and retardation in 1903, 1907, 1913, 1921, 1930, 1937, 1953–54, 1957–58, 1969–70, 1973–75, and 1980–82. Such cyclical phenomena, although not in synchrony, were similarly experienced in other nations—developed and developing, capitalist and socialist.

BACKGROUND

Before mathematical formulas representing these two approaches took hold, economics, then known as the study of political economy, evolved through several stages.

Concepts of "political economy" emerged from medieval philosophy during the seventeenth century with the principle that a nation, like an individual, could measure its wealth in terms of the amount of gold it held. This attitude was dominant for several centuries. As "mercantilism" it was espoused by Jean Baptiste Colbert, finance minister for Louis XIV, who so ordered his country's economy as to produce the greatest supply of goods for export. The accumulated gold was expected to pay for the best professional armed forces. This philosophy failed to motivate production, however. France, at one time the world's richest country, became poor in spite of its huge gold holdings. Contemporary England prospered under a different philosophy.

The eighteenth century brought Le Tableau Economique, opening an era dominated by the Physiocratic School. It proposed the end of almost all feudal, mercantilistic, and government restrictions. It emphasized the accumulation of productive capital.

As money replaced barter in the nineteenth century, revolutionary new ideas of marginal values suitable for industry were conceived to create what we now call "classical economics." This era will be remembered for Adam Smith's The Wealth of Nations and laissez-faire. Value and price became the dominant concepts in economics. This approach emphasized supply and the microeconomics of the time—the reactions of individuals and firms. Money was seen as a "veil of reality." From this evolved the labor theory of value, and from this soil came the writings of Karl Marx.

Alfred Marshal (1842–1924), a lecturer at Cambridge, later attempted to present a modern version of these old doctrines in 1940.[3] He was, in fact, the last classical economist, combining theories of microeconomics and macroeconomics within classical concepts.

In the background of economic thinking were the writings of Thomas Malthus (1766–1834), an English clergyman whose conclusions were based on the geometric increase in population in a world that increased its product at an arithmetic rate.

All of these philosophies were a part of Kondratieff's background and even today play a part in modern thinking. Malthus' opposition to "the poor laws" based on the conclusion that aid provided no real relief because it entrenched poverty, is voiced in the twentieth century, particularly with regard to foreign aid. The Club of Rome's report on "Limits of Growth" is a subliminal part of this contemporary economic reasoning.

THE KEYNESIAN APPROACH

The period of 1940 to 1967 was the golden age of economics, with a mind-set based on John Maynard Keynes' 1936 text, General Theory of Employment, Interest and Money. His paradigm dominated economic thinking for 40 years.

The General Equilibrium Theory was first defined by Arrow (1954) and Debrieus (1955).[4] They viewed the economy as made up of firms and households. Individual households select from the menu of priced goods and services offered by firms those they can consume and afford, and those they prefer. Equilibrium exists where decisions of firms and households are compatible. Prices are set where there is a profit-maximizing choice of firms and a preference-maximizing choice of households, so that demand is equal to supply available plus the amount produced.

In a free economy, many individuals make individual economic decisions which, in light of their knowledge, they consider to their advantage. Social good does not set their dominant guide lines.

Keynes' "general theory" approach to cycles offered a sense that these decisions could be manipulated through increasing and decreasing government spending, money supply, and interest rates.[5] Mathematical models of the economy in equilibrium were constructed during the following years in an almost endless array, reflecting ideas about the way people act under various economic circumstances.

Similar principles of equilibrium were voiced early in the study of economics—an equilibrium between supply and demand, between values and the means of obtaining them. Although equilibrium is often perceived as stability, in an economy it is dynamic as populations increase, move, and constantly expect more. Your nineteenth-century great-grandparents could hardly believe the level of twentieth-century expectations.

Keynes in 1936 voiced the radical proposition that supply and demand were not entirely responsible for setting prices, and that something additional influenced price levels. He saw wages in a light different from preceding economic dogma. Until his attack on this classical postulate, it was accepted that "the utility of the wage when a given volume of labor is employed is equal to the marginal disutility of that amount of disemployment"—that people were employed when it was profitable to employ them. For years economic theorists accepted the concept that unemployment was a function of unrealistically high wage levels.

Keynes also noted that inflation had so distorted the relationship between nominal wages and real wages that generally, in practice, when nominal wages were rising, overall real wages were declining, and the contest about money wages was principally a struggle about the distribution of the aggregate real wage among various labor groups. Thus the real wages in highly unionized industries rose at the expense of real wages of the labor force in general, especially among those in slowly changing ("sticky") wage categories.

The Keynesian solution to the problems of the political economy was to control total demand, using government budget deficits to stimulate and surpluses to sedate the economy. He saw depressions and inflation as the product of changing demand patterns. These, within limits, were seen to be affecting supply and demand for labor. The disequilibrium theory (that the components of the economic system tend to balance out and seek equilibrium) is a modern variation by Keynesian economists of an older theorem.

The monetarists, whose ideas evolved from this concept of disequilibrium, hold that level of spending (the demand for money) is the dominant factor in creating changes in the level of nominal (not adjusted for inflation) income, and therefore of total spending and the growth and health of the economy.

Keynes's general theory points out that economies stagnate because of lack of investment by business or government. (This is basic in the long-wave theory, as we will see.) It was this spending (demand) that ignited the economy's expansion. Thus his whimsical comment:

> If the Treasury were to fill old bottles with bank notes, bury them at suitable depths in disused coal mines which are then filled up to the surface with town rubbish, and leave it to private enterprise on well tried principles of *laissez-faire* to dig the notes up again ... there need be no more unemployment and with the help of the repercussions, the real income of the community would probably become a good deal larger than it is. It would, indeed, be more sensible to build houses and the like; but if there are practical difficulties in the way of doing this, the above would be better than nothing.

Keynes's view depended primarily on creation of demand by government regulation of money and supply, but held that monetary authority must also respond to other factors in the equilibrium, especially interest rates.

MACROECONOMIC MODELS

The accent of economic thinking during the post-Keynesian era has been on the establishment of standard macroeconomic models. These models have been examined in static and dynamic forms, with evaluation of endogenous variables (forces that are created internally) and exogenous variables (outside forces that would be exerted by accident). Some elements, such as the capital–output ratio, were viewed as stationary states affecting the economy.

The model in its simplist form is an equilibrium at any point in time, linking aggregate output and its components:

Production = Real rate of consumption
+ real rate of investment
+ real rate of government expenditure
− real rate of depreciation of capital

More complex formulas, some containing many thousands of equations, are used by the data banks *Chase Econometrics, Data Resources,* and *Wharton Econometrics.* They involve linear equations, differentials, vectors, optimization, regression, recursive projections, and so on, made practical by the computer. These models are used in the solution of analytical problems to determine policy and to maximize goals for any of the facets of the economic picture: employment, prices, long-term development, and so on.

The national economy is viewed as consisting of three sectors:

1. Firms, which employ labor and capital.
2. Households, which own money, business liability and equities.
3. Government, which collects taxes, issues money and bonds, and purchases goods.

Within this equilibrium are at least six endogenous variables: production, labor supply, consumption, investment, prices, and interest rates. The classical model assumes that each of these elements reacts in specific ways to changes in the other elements (e.g., higher wages increase the labor supply, higher interest rates increase funds for investment, higher production creates more employment and need for more capital investment, etc.). Models hold that different values resulted from the application of individual theories. This general concept was accepted by virtually all analysts during the past five decades, subject to adjustments for expectations, imperfect foresight, and uncertainty.

Under the umbrella of these formulas, economists have manipulated the economy, or attempted to, in such a way that economic growth, full employment, stable prices, and production generally met the demand for goods and services in a balanced way. The acceptable manipulative tools suggested were government spending and deficit financing, increases in the money supply, the adjustment of interest rates, lowering and raising taxes, and various make-work measures. Wage and price controls were abandoned as counterproductive.

The hope of economists was based on the proposition that business cycles could be rationalized as responses of a stable dynamic model to random disturbances in order to limit oscillations that result from exogenous variables.

RATIONAL EXPECTATIONS

Four approaches are currently dominant: the Keynesian, the monetarist and rational expectations, and supply-side equilibrium models, either separately or integrated in various combinations. The reluctance of the economy to act as it should is explained as the result of individual rational expectations.

Recent efforts to measure rational expectations as a guide to economic direction falls into the trap of public discounting. Consumers, investors, and speculators are constantly second-guessing the conclusions of a multitude of other sophisticated investors and entrepreneurs who anticipate what others will anticipate and discount the effects of discounted effects.

Typically, a chart on the desk of many bond salesmen negates what one might consider rational expectations, often the opposite of logical reasoning.

Macroeconomics may or may not have mitigated economic cycles since the 1940s. The world has not recently seen drastic postwar depressions like 1920 and 1932, but intervening wars and an unprecedented inflation have affected normal tools for measuring and forecasting the direction of the economy.

ECONOMICS IN DISARRAY

These paradigms have dominated economic thought for 40 years. The economic world has been made up almost entirely of Keynesians, near-Keynesians, anti-Keynesians, or new Keynesians, each with a view that governments and modern monetary techniques could avert the hardships of periodic business declines. The approach has been vulnerable. Professor Robert Mundell of Columbia University concluded by 1974 that Keynesian policies do not work, and since 1974 most economists have voiced similar reservations.

In total these approaches left a sense of failure of human capacity to control or regulate the elements that mean most to ordinary people—growth in production and productivity, fairness and stability in employment and incomes, and a safety net for those who cannot keep up. Keynes held that productivity was a function of demand. "We can take productivity for granted, provided that employment and demand remain high," he said on several occasions.

The United States put the Keynesian approach into disarray between 1967 and 1980. The economic realities refused to respond properly to pump priming (government spending in various guises to stimulate the economy) and increasing money supply as remedies for

Table 1.1. Security Markets: Cause And Effect As Discounted By Analysts

News Indicator	Effect On Bond Market Prices	Reason
Agricultural prices are up	Market moves down depending on amount	Inflationary value of consumer dollar decreases.
Consumer price index rises	Market moves down	Inflationary. Fed will restrain by contracting money supply.
Gross national product is down	Market moves up	Shows a slow-down in the economy and, therefore, the Fed will loosen money by allowing rates to come down.
Housing starts are up	Market moves down	Shows a growth in the economy and in new housing. Prices rise and mortgage rates will rise. Fed is less accommodating and attempts to tighten by allowing rates to rise.
Industrial production is down	Market moves up	Indicates a slowing of the economic growth and, therefore, the Fed is more accommodating in allowing interest rates to drop to stimulate the economy.
Money supply figures are up	Market moves down	Excess growth in money causes inflation; therefore, generally creates fear that the Fed will tighten money growth by allowing short-term interest rates to rise. This will cause lower prices in the bond market.
Personal income is up	Market moves down	The higher one's income, the more one consumes, causing more demand and higher prices of consumer goods (inflationary).
Retail sales are up	Market moves down	High retail sales are an indication of economic growth and the Fed is less accommodating.
Unemployment figures are up	Market moves up	High unemployment indicates lack of expansion, which will lead to lower interest rates within the economy and is, therefore, good for the bond market.
Wholesale price index is up	Market moves down	Demand for goods rises and prices also rise, an inflationary indicator. Fed is less accommodating in allowing rates to go lower.
Fed buying bills	Market moves up	Fed adds money to the system, lowering interest rates due to their feeling that the growth of money is not expanding at an accelerated rate.
Fed is tightening	Market moves down	The Fed fears that excess growth in money supply prompts the Fed to allow the Fed funds to rise, causing other short-term interest rates to rise.
Fed is raising discount rate	Market moves down	An increase in interest rates between banks and the Fed means that an increase in rates to customers follows. Higher interest rates push stock and bond prices down.

Source: Compiled by the author.

increasing employment. The models of the economy produced by macroeconomic concepts of equilibrium came to be increasingly adjusted by new, more complex formulas that led to a new philosophy based on rational expectations.

Lester Thurow, in his recent *Dangerous Currents*, put it this way:

> Economics is in a state of turmoil. The economics of the textbooks and of the graduate schools not only still teach the price-auction model but is moving toward narrower and narrower interpretations. The mathematical sophistication intensifies as an understanding of the real world diminishes.[6]

The macroeconomic models essentially fail to consider the non-profit motivation of many personal and business transactions—the emotional forces involved. But he hoped:

> Economic models are being constructed that are designed to better reflect the world as we can see and measure it and also enhance possibilities of exercising economic control.[7]

The economic history of the post-1970 period further denigrated the hypotheses of macroeconomics. In recent commentary, Paul Samuelson is quoted as calling it a "shambles" because its laws failed to predict stagflation or urban decay. During the Reagan term not the rates of growth, interest, prices, or employment were forecast with even remote accuracy.

Macroeconomists failed obviously in accounting for unemployment. They assumed that labor supply is a function of voluntary choices, that workers give up gainful employment to have more leisure time, to find better jobs, or as the result of false expectations, of misperception of the rate of real wages, of real interest rates, or of better wage opportunities. This is a far from realistic picture of unemployment in modern society.

Ludwig von Mises wrote:

> The fundamental deficiency implied in every quantitative approach to economic problems consists in the neglect of the fact that there are no constant relations between what are called economic dimensions. There is neither constancy nor continuity in the valuation and in the formation of exchange ratios between various commodities. Every new datum brings about a reshuffling of the whole price structure.[8]

Economic cycles appear to be rooted in the way people relate to circumstances—a sort of sociobiological force comparable to the gravitational-centrifugal balance on which the universe rotates.

Before the Keynes theory and equilibrium models became gospel, the economic world accepted the business cycles as an inevitable result of normal forces; production expanded to oversupply, prices fell, production slowed, unemployment grew, wages fell, capital investment slowed, interest rates fell (to a point where low costs and pent-up demand spurred further buying, investment, and employment) in an inevitable simplistic cycle.

After Keynes, the traditional studies of business cycles were relegated to a back burner, as an area for relatively few technicians and cultists—almost as if the cycles were part of a discarded myth conceived in an era when people had no knowledge of the realities of pump-priming, money supply, and stagflation.

MONETARISM

Keynesianism faced its great setback during the 1970s. Pumping funds into the economy during the Carter administration via loan guarantees (for housing, farms, education, electrification, etc.) and social service spending brought not economic stimulation but stagflation.

The variety of opinion among economists who use macroeconomic stimulation techniques was evident during the Reagan years, when advisors suggested that control of economic fluctuations be limited largely to control of the money supply. A policy of increasing funds in regulated measure was adopted. This path had proved unsuccessful at various times in history and was decried in most academic circles. (A historic attempt at achieving expansion by spending, followed by Louis XV under the ministry of Aiguillow-Maupeon Terry, had been a disaster.)

Monetarist theoreticians such as Milton Friedman, Fred Kalkstein (chief economist at Janney, Montgomery Scott), Lawrence Kudlow (former economist at the Office of Management and Budget), and others were predicting in the early 1980s that there would be an inflationary explosion. Friedman forecast in December 1982 that there would be a recession in 1984, as the Federal Reserve would be obliged to cut back on money growth and that this money growth reduction would bring about a recession. He warned that immediately after the elections there would be a real possibility that the government would attempt to impose wage and price controls to contain the inflation he believed would then be raging. A rate of inflation of 8 to 10 percent was forecast by this group for 1985. The prediction was reinforced by the inflationary forecast of Geoffrey Moore and his Center for International Business Cycle Research at the Columbia Business School.

Moore was associated with Lawrence Kudlow, whose leading index of inflation, composed of commodity prices, total employment and total credit demand, surged 22 percent during the first 18 months of the recovery. This was almost double the index's rate of increase at a similar juncture in the 1973–1975 and 1975–1979 expansions. Part of much of this monetarist analysis has been a prediction of a recession.

Karl Brunner, the monetary economist of the University of Rochester in New York, was so worried about Federal Reserve policy that he came to believe the Fed would bring about the defeat of President Reagan in 1984. This would be followed by a wild inflationary explosion under President Mondale, culminating in a financial collapse and a major recession.

Some monetarists argued strongly that it was desirable to increase holdings of gold. They also argued, by inference, against bonds and in favor of Treasury bills.

Their conclusions were wrong. In 1984, the consumer price index rose at an annual rate of 3.3 percent in 1983, 4 percent in 1984 and 3.8 percent in the last six months of 1985.

The inflationary disaster did not occur. The problem remained to provide a nexus between economic theory and business decisions.

While macroeconomics and monetarism dominated the scene, business cycles did not disappear entirely from economic thought and research. Scholars such as W. C. Mitchell, Arthur Burns, Joseph Kitchin, J. M. Clark, A. C. Pigou, Warren Persons, Carl Snyder, Joseph A. Schumpeter, Alvin H. Hansen, Edward R. Dewey, and Edwin Dakin have made enormous contributions to understanding them. The National Conference Board provided substantial funds and study.

BUSINESS CYCLES

There is little mystery in the basic business cycle. Demand for something causes someone to produce it. Inasmuch as measuring demand is not definitive, too much is produced. This oversupply forces prices down, increasing demand, until demand exceeds supply.

We think we know why this happens. The classic theory is part of the widely accepted understanding of economic equilibrium, an auction block on which prices determine supply and demand.

The reality is a bit more complicated, involving money, capital, savings, investment, interest rates, wages, comparative costs of different products, imports, exports, trade facilitation and restrictions, taxes and government spending, and perhaps a score of other elements, real or imagined, creating a cycle moving in the direction of dynamic demand.

THE CORN–PIG AND CATTLE CYCLES

A typical visible simple cycle is the corn–pig cycle, which continues decade after decade. When corn is cheap and pork is priced high, farmers buy corn to raise more pigs, until there is a glut of pork bellies on the market and the price of corn used to feed the pigs moves up to higher levels. At a marginal point, when it no longer pays to raise pigs, they are slaughtered heavily, forcing down the price of pork. Low port prices induce fewer pigs to be raised, allowing the price of corn to fall. When the glut of pork bellies on the market has been sold, there is a shortage of piglets, the price of meat rises again and the cycle is repeated. The size of the corn crop, and the weather that helps determine the size of the crop, complicate this calculation.

In a corollary context, the expectation of higher incomes when grain prices are high leads farmers to borrow to buy more land and equipment and extend themselves further, thus helping to raise interest rates. In this oblique fashion they affect the credit structure and accentuate upswings or downswings in business. When prices of grain fall, farmers' income is pressed to pay interest. Some default; land prices fall.

A descriptive report in *Business Week* published at the end of 1983 makes this picture more concrete:

All agricultural commodities go through a production–price cycle in which high prices induce expanded output which results in falling prices, production cutbacks, a return to high prices—and a repetition of the cycle. But each cycle is strengthened or mitigated by other economic cycles.

In 1976, the cattle cycle was in a down phase. Then consumer price inflation fell below 5 percent from double digit figures two years earlier, retail meat prices dropped 12 percent. Cattle herds went to the slaughter house—to a point where cattle was in short supply in 1977. And in 1978 and 1979 meat prices rose 35 percent contributing to a double-digit inflation.

In 1983 the cycle was interrupted by exogenous elements. A drought caused the price of feed to go through the ceiling. At the same time forage was depleted. Dietary habits changed as a result of publicity about cholesterol. Producers reduced their herds by 600,000 head. The same elements affected the hog cycle.

Altogether this resulted in stable, moderated meat prices in the winter of 1984. But history tells us that herd rebuilding—and a new cycle—will begin before the year is over.

By mid-1984, meat prices could go hog-wild again. If inflation does start to rise handily next year, one of the culprits could be the so-called cattle cycle.[9]

Although most people need to identify the stage of a cycle to make judgments regarding price trends, the cycle for any product is additionally obscured because the demand and supply for each product are in competition for dollars with those of every other product.

Business cycles do not affect all industries uniformly in either time or dimension. It is this rotation of prosperity that makes difficult an analysis of cycles on a wide basis.

AGRICULTURAL CYCLES

Until 1940 agricultural products and raw materials were dominant in setting all prices; since 1940 industrial product prices have predominated, offsetting declines in basic commodity prices. Moreover, large and erratic changes in energy prices distorted by monopoly practices have complicated this analysis.

Until 1866 the overall business cycle was largely a measure of harvests, and these were largely affected by the weather. When crops were good, bread costs dropped, wages fell, and industrial products became cheaper. A poor crop had the reverse effect, adding an inhibition of the ability of farmers to buy.

Figure 1.1. Sunspots And Production

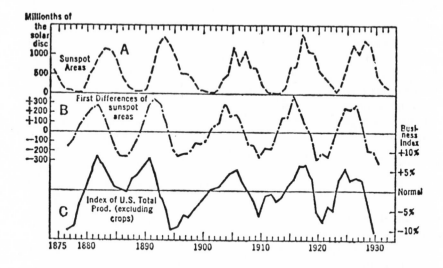

A: Sunspot areas; B: First differences of sunspot areas; C: An index of U.S. total production, excluding crops. B and C are 4-year moving averages. (After Garcia-Mata and Shaffner.)

Source: Edward R. Dewey and Edwin Dakin. Cycles (Foundation for the Study of Cycles, Pittsburgh, Pa., 1927).

Until about 1900 agriculture represented more than 50 percent of the U.S. economy. Farming accounted for one in four jobs in 1929 and 28 percent of exports. The proportions were less in Western Europe and larger in the rest of the world. In modern times, the plight of the farmer is often forgotten in analyzing cycles, but it still plays an important part in the condition of the economy as a whole in spite of the fact that agriculture now represents only 3.5 percent of the national product (and labor market). World prices for most agricultural and mined products started to decline in 1929. The drops were dramatic from September to December 1929. The result was deflation throughout the world.

However, agriculture still plays a part in business cycle dynamics. Declining farm income affects the buying power of a substantial segment of the population tied to a farm economy. Higher farm prices change the nature of consumer spending. Farm products are a major U.S. export. Farm loans and defaults affect the credit structure. A farm failure in the Soviet Union in 1982 had a major impact on farm income, food prices, the balance of payments, and the credit supply in the United States.

THE INTEREST CYCLE

Cycles become increasingly complicated as we get to look at them more closely. One basic cycle that affects all others is the one in interest rates, which is a complex of many factors, including savings; money supply; demand for money by government (federal deficits), by business for new plant and equipment, and by business for inventory accumulation; and consumer borrowing. The cycle in interest rates, in turn, affects the amount of spending for investment by business and consumers, as well as imports of foreign capital, which affects the price of the dollar in terms of various currencies, which affects the price and therefore the volume of imports and exports. And the price of each of the elements is itself subject to many factors each moving in its own cycle. Each component has a cyclical dynamics of its own and each business cycle must be disentangled for a clear view.

Two other elements distort the measurement of economic cycles: secular growth and the changing value of the dollar. Cycles weave their way around each other, especially around the growth pattern of increasing populations and productivity associated with technological development, a secular trend. And the dollar yardstick we use must be adjusted for its value changes to clarify the cyclical pattern.

For identification, economists distinguish four phases of a business cycle: a peak, a recession (decline), a trough (bottom), and a recovery.

There is no uniformity in the duration of each phase and only little uniformity in which sectors and industries are affected.

Moreover, the trend in any direction is never a smooth one; it is a series of oscillations of varying strength and duration which, when smoothed on a graph, look very clear. To the contemporary observer, the overall direction is seldom so obvious.

Most of the pressures that create dynamics for a cycle come from the cycle itself (endogenous factors). Internal elements (supply of money, interest rates) help keep the balance. But sometimes the equilibrium breaks down radically. The result may be a short period of adjustment, a moderate period of imbalance (a recession), or a long period of difficulties (a depression). Generally the longer the cycle has spiraled upward, the more precipitous is its decline. Sometimes the dynamic forces are exhausted by an occurrence not related to the cycle itself; an exogenous factor may cause the imbalance. In the real, dynamic world something always happens to upset the equilibrium and cause a panic.

The cycle is not married to a calendar. But there is a systematic, alternating sequence of cause and consequence that takes the economy through prosperity and depression. This may be tied to human rationalization leading to expectation of greater profit through pursuing certain economic actions. These actions are almost invariably undertaken in excess by many entrepreneurs, and each is not totally aware of what others are doing. It is the excesses of these actions that most commonly create an imbalance and a reversal of a long-term trend.

KITCHIN AND JUGLAR

In an analysis by Joseph Alois Schumpeter, three of these short (Kitchin) cycles are contained in a longer 7- to 11-year Juglar cycle, averaging 9 to 10 years. He noted that six Juglar cycles occurred in each long wave, although not always synchronously.

In recent years, four-year cyclical bottoms occurred in 1962, 1966, 1970, 1974, 1978, and 1982. In commenting on this cycle and the others, Schumpeter notes (in 1939):

> No claims are made for our three cycle (Kitchin, Juglar, Kondratieff) scheme except that is it a useful descriptive or illustrative device. Using it, however, in that capacity, we in fact got ex visu of 1929, a "forecast" of a serious depression embodied in the formula: coincidence of depression phases of all three cycles.[10]

One cycle analogous to the farm commodity cycle was identified in 1923 by Joseph Kitchin. This cycle is a relatively regular 40-month (3.3

years) fluctuation in prices, production, employment, and other factors created largely by fluctuations in inventories and the purchase of small equipment. It was used by Schumpeter in his analysis of Kondratieff's long-wave cycles, with which we will deal extensively later.

Clement Juglar (1819–1908), was the first to correlate clearly perceptions of economics, statistics, and history to use them in the understanding of mechanisms of alternating prosperity and recession. Juglar analyzed banking figures, interest rates, prices, marriage rates, and other evidence to support his notion of these major crises. He believed that he had discovered a single wave underlying the movements of world economies. This was an accepted thesis for a dozen years at the beginning of the twentieth century.

A physician, Juglar turned to economics because he saw cyclical movements as a demographic phenomenon. He felt cycles could not be avoided but that they could be predicted, and his predictions proved to be remarkably accurate. He noted that when consumers will not or cannot pay higher prices, entrepreneurs fail or go out of business, and demand for labor, materials, money, and space drop. Each movement creates a spiral that feeds on itself and it is measured in comparison with a previous level.

The cycle (later identified by his name) was of intermediate duration and based on investment in capital goods, equipment, machinery, and so on, and reflected as well fluctuations in prices, production, employment, and other similar series.

THE KUZNETS CYCLE

More widely accepted in recent years than the Kitchin and Juglar cycles is the 15- to 22-year swing in economic growth rates uncovered by Nobel laureate Simon Kuznets, a Russian-born professor of political economy who taught at Johns Hopkins and Harvard. The cycle is more evident in the United Sates than elsewhere. In structural building it reflects expansion of economic activity. It reflects variations in demand for goods and services of substantial character.

Kuznets worked closely with Schumpeter. Some economists (A.F. Burns, M. Abramovits) recognize the Kuznets cycle as associated with population growth and immigration. Others, notably Walt Whitman Rostow, hold that his cycle was material only for the period 1840 to 1914. However, construction as a factor in maintaining spending by the public, business, and government had become so important to the economy in the postwar era that ignoring its cyclical nature and its effects is no longer reasonable. Increased spending results not only from the expenditures for the construction itself, but also for corollary

Figure 1.2. Combination Of Long, Intermediate, And Short Cycles

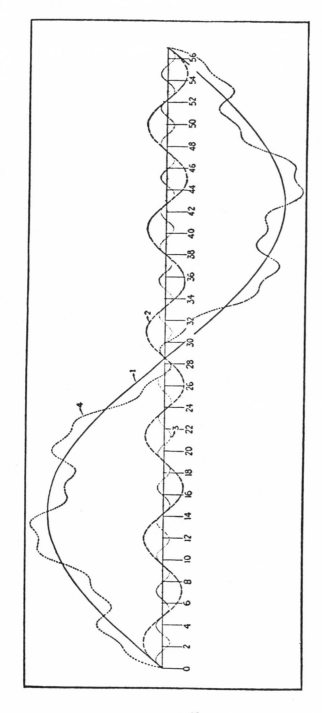

Source: Taken with permission from J. A. Schumpeter, *Business Cycles* (New York: McGraw-Hill Book Co., 1939), p. 213. Curve 1, long cycle; curve 2, intermediate cycle; curve 3, short cycle; curve 4, sum of 1–3.

stimulation to a wide range of other industries: lumber, cement, carpeting, paints, furniture, appliances, ceramics, glassware, and so on.

In Kuznets' schema, a technological hiatus existed in the depressions of 1814–1827, 1879–1885, and 1925–1939. The average length of the Kuznets cycle is 16 years—11 years of expansion and 5 years of contraction. An explanation of the elements in these cycles involves both demographic and economic variables. The maturing of a postwar generation, immigration, higher employment, a decrease in interest rates, and labor and material costs are all factors in stimulating and destimulating this cycle, largely through establishment of new households.

Inasmuch as mortgage interest payment usually constitutes two to four times the quoted cost of a home, changes in money rates, themselves subject to cyclical pressures, are a dominating force in home sales and construction. Government policy, in financing construction through its mortgage guarantee agencies and subsidies and tax abatements, adds to the problems in identifying the cycle.

It is interesting that Kuznets peaks usually precede Juglar peaks, probably reflecting the increased consumer demand stimulated by capital expansion.

Kuznets peaks	Juglar peaks
1955	1956
1972	1973

On the other hand, major peaks in economic activity have usually been preceded by downturns in the Kuznets cycle.

Kuznets	Long wave
1871	1873
1927	1929
1972	1973

2

The Long Wave

The short-term and intermediate-term economic cycles noted by Kitchin, Juglar, Kuznets, and others were easily perceptible fluctuations created by oversupply or excess demand for products, services, or money. These fluctuations receive consideration in almost all business planning.

There is another type of cycle, less perceptible because its duration is longer, its dynamics less obvious, and its origins less well defined. Economists who study it refer to it as the long wave.

This cycle of 50 to 60 years was identified empirically in modern society in 1810. Because statistical data prior to the twentieth century is relatively sparse, analysts have had difficulty in providing a provable, rational explanation of how it begins, why it acts the way it does, and how to control it. The studies of Nikolai D. Kondratieff are the best known in this direction, but earlier studies were published in England and Holland.

More than 100 years ago, Dr. Hyde Clarke described this longer cycle, which was different from others affecting the economies of Europe. In 1847 he published a paper in the *British Railway Journal* called "Physical Economy" describing fluctuations between 1793 and his own time. This long-wave period of 54 years included several famines and five apparent cycles of 10 to 11 years. Clarke offered no explanations; he merely recorded the figures. A crisis that began in that year after a 16-year period of expansion (a period of rising prices) ended with the Great Depression of 1873 in the United States and one in 1896 in Britain.

Half of a century later, Alexander Israel Helphand (1867–1924), a German socialist theoretician, writing as "Parvus," provided similar material that influenced Leon Bronstein (Trotsky), the Soviet leader and a frequent writer in economics. Parvus' pamphlet, published in

1901, outlined an economic wave: "when development in all areas of the capitalist economy—the state of technology, the money market, trade, the colonies—has come to the point that imminent expansion of the world market must take place, lifting the whole world production into a new, more comprehensive basis."[1]

Parvus saw this as a historic period, when the strong *Sturm und Drang* period of capitalism began. It is, he said, a period of short, sharp crises that evolve into a major, prolonged depression. This state continues until a new *Sturm und Drang* period begins. He went on to suggest a continuous series of cycles of expansion and contraction without mentioning either periodicity or self-correction forces. However, he thought that a new *Sturm und Drang* period started in 1896 because he saw then the effects of the development of electricity, the opening of new markets, and the large increase in the production of gold.

At the beginning of the twentieth century, several economists suggested that a long economic cycle was identifiable. In spite of the relatively limited history of economics and the difficulties in obtaining statistical material over an extended period of time, several other analysts suggested that a cycle of 50 or more years existed in the major trading areas of the world, England, Holland, Germany, and France.

In the Netherlands, two Marxists pursued similar studies. Wesley C. Mitchell credits J. van Gelderen (writing under the name of J. Fedder) with having noted the "large cycles" in 1913.[2] His analyses were confirmed by a compatriot, S. DeWolff, in 1924.[3] Arthur Spiethoff, a professor at Duke University, added to the literature in 1938.[4]

Van Gelderen concentrated on studies of industrial development, but he also used figures of production, finances, trade, and transport. He linked these to fluctuations of general economic conditions. His model was the 1850–1973 period of upward swings in Europe and the United States, followed by a 23-year period of slow growth, then another surge (he called it "a new springtide") in 1896, beginning a long wave of expansion. But van Gelderen avoided both the concept and the term "cycle." Looking for causes, he itemized the opening of new territories and new industrial activities (electricity, automobiles), which he saw as creating a consumption multiplier (a demand for new products and services, creating new jobs, new income) and a new prosperity.

However, at the same time he saw the seeds of a new recession as production in these sectors accelerated to a point of overproduction, ultimate shortages of raw materials, and rising costs, with declining demand, lower profits, and eventually, a break in the expansion pattern. As a Marxist, he could point to the inevitability of a breaking point in "the quantitatively and qualitatively uncontrolled course of the capitalist production process."

Figure 2.1. Four Kondratieff Waves

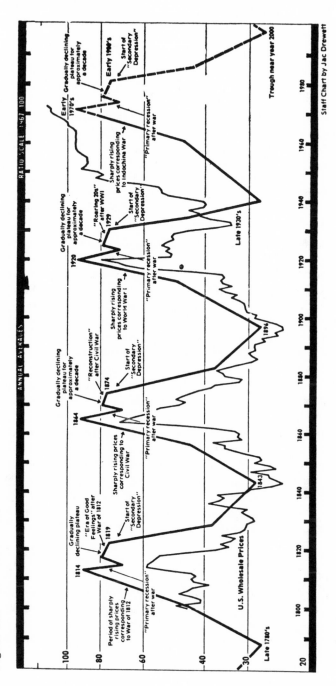

Source: Media General Financial Services, Richmond, Va., June 5, 1974.

23

DeWolff continued this line of study with two papers in Dutch and German in 1924 and 1929. He echoed a thesis previously mentioned by Marx, that it was the obsolescence of capital goods that was the chief cause of depressions, with the efficiency life of machines determining the duration of expansion periods. Marx had estimated this to be 10 years. DeWolff expanded this line, estimating the depreciation rate for capitalist infrastructure ("long-living fixed capital," e.g., manufacturing plants, bridges, roads, railroads, wharfs, etc.) at 2.615 percent per year, and decided on a 38-year lifespan. This coincided generally with the period from the peaks of 1873 to 1913 and the bottoms in 1894 and 1930. Like Marx, DeWolff believed that the frequency of capitalist crises would increase until a final collapse would destroy the system.

In the 1920s Lord Beveridge (father of the welfare state concept) released a study of wheat prices from 1500 to 1867. It represents a graphic cycle of peaks and valleys that top in roughly 54-year periods, with peaks in 1510, 1565, 1630, 1700, 1760, 1805, and 1848, and bottom out in 1548, 1570, 1610, 1675, 1785, and 1830. Imposed on a steady secular growth graph with a range four points above and below the normal, it showed a remarkable correlation. Other studies trace a similar 50- to 60-year pattern to the year 1250. A "History of Agricultural Prices in England 1260 to 1922" indicates cycles of 50 to 60 years averaging 54 years.[5]

KONDRATIEFF

Thus the long-wave cycle that bears his name was not originated by Kondratyiev (anglicized to Kondratieff). Born in 1892, Nikolai Dmitryevich Kondratyiev became an agricultural economist and in 1916 began to work in the economic sector of the Union of Zemstvos, headed by Chayanov. From there he was appointed vice-minister of food under the short-lived government of Alexander Kerensky in 1917. There he was responsible for providing consumer goods for the peasants. He worked at the Agricultural Academy in Moscow for a few years and there attained sufficient stature to be appointed by Lenin to establish a Conjuncture Institute to study the cycles in capitalist economies. For eight years he directed a group to study these fluctuations.

The concept of a long-wave cycle was first suggested by Kondratieff as early as 1910. It was not until 1919, however, that he began serious work on his long-wave theories. As soon as he had the status of the Conjuncture Institute and its funds for amassing material, he was able to publish "The World Economy and Its Condition during and after the War" in 1922.

Kondratieff's mentor (and probably the sponsor of his rapid rise in the Soviet hierarchy) was Professor Mikail Ivonovich Tugan-Baranovskiy, recognized as Russia's greatest economist. Tugan-Baranovskiy had been a minister in the rightist Ukrainian government which fought the Bolshevik regime. When Tugan-Baranovskiy died in 1919, Kondratieff prepared the eulogy, a paper that was part of the indictment that led to his own downfall.

In January 1924 Kondratieff, in collaboration with N. P. Markov, was assigned to analyze the Five-Year Plan for Agriculture created by Gosplan, the national planning unit that created production and distribution quotas. The two worked on the plan for a year and published several papers, including 16 special production plans. The plan was overfulfilled, except in its target for grain. At the time the grain quota was established, Kondratieff, a David Stockman of his time, had attacked the Five-Year Plan proposed in 1926–1927, insisting that it was possible to install collective farms without liquidating the *kulaks*, and suggesting that working out the control figures for the whole economy should provide for some margins of error. He believed in the New Economic Policy (NEP), which would have provided motivation for increasing production, even in the extension of NEP, which favored the more well-to-do peasants, who were the more efficient. And Kondratieff was not in favor of a state monopoly of foreign trade. Moreover, he belittled the quantitative rather than qualitative aspects of long-term plans, which he sarcastically called "bedspreads," and considered unrealistic.

It is possible and even certain that forecasts for the more distant future will become poorer and more modest. One of two things: either we want serious and realistic plans, and in that case we must base them exclusively on assured scientific foundations; or we shall continue to engage in all kinds of "bold" calculations and computations for the future without sufficient foundations, and then we must accept from the start that the calculations are arbitrary, that such plans lack reality. But what is the purpose of and value of such plans? At best they remain harmless, because they are dead from a practical point of view. At worst they will be harmful, because they may introduce serious errors into our practice.

As the leader of a new *narodnik* group called the Working Peasants Party (TKP), Kondratieff was more to the right than most of his colleagues and so invited a hostile press that linked him with several non-socialist extermists (Litoshenko, Yurousky). Kondratieff had already at that time built up a substantial reputation as a maverick (a sort of David Stockman) among communists. In 1917, at 25, he leaned to the right among the SRs, the Socialist Revolutionaries who seeded the revolution. The left wing of the party had supported the Bolsheviks; the right wing believed in nationalization of the land and redistribution among those who worked it.

He first worked with the Petlyura government in the Ukraine. Later he received the title of Director of the Market Institute, which he held from 1920–1928, where he opposed the state's monopoly of trade and its market manipulation. He pleaded for slower industrialization, holding that the nation's economic health depended on a harmonious interplay and integration between industry and agriculture, with a concept of "restorative prices," an overall policy later adopted by the Trotskyists.

During this period he was also a professor at the Timiryazez Agricultural Academy and an associate of the USSR Popular Commissariat of Finance and the Popular Commissariat of Agriculture.

He was exposed to some of the rationale of Western ideas when he visited the British Exhibition in 1924 and came to the United States for economic talks in 1925.

Krylenko, who prosecuted at his later trial, spoke of Kondratieff as one of the principal defendants, and characterized him as the leader (with Chayanov) of a counter-revolutionary kulak group. The charges were supported by the Agrarian Institute at the Communist Academy and by the Inter-Agrarian Institute.

As soon as the Soviets took over the government of Russia, they set about to prove, in economic terms, that capitalism was in crisis and to determine just when this crisis would lead to the collapse of capitalism. For this purpose a "Conjuncture Institute" was created. Kontratieff was appointed to be its head.

The study of the long wave was continued by Kondratieff during the winters of 1924–1925 and 1925–1926 in spite of other heavy duties as director of the Conjuncture Institute. In mid-1922 he began publication of *Ekonomichesky bulletin Konyunktur Nogo Instituta* (*Economic Bulletin of the Conjuncture Institute*) and served as its editor. After 1925 Albert Weinstein was added as collaborator.

By 1924 the study had grown to 80 pages and consisted of four parts: the overall domestic economic indicator of the Conjuncture Institute, domestic indicators of the state of the national economy of the USSR, foreign sections, and articles of general and theoretical nature.

His conclusions were, simply:

1. During price upswings in the capitalist economies, prosperity years were most common.
2. During downswings, agriculture suffered more and long depressions than did industry.
3. Major technical innovations were conceived in downswing periods but were developed during upswing periods.

4. Gold supply increased and new markets were opened at the beginning of an upswing.
5. The most disastrous and extensive wars occurred during periods of an upswing.

His hypothesis held that there is a complete interrelationship between political and social developments, wars and revolutions, and economic and financial behavior. As he saw it, the United States had experienced three complete long waves, all strikingly similar in their overall economic, social, and political patterns. These long cycles each had a well-defined rising wave and falling wave. The rising waves, as measured by the wholesale price index and interest rates, lasted on the average about 21 to 25 years. The falling waves lasted a little longer, 29 to 32 years.

Undoubtedly, Kondratieff's reasoning was restrained if not colored by the comments of his critics, even at the beginning. In a rare explanation, responding to the question as to why capital goods investment increases in "clusters" at 50- to 60-year intervals to stimulate the economy, he responded that at the trough of a recession (or the beginning of an expansion phase), large sums of capital were available at low interest rates. When these funds were depleted by investment, interest rates went up, restraining new investment and exerting pressure for a downturn, thus creating a decline. A period of business decline stimulated the accumulation of savings, setting the stage for a new upswing.

In the 1928 paper, however, there is a concession to Marxist outrage, that an upswing need not necessarily follow a depression and that "organic change" could destroy the dynamics of the cycle.

Kondratieff figured as the star witness and defendant in the Menshevik trial in March 1931, before the breakup of the Working Peasants Party, and his long-wave hypotheses went on trial with him. He had suggested that the commanding position in the development of the national economy should be assigned to agriculture, and his group had expressed resistance to Stalin's program for "annihilation of the kulaks as a class." After a full year in prison awaiting a day in court, he "acknowledged" that he now thought that his previous position was "criminal." At the trial, the analysis of cycles in the United States and Britain proved to be most irritating to the Soviet judges, who felt that it was anathema that Soviet citizens should be made familiar with foreign conditions.

His deviation in interpreting Marx was based on a letter to Zasulich, the leader of the Social Revolutionary Party. The SRP followed the narodnik (populist) tradition urging that expropriated lands be distributed to the peasants who cultivated it. Lenin believed it should be collectivized.[8]

The Conjuncture Institute was dissolved; the institute's bulletin was transferred to the Statistical Office and was soon allowed to die; Kondratieff was himself imprisoned.

According to Solzhenitzyn in his *Gulag Archipelago*, Kondratieff was sentenced to solitary confinement, became mentally ill, and died. The Working Peasants Party, with some 200,000 members, was scheduled for a mass trial in 1931, but the trial was canceled by Stalin.

THE RECEPTION

Much of what we know of Kondratieff's comments results from the writings of a critic, George Garvy, in the November 1943 *Review of Economic Statistics*. Apparently the substantial criticism among Soviet economists flowed toward the implication that downswings in capitalist cycles were self-correcting and that the lull between 1914 and 1920 would have been followed by an expansion and prosperity if the war had not intervened. The Marxist version of a capitalist collapse was nowhere indicated. This, of course, was the bourgeois view and socialist heresy. That the wave was also implicit in the writings of Marx carried no weight.

THE THEORY

In describing the origins of his theory, Kondratieff wrote:

I arrived at the hypothesis concerning the existence of long cycles in the years 1919–20. Without going into a special analysis, I formulated my general thesis for the first time shortly thereafter in my study, *The World Economy and Economic Fluctuations in the War and Post-War Periods*. During the winter and spring of 1925, I wrote a special study, *Long Business Cycles*, which appeared in Volume I of *Voprosy Konyunktury (Problems of Economic Fluctuations)*, published in Moscow by the Institute of Conjuncture in 1925.

The first paper was read at the Institute of Economics of the Russian Association of Research, Institute of Social Science (later merged with the Academy of Sciences). A week later Oparin read a critical counter-report. Both were later published as a book (*Long Cycles*), translated in the *Review of Economic Statistics* in November 1935, and in an abridged translation in *Archiv für Sozialwissenschaften und Sozialpolitik* in 1926. This was reprinted in *Readings in Business Cycles Theory*, after being selected by a committee of the American Economic Association of Philadelphia in 1944. Kondratieff noted:

The idea that the dynamics of economic life in that capitalistic social order is not of a simple and linear but rather of a complex and cyclical character is nowadays generally recognized.

The Review of Economic Statistics carries a translation of peculiarly important articles by Kondratieff which, under the title "Die langen Wellen der Konjunktur," appeared in the *Archiv für Sozialwissenschaft und Sozialpolitik* in 1926.

The evidence we have presented thus far permits some conclusions: (1) the movements of the series which we have examined running from the end of the eighteenth century to the present time show long cycles. Although the statistical-mathematical treatment of the series selected is rather complicated, the cycles discovered cannot be regarded as the accidental result of the methods employed. Against such an interpretation is to be set the fact that these waves have been shown with about the same timing in all the more important of the series examined.

Kondratieff worked out his theories on the basis of wholesale prices, interest on British consols and French rentes, deposits at French savings banks, French trade, per capita coal, lead and wage data of English farm and textile workers and French coal miners, pig-iron production in the United States, coal consumption in France, gold production, and other production series from 1780 to 1926. He used a nine-year moving average to eliminate minor fluctuations. His charts showed great European prosperity for 25 years from 1789 to 1814, then a fall into a 35-year decline. He traced a commodity price depression and a recovery that lasted from 1896 to 1920. He found a very high correlation in the price movements in the United States, England, Germany, and France, except that the Civil War in the United States caused a special price rise, and the Napoleonic War and World War I had similar special effects. But by and large, the graphs of price indexes showed a marked uniformity.

Kondratieff's average time span for the first three cycles was 53.3 years. His original work did not extend beyond 1920; his 1924 writings appeared in the *Quarterly Journal of Economics* (vol. 39, August 1925, p. 518) and in 1953, and his final report on the data appeared in 1925. It was reprinted in German in 1926, and in English in 1935 ("The Static and Dynamic View of Economics" and the "Long Wave in Economic Life").

Kondratieff concentrated on value-dominated statistical series: money, interest rates, and wages. These do not necessarily move in the same periodicity as other factors in the economy, but they provide a thermometer measured in prices which move in rhythm with other series and essentially reflect the underlying forces in a capitalist

Figure 2.2. Price Indexes, 1775–1975

Warren and Pearson wholesale price index
for all commodities (1910–1914 = 100)

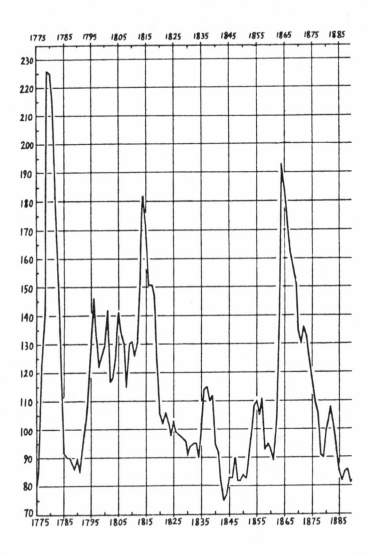

Bureau of Labor Statistics wholesale price index
for all commodities (1967 = 100)

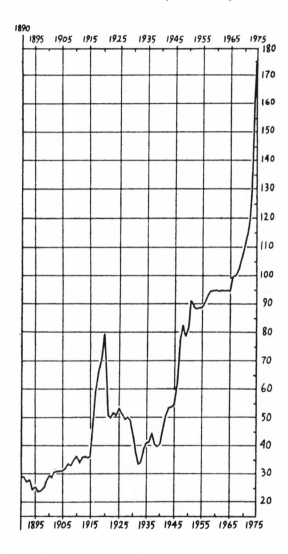

Source: Bureau of the Census, *Historical Statistics*, pp. 199–202.

economy, rising and falling with supply and demand, which provide the basic dynamism of the economy.

Most other studies made at that time and since have used the fluctuations of wholesale prices and interest rates as the barometers of changes:

> We can only say that the rhythm of the long cycles reflects the rhythm in the process of the expansion of society's basic capitalist goods. However, that process is not rhythmic because rhythmicality is metaphysically inherent in it, but because, being associated with the process of the assimulation and investment of capital, and taking place under the concrete conditions of the capitalist society, by virtue of the concatenation of its elements analyzed above, it cannot flow uninterruptedly at one and the same rate.

Thus each cycle is different because each phase is the

> consequence of conditions cumulatively amassed during the preceding time internally... Each new cycle takes place under new concrete historical conditions, of a new level in the development of productive forces, and hence is by no means a simple repetition of the preceding cycle.
>
> In asserting the existence of long waves and in denying that they arise out of random causes, we are also of the opinion that long waves arise out of causes which are inherent in the essence of the capitalist economy.

As Kondratieff saw it, the long wave is usually made up of five intermediate cycles of two to four years, broken by mild recessions. Schumpeter found four to six Juglar cycles in each long wave. However, the cycles are now seen as not necessarily uniform in size, shape, or duration, but do seem to follow a fairly specific pattern. In his second paper Kondratieff noted a three-year cycle later defined and discussed by Joseph Kitchin.

Kondratieff notes short cycles in introducing his own approach:

> References to fluctuations in business conditions lasting about three or three-and-one-half years are also to be found in the work of other authors; for example, Lacome. Again, American statisticians and economists—in particular those associated with the Harvard Bureau—although they reject the idea of a strict periodicity in the fluctuations of the market, note that in America the capitalist cycle has an approximate duration of three-and-one-half years. The cycles studied by them more or less correspond to what in Europe was studied under the name of the seven-to-eleven-year cycle. Thus the indications of the existence of shorter cycles have, it seems to me, a twofold character. On the one hand, that short cycle looks like a special type of fluctuation in business conditions. On the other

hand, it looks like the same type of business cycle that was known earlier, but more compressed in time. I do not, however, intend to dwell here upon the question of the existence of these short or small cycles, or of their nature. In this paper, I have in mind a special, third type of cyclical fluctuations: long cycles.

The short cycles and intermediate cycles are strung as they were on the waves of the long cycle.

FOUR STAGES

Kondratieff held that long waves showed the same regularity as short waves, with similar distinguishable dramatic changes. He cites "four empirical patterns which may be discerned in a more or less attentive examination of the specific course of development of economic life."

However, the long rise is characterized by short depressions followed by intense upswings. During a downswing, the converse is true, with agriculture suffering most sharply. Kondratieff insisted that the swings were due not merely to gold production or prices. He saw prices as an integral part of major cycles and their dynamics.

Later, Marxists like Ernest Mandel (in 1980) suggested that each upswing was dependent on exogenous factors: wars, migrations, industrial revolution, and so on. But later analyses have been able to illuminate a set of dynamics that outlines and rationalizes the long waves.

Even before Keynes, Kondratieff was concerned with equilibria in the economy based on Albert Marshall's distinction between short-term and long-term equilibria. He saw these factors in minor cyclical equilibrium in the economy (with major cycles based on fluctuations in a third order of equilibrium) and viewed all elements in the economy as tending to approach this position of equilibrium, at levels which, he noted, constantly change.

> The wavelike fluctuations are processes of alternating disturbances of the equilibrium of the capitalistic system; they are increasing or decreasing deviations from the equilibrium level.

Kondratieff saw cycles as part of the dynamism of the capitalist system.

> Capitalism is by nature a form or method of economic change and not only never is, but never can be stationary. And this evolutionary character of the capitalist process is not merely due to the fact that economic life goes on in a social and natural environment which changes and by its change

alters the data of economic action; this fact is important and these changes (wars, revolutions, and so on) often condition industrial change, but they are not its prime movers. Nor is this evolutionary character due to a quasi-automatic increase in population and capital or to the vagaries of monetary systems of which exactly the same thing holds true. The fundamental impulse that sets and keeps the capitalist engine in motion comes as short and intermediate waves that are international in nature, similar to short series but of differing character.

THE EXPANSION

In the beginning of a long wave, Kondratieff says, profound changes in economic life take place, principally in the diffusion of technology, in the exploitation of important discoveries and inventions previously developed, the inclusion of new countries in the system of the world economy, and changes in gold production and monetary circulation. Most social upheavals (wars and revolutions), he found, take place during the long upswing, one in the early stages, one near the peak. The cycles are not limited to certain economic activities but impact on the whole company.

The beginning of a new wave is a period of diffusion of technology and consequently of high investment. This expansion of investment, production, and affluence causes prices to rise. The increased volume of goods requires a higher velocity of money, thus creating a price structure at a higher level of prices. This growth requires about 25 years to complete. During this period unemployment falls and wages and productivity rise. The mood is one of accumulation and high consumer spending, while technology, accumulated during previous years of decline and depression, is refined and absorbed. The spurt in investment has a high multiplier effect, bringing about substantial new construction, the creation of durable goods, increasing employment on many levels, and a ripple effect due to increased personal income.

Kondratieff noted that periods of rising waves of long cycles are rich in social upheavals and radical changes in the economy.

It is clear from the foregoing preliminary remarks that the rising wave of a long cycle is associated with the replacement and expansion of basic capital goods, and with the radical regrouping of, and changes in, society's productive forces. But this process presupposes tremendous investments of capital. And in order for them to be made, it is obviously necessary that the capital be available. This, in its turn, is possible only if certain prerequisites are present. The first requirement is that the accumulation may be in part physical and in part monetary, in the broadest sense of the word. But however sizable the accumulation built up, we never have the formation of such huge amounts of capital that their outlay can be subsequently continued for decades and more. That is why the possibility of big, long-term investments of capital presupposes a second prerequisite; that the process of accumulation continue, and at such a rate that its curve is higher than the curve of current investment. But this accumulation can take place in various strata of the capitalist society. And if the accumulated capital were in a scattered and diffuse state, big investments and the radical reconstruction of the economy would be impossible. Thus the third prerequisite to such reconstructions is the concentration of capital at the disposal of powerful entrepreneurial centers."

Stimulation comes, says Schumpeter, from the new consumers' goods, the new methods of production or transportation, the new markets, the new forms of industrial organization that capitalist enterprise creates.

The upswing of the first long wave embraces the period from 1789 to 1814, i.e., 25 years; its decline begins in 1814 and ends in 1849, a period of 35 years. The cycle is, therefore, completed in 60 years.

Kondratieff notes that at the beginning of an expansion there may be an additional stimulation provided by a "limited war" (noted in cycles as a "trough war") undertaken at the option of the government with popular support (sometimes characterized as "inspired"). These wars have created a minimum drain on an expanding economy. In the United States the Revolutionary War, the war with Mexico in 1848, the Spanish-American War in 1898, and the war in Korea in 1950 may be seen as falling into this category.

Later, Mensch and others note, as the expansion begins to reach maturity, there is a tendency for government to increase defense spending to provide additional stimulation. This creation of demand does not flood the marketplace with competitive product and has a high multiplier effect. Public acceptance appears to have always been ready (or to have been made ready) by increasing belligerency in response to the world situation. Historically this belligerency has been followed by "peak wars" near the climax of expansion. Inasmuch as the economy has been at a higher level during these periods, these wars have been more costly (sometimes called "absolute wars"). In past cycles these are identified as the War of 1812, the Civil War (1861–1865), World War I (1917–1918), and Vietnam (1965–1975). (World War II is seen as "the end of the truce following 1918" and due to cyclical forces abroad, and does not change the calendar pattern.) The expansion period of the first Kondratieff wave included both the American and French revolutions and revolutions and reforms in Holland, Italy, Switzerland, Germany,

Spain, and Portugal, as well as two partitions of Poland. Kondratieff saw it in this way:

> The rise of the second wave begins in 1849 and ends in 1873, lasting 24 years. The decline of the second wave begins in 1873 and ends in 1896, a period of 23 years. The length of the second wave is 47 years. The upward movement of the Third Wave begins in 1896 and ends in 1920, its duration being 24 years. The decline of the wave begins in 1920.

The second wave saw the 1848 revolutionary movements in France, Germany, Austria, and Romania; the unification of Italy (1850–1879) and of Germany (1862–1870); and the Civil War in the United States.

The third wave involved Japan and China, Turkey and Greece, the United States and Spain, Italy and Turkey, the Balkan War and World War I, as well as revolutions in Russia (1905, 1917), Turkey (1908–1913), and Germany (1918–1919).

THE PEAK

Expansion eventually reaches a peak. The economy enters a period where affluence begins to cause a shortage of goods and production becomes strained. There is a change of attitudes toward work. Inefficiencies develop, causing prices to rise. Money is diverted from capital investment to consumption. Cost increases cause profits to fall, cresting at an inflationary recession (stagflation). Kondratieff saw the imbalances of this period as historically associated with what has been termed a "peak" or "absolute" war near the point of maturation (the War of 1812, the Civil War, World War I, and the war in Vietnam). These wars bring about a period of affluence and produce strains on the economy that are reflected in rapid inflation. Adjustments at wars' end are, typically, a decline in government spending to accumulate funds to pay war debts, large additions to the labor force due to demobilization that are not quickly assimilated, a rapid rise in unemployment, a drop in output, and a recession. This "primary" recession lasts two to five years, but it brings about a change in the popular mood felt for many years afterward.

Some analysts define the conditions existing during long periods of prosperity as a "numbing of the senses" involving, among other things, a reluctance to change any of the prevailing trends or to take adequate precautions against excesses.

One hypothesis suggested by Thomas Robert Matthews and found in writings by William T. Foster, Waddell Catchings, and John Hobson holds that during expansion too large a proportion of income is devoted to capital formation, creating a tendency for productive capacity to outrun consumer demand. Others, like C.H. Douglas, maintain that declines are the result of a deficiency of purchasing power. But a relatively new approach sees the peak reached with the maturity of those industries created by basic innovations in past years.

Prosperity in the long-wave process accedes to recession when the rate at which basic innovations appear has remained at a low level for a period sufficient for stagnation to dominate over the invigorating forces of the economy. Thus stagnation is rooted in the exhaustion of possibilities for adapted improvement in the technologies that originally seeded the expansion.

According to this view, the prosperity we experience for these few years is not the conversion period to a new growth phase, but the blow-off of the old one.

THE FIRST ADJUSTMENT

The historical record shows that each major war is followed by a short, sharp period of adjustment, a recession. But Kondratieff pays little attention to this. Having reached a peak during the last years of an "absolute" war, with a high rate of debt accumulation by the government, demand accumulation by the public, and labor shortages (with wage increases), the economy must adjust for more balanced budgets, sometimes for reduction of the public debt, and demobilization. Such adjustments occurred in the United States in 1816, 1867, and 1920. However, the accumulated demand soon brings about a recovery, and the economy enters a plateau period of gradual, almost unnoticed decline.

THE PLATEAU

By Kondratieff's standards this following period is the initial phase of the long-wave decline. From the contemporary view, this period of seven to 10 years appears to be one of relative stability. Emotions restrained during the preceding war emerge in a form of public ebullience, a loosening of moral constraints, and an increase in gambling and speculation. Historically these periods have been noted as "The Era of Good Feeling" (1815–1823), "The Gilded Age" (1867–1872), and "The Roaring Twenties" (1922–1929). During this period, accumulated demand becomes satisfied, there is an increase in new household formations, birthrates increase, and consumer spending and speculation lead to the accumulation of increasing debt.

A similar period followed the peak of 1973, sustained by a Keynesian approach, with large injection of funds into the money supply to sustain large federal deficits. During the Carter years this resulted in stagflation. During the Reagan years even larger deficits financed defense spending, with less inflation and less unemployment.

This period is characterized by growth in selected industries, development of new ideas (both technological and social), and strong feelings of affluence, terminating in a feeling of euphoria. Inflated prices plus strong consumer spending results in a rapid increase in debt.

This time following the peak in prices and production is sometimes called "the secondary prosperity." It starts with and is fed by expectations of "another leg," ever increasing income, and extrapolation of the graph of the rises during previous years to unprecedented heights. Expectations of ever increasing sales leads to inventory accumulation. Both consumers and businesses increase their debt to accumulate assets on thinner margins. Farmers borrow on the increased value of their lands to buy more land. It was in this climate that investment trusts were formed in the 1920s to buy stocks on margin and sell their own stocks to the public, which bought them on margin. In the 1980s highly leveraged business acquisitions increased the public total debt level.

The end of the plateau period is evidenced by an increase in business failures and foreclosures. Public confidence remains high, with professional pessimists becoming more numerous.

THE PANIC

As the economy becomes more fragile, business failures and bank failures increase, and finally one failure appears to trigger a reversal in this public confidence. In historic perspective, the event may appear insignificant: a presidential challenge to Britain about the Venezuela border, the failure of a well-known bank or other business, or a sharp drop, albeit temporary, in security or commodity prices.

The history of peaks and panics shows an almost uncanny consistency. Using wholesale prices as an index (in 1957–59 dollars), the peaks and troughs occurred at intervals of 50 to 56 years:

Peak years	Trough years
1814 at 62.3	1843 at 25.4
1864 at 74.7	1896 at 25.4
1920 at 84.5	1952 at 35.6

THE DECLINE

Whereas the upswing in a cycle is inhibited by a shortage of resources, or a reluctance of entrepreneurs to commit savings, a decline is inhibited only by inertia—the desire of entrepreneurs to stay in business even though their ventures cease to be immediately profitable. Additionally, inasmuch as downturn is initiated by an overcapacity, the early withdrawal of this overcapacity serves to remove some of the pressure on liquidation.

The public impact of each wave may be substantially different. Unemployment was moderate in recessions from 1780 to 1815, but was high before 1825 and after 1834, as industry increased its share of the economy.

During the early part of the nineteenth century, exports played an important role in the economy. As a result, the requirements of Europe and the state of its economies were especially important in accenting or mitigating movements of the economy.

Kondratieff, a product and instrument of a labor-oriented economy, would not have mentioned the cycle in labor attitudes as a factor in the long wave, but it does play some part, principally as a retardant to change in production methods. This was eponymized by the Luddites in the nineteenth century.

Kondratieff also found "that the downward waves of these cycles are accompanied by a long depression in agriculture." During the first wave, prices of agricultural commodities dropped further than the prices of industrial products. He finds only tangential proof of the decline following the Napoleonic Wars but refers to the indices of prices of wheat, flax, and wool for the second-wave period:

Year	Wheat	Flax	Wool
1869–1877	105	101	104
1878–1886	93	90	108
1887–1895	79	91	99

During the third wave he noted the great depression in agriculture in the United States and Europe taking place at the time of his writings.

The beginnings of a downturn usually reveal corruption and mismanagement that pass unnoticed or investigated in the euphoria of booming business. During times of prosperity, it becomes uneconomical to prosecute small defalcations. Larger ones are papered over to avoid rocking the boat.

In national affairs, scandals that followed the 1873 crisis involved Grant's secretary of war, William W. Belnap, and Orville E. Babcock, his private secretary. Before Warren G. Harding's "sudden death" in 1923, scandals involved the Veterans Bureau, the Office of Alien Property, the Justice Department, and the Interior Department. Two cabinet members, Henry M. Daugherty, the attorney general, and Albert B. Fall, the secretary of the interior, were involved in the Teapot Dome scandal.

The recession occurs because of an imbalance in the economy. Rapid rises in prices and changes in production correct this imbalance temporarily. Changes in price structure, in the mood of the people accustomed to free spending, establish a period of relatively flat growth. At this point the economy becomes consumption oriented. The popular mood moves toward isolationism.

This period is characterized by growth in selected industries, development of new ideas (both technological and social), and strong feelings of affluence, terminating in a feeling of euphoria. Inflated prices plus strong consumer spending results in a rapid increase in debt.

In this view, the downswing following World War I was particularly severe. A 23-month downturn, beginning in 1920, was the sharpest in history, and the Great Depression of the 1930s that began in August 1929 continued for 43 of America's most economically trying months.

Eventually wealth consumption expands beyond its limits, the economy stretches far, and like a rubber band it snaps. Debts become burdensome. Bankruptcies abound, and the economy slips into a severe depression.

The excesses during the plateau period cause a collapse of the price structure. The economy goes into a period of sharp retrenchment, generally for a three-year collapse, followed by a 15-year deflationary workout period. (Krondratieff and others viewed these depressions as cleansing periods that allowed the economy to readjust from a period of excesses and to lay a base for future growth.)

The depressed state of the economy during this period stimulates the search for means of cutting production costs and a search for inventions that will facilitate such cost cutting. Interest rates begin to decline due to the decline in capital expansion. Wages and material prices fall. The period leads to the emergence of factors facilitating increased accumulation of capital in the hands of banking and other business enterprises. The accumulation is seen first among those segments of the population who have fixed incomes and benefit from a downward trend in prices. It also comes at the expense of agriculture.

It is during this trough period that Kondratieff saw an accumulation of inventions that remained undeveloped or unused. Later commentators saw here clusters or swarms of inventions, renewing the cycle. History indicates that the "clusters" surround a single major seminal development.

Although it has not yet been widely accepted as dogma that innovations arrive in swarms, that thesis has been voiced by economists of note (Mensch, Schumpeter, Dewey). The thesis is extended to define innovations not merely as inventions but as the development of technology and the diffusion of these developments into the economy. When a basic seminal invention is put into productive use, it is usually followed by others applying the same or similar principles in different industries.

None of Kondratieff's original papers offers a fully satisfactory explanation of why long-wave cycles occur with such uniformity, nor do they give any hypothesis beyond the historical statistics. This became the source of much of the critical comments.

To repair this failing, Kondratieff presented another paper in 1926 at the Economic Institute in Moscow, offering "a first attempt to give a tentative explanation of the long cycles," and with critics still not satisfied, still another restatement was published in 1928. His second and third papers proposed a theory of investment as part of the dynamics.

Kondratieff mentions war as a factor but makes no attempt to expand on his observations that wars (or inventions) were a feature of upswings. He merely chronicled the events as historical inventory. He makes the point that cycles were not isolated factors in history but are part of connected elements in technological progress and political and social history, and are based on endogenous factors.

IDENTIFYING THE WAVES

Kondratieff identified the cycles as follows:

First Kondratieff
   Prosperity 1782–1792 (10 years)
   Prosperity 1792–1802 (war 1802–1815)
      The rise lasted from the end of the 1780s or beginning of the 1790s until 1810–17.
   Decline 1815–1825 (10 years)
   Depression 1825–1836 (11 years)
   Recovery 1836–1845 (9 years)
      The decline lasted from 1810–17 until 1844–51 (41 years).
Second Krondratieff
   Prosperity 1845–56 (16 years)
      The rise lasted from 1844–51 until 1870–75 (31 years).

Prosperity 1856–66 (10 years)
Decline 1866–72 (6 years)
Depression 1872–83 (11 years)
Recovery 1883–92 (9 years)
    The decline lasted from 1870–75 until 1890–96 (26 years).
Third Kondratieff
Prosperity 1892–1903 (11 years)
    The rise lasted from 1890–96 until 1914–20 (30 years).
Prosperity 1903–1913 (war 1913–1920) (10 years)
Decline 1920–1929 (9 years)
    The decline probably begins in the years 1914–20.
Depression 1929–1937 (8 years)
Recovery 1937–1948 (1 year)
Fourth Kondratieff
Prosperity 1948–57 (9 years)
Prosperity 1957–66 (11 years)
Decline 1966–73 (7 years)
Depression 1973–74 (2 years)

Later commentators made some variations in the dating.

Table 2.1. Long Waves: Expansion Periods

Author	1st Wave	2d Wave	3rd Wave	4th Wave
Schumpeter (1939)	1787–1813/14	1842/43–1869/70	1897/900–1924/25	
Rostow (1978)	1790–1813	1848–1873	1896–1920	1933–1973
Van Duijn (1982)		1845–1872	1892–1929	1948–1973
Mandel (1980)	1826	1847–1873	1893–1913	1939/48–67
Duprez (1947, 1978)	1789/92–1808/74	1846/51–1872/3	1895/6–1920	1939/46–1947
Clark (1924)		1850–1875	1900–1929	
Von Ciriacy Wantrup (1936)	1792–1815	1842–1873	1895–1913	
DeWolff (1929)	1792–1815	1842–1873	1895–1913	

Source: Compiled by the author.
    The timing of the cycles is based on wholesale prices. All are based on "smoothed" price changes. One is an adaptation for wholesale prices in gold dollars, and one for wholesale prices in nominal dollars.
    In 1985 prices viewed in terms of gold show a substantial deflation not reflected in nominal prices.

Table 2.2. Peak And Trough Rates Of Kondratieff's Long Waves And The Long Waves In Wholesale Prices Of Four Countries

Nature Of Turn	Turns In Kondratieff's Long Waves	Turns In Long Waves Of Wholesale Prices			
		United States	Britain	Germany	France
Trough	Late 1780s or early 1790s	1789	1789	1793	
Peak	1810–17	1814	1813	1808	1820
Trough	1844–51	1843	1849	1849	1851
Peak	1870–75	1864	1873	1873	1872–73
Trough	1890–96	1896–97	1896	1895	1896
Peak	1914–20	1920	1920	1923	1926
Trough		1932	1933	1933	1935

Source: Compiled by the author.

The cycles in other nations were traced approximately (Table 2.2). Peaks and troughs in wholesale prices are not the most reliable indices of all aspects of the economy or for each leading indicator, but they provide the most visible means of identifying the cycles themselves.

Based on a calendar approach to the Kondratieff theory, the data available since 1920 would indicate a fourth long wave, which can be identified as

Rising	1949–1973	24 years
Declining	1973–2003	30 years
		54 years

The effects of World War I created some doubt as to the major turning point in the period—1913, 1920, or 1929. Prices declined after 1815 and 1920, but from an inflated wartime level.

The first Kondratieff period saw the expansion of cotton textile and pig iron industries growing from the Industrial Revolution. The second saw the huge expansion of the railroads, which in turn opened new areas to settlement and farming. The third saw the development of electricity, the telephone, and the radio. The fourth witnessed a huge expansion of the automobile-related industries. Around us is, presumably, a fifth wave, the electronic explosion, centered on the transistor and the microchip, the computer, and expansion of automated production. It is not difficult to see contemporary patterns that seem to coincide with the long wave, or resemblances to the great upswing in production that followed adjustments after World War II.

In recent years the cycle has been refined by a school of analysts into a series of four irregular idealized cycles carried back to 1780, with bottoms in 1790, 1843, 1896, 1949 (actually 1932), and one projected for 2003. The revised graph follows the postwar actual rises of prices to peaks in 1793, 1812, 1865, 1920, and 1973 (the oil embargo), each immediately followed by a sharp primary postwar recession and a drop in prices, a quick partial recovery, a gradual declining plateau beginning in 1819, 1867, 1923, and 1974, followed by precipitous drops beginning in 1826, 1873, 1920 and a sharp decline in the inflation rate in 1974. The underlying trend is relatively clear in the U. S. Department of Commerce graph of wholesale prices.

HOW HIGH, HOW DEEP?

How far is up? How far down does a cycle take the economy?

The record shows that changes around the peaks are more spectacular than changes of the trough periods. In most cases, peaks have been associated with long, expensive, disruptive wars followed by a recession. The wars themselves are viewed by Kondratieff as part of, and a consequence of, economic dynamics.

It is notable that the depth and severity of crises appears directly proportional with the prosperity that preceded them, and that there is great similarity between the situations preceding each crisis and the crises themselves (e.g., 1826–1834 is comparable fo 1920–1933, as to preceding factors and difficulties, including a persistence of gloom). In general, downswings are more severe and last longer than upswings. The impact at the bottom of second postwar downswings is the most difficult.

Based on an index of 100 for 1957–1959 wholesale prices, the peaks in the first wave are shown in the accompanying table. Prices at the troughs show considerable deterioration. However, deflation does not approach the extent of peak inflation. The trough figures are shown in the second table. A more volatile index of the economic cycle, especially its personal effects, is seen in the fluctuations of the unemployment rate described in the third table.

The three deepest depressions during this period were 1825–1830, 1873–1878, and 1929–1934. Each of these entailed coincident phases of shorter cycles, which increased the intensity of the depression.

First Wave

	Year	Index
First peak	1809	45.4
	1814	62.3
	1819	47.7
Second peak	1859	34.3
	1864	74.7
	1869	56.9
Third peak	1915	38.0
	1920	84.5
	1925	56.6

First Wave

	Year	Index
	1838	37.2
First trough	1843	25.4
	1848	26.5
	1891	30.6
Second trough	1896	25.4
	1901	30.2

Unemployment Rate

1894	18.8	1933	24.9	1970	4.9
1897	14	1938	19	1975	9
1923	2.4	1944	1.2	1979	6.3
1924	5	1954	5.5	1982	10.2
1926	1.8	1961	6.7	1985	7.2

HOW LONG?

It should be noted that cycles, especially long waves, are an irregular phenomenon. Although there is no obvious reason why each major cycle should include the same number of Juglars in a long wave or Kitchins in a Juglar, that appears to have occurred in most waves—three Kitchins in each Juglar and six Juglars in each Kondratieff. However, there is no reason to expect such regularity. On the contrary, it would appear that such regularity is contraindicated by the variety of the causative factors and the variation of the cycles phases (somewhat less than 40 months, somewhat less than 10 years, and somewhat less than 60 years). And it must be remembered that short cycles are superimposed on trade cycles, seasonal cycles, product cycles of varying measures, political cycles resulting from elections each four years apart, building cycles, investment cycles, and other forces of infinite complexity.]

UNDERLYING PRESSURES

It is easier to relate the long-term waves to the effects of wars which create inflation as a financing measure, and balanced postwar budgets and adjustments, followed by further adjustments in a secondary recession.

Kondratieff did not try to establish a new paradigm in economics. He accepted contemporary theory, then merely pointed to empirical evidence. Each of the accepted paradigms during its time had much to say for its philosophy; many continue to be accepted and acted upon today. The mercantilists (dominant from 1500 to 1750) accented accumulation of material assets (bullion) through protectionism, a policy not entirely dormant today. The Physiocrats (1750 to 1780) viewed agriculture as most important and espoused free trade. Francois Quesnay denigrated the value of service industries. Ricardo had faith in the long-run equilibrium. Adam Smith held the spotlight on laissez-faire (deregulation in contemporary terms) and on equilibrium created by prices as a stimulant to production. Keynes saw government spending and money supply control as the flexible element required to stabilize prosperity. He depended on monetary policy assisted by fiscal measures.

Kondratieff recognized all the approaches, noting especially the forces that drove the economy toward equilibrium and those that increased costs during expansion and reduced them during declines. The marginal factor in his thinking was investment in innovations.

Comment And Criticism

The response to Kondratieff's long-wave study, even if political considerations had not been a factor, would have involved deep and devastating criticism. Hardly any study presenting a new viewpoint or an economic formula would escape skeptical scrutiny from the army of economists in both the government bureaucracy and a competitive academia, particularly a paradigm tied so closely to a calendar. The climate in the Soviet hierachy was such that it was politically safer to destroy a new concept, and it was virtually self-indictment to accept a new concept by a colleague. The Soviet critics were universally more eager to demolish the Kondratieff hypothesis than to find any truth in it.

The Kondratieff conclusions, which started to have an impact on American thinking in the 1930s, found little following among contemporary economists and business analysts, most of whom had become attached to the new Keynesianism, monetarism, or some other form of econometrics that related economic development to government fiscal and monetary policies. (Actually, Kondratieff illuminated the effect of investment as an expansion stimulus.) A decade later, Kondratieff's rather modest assertions were reinformed by the more extensive work of Joseph Alois Schumpeter, Edward R. Dewey, Arthur Burns, Wesley Mitchell, Charles Clark, A. H. Hansen, Willard L. Thorp, S. DeWolff, and others, and received occasional commentary in the popular press.

The "54 year" label led to a superficial popular calendar orientation to the Kondratieff waves rather than directing attention to the dynamics. Several German analysts noted the underlying dymanics inherent in a history of sigmoid or parabolic expansions of industry and the seminal nature of some innovations.

COMTEMPORARY REACTION AT HOME

The very first presentation of the long wave left Kondratieff under attack from almost all his colleagues. He first published his theory of long cycles in 1922 in discussing economic conditions following World War I. The conclusions were stated tentatively; "We consider the long cycles in the capitalist economy only as probable." The presentation attracted considerable comment, mostly criticism of his methodology, much on political heresy, and some on empirical grounds.

This led Kondratieff to further studies in defense of his position. Other papers followed, notably an introductory paper, "On the Notion of Economic Statics, Dynamics and Fluctuations" (*Sotsalis-tickeskoe Khoziaistvo*, no. 2, 1924, pp. 349–81). This led to a revival of discussion of the long wave, both in the Soviet Union and abroad. One economic review, *Planoval Khoziaistvo*, published half a dozen analytical papers on the theory during 1925–1926, almost all unfavorable. Criticisms dealt principally with the absence of a theory explaining the dynamics of such cycles. Of the many commentaries, only two endorsed the work.

In spite of the criticism Kondratieff persisted, presenting an almost identical thesis in February 1926, filling in only a few gaps in the presentation, and extending the statistical series to include intervening years. Only one concession was made to critics: he included a section dealing with a "first attempt to give a tentative explanation of the long cycles." This aroused more criticism.

The new paper was largely ignored, but criticism of the original presentation continued. One economist, using a staff of nine assistants, presented a contravening report at the next meeting of the Economic Institute which attacked Kondratieff's sources, methods, and conclusions.

METHODOLOGY

The methodology followed by Kondratieff was open to obvious legitimate criticism. Although, with a single exception, the price and value series all revealed major swings, only 11 of 21 production and consumption series studied followed the predicted long cycles. Of the seven French physical quantity series, only two showed long cycles, and one of these (oat acreage) was an inverted cycle. There were no long cycles in wool and cotton production. Of eleven physical quantity series studied, only eight showed a cyclical pattern, and figures were available to show only one complete cycle. Only four series actually exhibited the two-and-one-half cycles hypothesized in 1920.

The four series that encompassed pre-nineteenth century activity were price cycles, a these price figures demonstrated his conclusions. In fact, however, a close examination of the production cycles reveals that rounding of the figures covers substantial deviations from the anticipated cyclical curves. Moreover, the selection of turning points appears arbitrary, some varying by 1 to 4 years from the statistical figures.

On technical grounds, the critics also attacked: (1) the logic of the composition of time series (methods of mathematical statistics had not yet been widely accepted); (2) the significance of the conclusions, especially those not related to equilibrium theory; (3) the regularity of the waves; and (4) the explanation of long-cycle generation.

Oparin and Eventov were the severest critics. They held that it was necessary to justify the use of mathematics for research in economics.

Soviet critics would not accept the time lag (20 years) between inventions and their integration into production. Several held that capital replacement, because of the variation in the lifetime of capital installations, was a continuous process. Several pointed to the time lapse required for replacing the Suez Canal or the Pacific Railway lines.

The lines of criticism were legion—and lethal.

The Apologetic Basis

Basic to the reluctance of the economic establishment to give credit to Kondratieff was what was called its "apologetic character." It described the long-wave concept as implying the existence of a continuous evolution of the capitalist economy, with long and short swings as temporary deviations from this process. If the downswing of a new long wave began in 1914–1920, the postwar situation was to be viewed in a new light. Marxist theory programmed this as a period of wars and revolution preceding disintegration of capitalism. If this was held to be a new phase of a regularly recurring long swing, the new idea was virtually treason in the Soviet Union. And in truth, bourgeois economists had confirmed the same logic.

Fellow economists in the USSR were unrelenting in their attacks. Criticism was generally based on political grounds—especially on Kondratieff's findings that the cycle, in a capitalist system, was self-correcting. This was seen as a direct contradiction of the Marxian precept that continuing declines in capitalist economy would bring about the annihilation of the system. Undoubtedly much of the venom in these attacks was motivated by personal considerations. In a bureaucratic milieu, one-upmanship is essential to advancement.

Some critics (e.g., Guberman) attributed price changes to the increase in the productivity of labor, others to increases in gold supply. Still others insisted that each step in a statistical analysis required an underlying theoretical premise. On this basis they would not accept the smoothing out of short-term and secular trends.

Other critics (W.A. Bazarov, L. Eventov, V. Bogdanov) attacked the whole mathematical methodology. "The historical evolution of capitalism," Bogdanov held, "is determined by certain external factors. These factors must be looked upon as being, to a certain extent, accidental and independent of the internal rhythm of the capitalistic economy."[1]

The significance of the results received more moderate attacks. Several economists accepted the concept of long swings but denied their cyclical character. Oparin noted that not all available time series were used and questioned their selection. He noted that Kondratieff used long waves in British lead production but ignored world production. Oparin concluded that long waves applied only to prices and interest rates. He was echoed by Granovsky and Guberman.

The Third Paper

Another opportunity to defend the theory inspired a paper presented on the "Dynamics of Industrial Agricultural Prices" (*Voprosi Konjunktury*, vol. 4, 1928, pp. 5–85). In this paper Kondratieff repeated all he had said before and added a study of long waves in two commodity groups and their relation to long swings in the economy.

In his three papers, Kondratieff used substantially the same statistical series, each (except prices and interest rates) adjusted for population changes. A trend curve of per capita data was created by the least-squares method. The curve followed a nine-year moving average to smooth out random movements, short cycles, and small deviations. Turning points were derived from the unsmoothed data, and announced as a temporary and approximate expedient, pending further studies. A study of the material proved less convincing than the smoothed summaries that had been published.

The analysis that excited the ultimate criticism and led to political exile for Kondratieff was the affirmation in his second paper that

> each consecutive phase is the result of the cumulative process during the preceding phase, and as long as the principles of the capitalist economy are conserved, each new cycle follows its predecessor with the same regularity with which the different phases succeed each other.

In other words, the cycles are self-correcting.

An especially interesting (and daring) statement, in view of then unknown cyclical swings in the economies of East European nations paralleling those in the West, was made in his first paper:

We do not have sufficient data to affirm that cyclical swings of the same character are also proper to non-capitalistic countries. If they are linked to the captilist economy, we can affirm that the collapse of capitalism will bring about the disappearance of the long waves.

Another economist, Gernzstien, claimed Kondratieff's segment of 1815–40, a period of falling prices, was merely a product of a long peace and that the Industrial Revolution caused the period of high productivity. A second period of declining prices was attributed to rapid industrialization in the United States and Germany. The decline in Britain's growth is seen as a consequence of industrialization on the continent. And the 1890–1914 price increases were attributed to decline in productivity growth, especially in agriculture.

All critics rejected the "cluster of inventions" concept as an unrealistic factor in recoveries, as well as the claim that they occurred principally in trough periods, or that they could be reconciled with lower prices.

That agricultural product prices declined during depressions was generally accepted, but critics found a common cause in denying the difficulties in meeting interest and mortgage payments contracted during periods of higher prices.

Underlying all the criticisms was an objection to the regularity of long waves, especially their periodicity. Critics noted that successive phases varied not only in quantity but also in quality. Trotsky, who had taken a keen interest in long-swing theories even before the Kondratieff papers, concluded that these swings were due to concrete, unique, political and economic circumstances:

> The historical evolution of capitalism is determined by certain external factors. These factors must be looked upon as being, to a certain extent, accidental and independent of the internal rhythm of the capitalistic economy.
>
> As for those large phases of the trend of the capitalist evolution (of 50 years) for which Professor Kondratieff incautiously suggests use of the term "cycles," we must stress that their character and duration are determined not by the internal dynamics of the capitalist economy, but by the external conditions which constitute the framework of capitalist evolution.
>
> A cycle means fluctuations within the framework of a fundamentally unchanged system, whereas in the case we are considering, each new wave of technical change results in the shifting of the economic system to a new, qualitatively different stage of organization and technique, with a resulting number of important social-economic changes. The waves of technical progress must be interpreted, not as cycles, but as phases of a reversible historical process of the development of a productive force which proceeds by jolts and is accompanied by crises.[2]

Others returned to stressing the Marxist concept of the evolutionary character of changes in the capitalist economy from semi-feudalism to monopoly, involving different rates of growth.

Marx had earlier noted the cyclical nature of capitalism and proposed that cycles were caused by periodic reinvestment of fixed capital after 10-year life spans. Kondratieff both expanded the time span and noted the varation in durability of different kinds of capital goods, particularly in the "big plants, important railways, canals, large land improvement projects, etc.—[and] the training of skilled labor."

With regard to causation of long cycles, critics perceived that regeneration resulting from endogenous forces was contra-Marxian. This generated accusations that Kondratieff was attempting to develop a super-Marxian view of history and thus a subversive dogma. On this point he was attacked by Bogdanov and Svetlov. They insisted, as others had, that swings in economic life had exogenous causes.

It was not long after the third paper that Kondratieff was removed from his position in charge of the Conjuncture Institute, and his theories were officially denigrated in the next Soviet Russian Encyclopedia in six words, "This theory is wrong and reactionary."

The Official View

The Soviet encyclopedia published some years later clearly condemned the "Theory of Long Cycles" in all its editions:

Theory of Long Cycles, one of the vulgar bourgeois theories of crises and economic cycles. It was first formulated in the 1930s by the Russian economist, N.D. Kondratiev. In bourgeois economic literature long cycles are usually called "Kondratiev cycles." The theory was further developed in the works of C. Clark (England); W. Mitchell, A. Burns, and their supporters from the National Bureau of Economic Research (United States); and F. Simiand (France), among others. The essence of the theory of long cycles is the assertion that there supposedly exist "long cycles" (50 to 60 years), which are characterized by an alternation of increasing and declining economic activity. The cycle consists of the "capital starvation" and "capital saturation" phases. During the first period there is a rise in the rate and scale of new construction, an increase in employment in the manufacturing industry and service spheres, a maintenance of the employment level in agriculture, an elimination of chronic unemployment, an increase in the export of capital, a rise in investments into nations and sectors which are the suppliers of mineral and agricultural raw materials, a rise in loan interest rates, and so forth.[3]

The offical description then goes on to explain the cyclical trough as a phase of weak investment demand replaced by a capital saturation phase lasting 25 to 30 years, during which manpower shifts from producing raw materials into manufacturing, with services declining, capital exports falling, and interest rates dropping. The official analysis cites fluctuations in commodity prices as the chief explanation offered by proponents of the theory. Two long cycles are recognized, from 1850 to 1900 and from 1900 to 1940. A third is seen as beginning in 1945 with an economic crisis of overproduction (basic to the Marxian philosophy) diffused in the fluctuations of the long wave. The Soviet view is that

> The concept of the long cycle in theory is directed against the basic Marxist thesis concerning the inevitability of economic crises under capitalism, and that it conceals the unsolvable contradictions of capitalist society.

Regarding Western opinion, the article continues:

> After World War II, its theses have been shaped by a number of bourgeois economists and used by them for forecasting the development of the capitalist economy.

Several Soviet references are offered. Western sources mentioned are A. Clark (*The Economics of 1960*), Arthur F. Burns (*Prediction, Trends of the United States since 1870*), and the National Bureau of Economics (*Potentials of the United States in the Next Decade*, New York: 1965).

IN THE WEST

Some years later, Western economists gave considerably more acceptance as well as negative criticism to Kondratieff's studies. But Harvard professor Joseph Schumpeter provided an affirmation with a massive book, *Business Cycles*.

Wesley Claus Mitchell a few years later acknowledged the empirical evidence, but deplored the lack of an explanation. Ernest Wageman accepted the evidence of long waves in the volume of money in Germany and suggested wars, gold supply, and colonization as possible explanations. A. G. Hansen (*The Business Depression of Nineteen Hundred Thirty: a Discussion in American Economic Review*) attributed the Great Depression to the Kondratieff long wave. In the same issue, Willard L. Thorp accepted and summarized Schumpeter's analysis.

George Garvy

One of the earliest translators and non-Russian critics of Kondratieff was George Garvy, chief of the domestic research division of the Federal Reserve Bank of New York. Born in Riga in 1913, he was educated at the University of Berlin, the University of Paris, and Columbia, and was fluent in Russian. The Kondratieff study was his doctoral thesis. In it he pointed out that only 11 of 21 series Kondratieff studied were used to reach his conclusions. He then recited the litany of Soviet criticisms. He reported:

> Does the evidence presented by Kondratieff support his hypothesis with sufficient strength: The Russian economists unanimously and emphatically answered his question in the negative.

Garvy's exhaustive analysis, "Kondratieff's Theory of Long Cycles" appeared in November 1943. In this work he is particularly critical of Kondratieff's statistical work and the arbitrary manner of selecting turning points.

But he noted that most of the Russian critics were more eager to demolish Kondratieff's theoretical explanation of the long cycles than to find any truth in it:

> The theory offered by Kondratieff to explain the cyclical recurrence of long cycles has no empirical foundation. He did not show that investment of "basic capital goods" clustered around time points, separated by periods of from 48 to 60 years. As Bogdanov and Gernzstien pointed out, the process of reinvestment is an economic and not a purely technical one . . . even if the investment process, which depends not only on actual wear and tear but also on the obsolescence rate, the cost of maintenance, interest rates, wages, technical progress, and rate of operation, would be continuous.

He added:

> Although the hypothesis of cyclical swings of long duration, upon which shorter cyclical movements are superimposed, should be discarded, the view that the capitalist economy has passed through several successive stages of development characterized by different rates of growth and geographical expansion deserves attention.[4]

Joseph Schumpeter

The major support for Kondratieff's ideas came from Joseph Alois Schumpeter (1883–1950), a professor at Harvard University (1932–1950), at the University of Bonn (1925–1932), and one time Minister of Finance of Austria (1919–1920). Known as a great teacher and historian of economics, he traced the economies of the United States, England, and Germany in terms of Kitchin, Juglar, and Kondratieff fluctuations in a two-volume masterwork, *Business Cycles,* published in 1939. He used a sharply detailed record of the economies of the United States, England, and Germany to provide empirical support for three long waves from 1889 to 1937 (which we here have attempted to replicate).

Schumpeter developed this theory of business cycles around Kondratieff from models made up of five or six Juglars, each of 9 to 10 years, and several non-coordinate shorter-term Kitchin cycles. The same elements that were involved in these cycles (changing interest rates, changing levels of prosperity) and the industrial evolution that causes people to change their dwellings are involved in the long waves. He found that this pattern did not always exist, but in each instance, where it did not exist, some special factors intervened. Later studies by Burns and Mitchell found that the short cycles varied greatly in duration.

Schumpeter viewed the entrepreneurial frontiersman as the dynamic influence on the economy, who "incessantly revolutionized the economic structure from within, incessantly destroying the old one, incessantly creating a new one. The process of Creative Destruction is the essential fact about capitalism." This process necessarily created crises, booms, and recessions, ultimately expressed for him in the Kondratieff waves.

Although Schumpeter recognized that actually there were an indefinite number of cyclical movements in continuous operation, he selected three waves to be studied for the component periods. Five periods, he said, would have been better but would have unduly encumbered the voluminous work. And even more might have been selected to scrutinize the suspicious implications of the new theory than to analyze critically the evidence presented. He goes on:

> The principal points discussed by Kondratieff's Russian critics on the following matters are:
> 1. The logic of the decomposition of time series, particularly the implications of the elimination of the trend.
> 2. The significance of the results of Kondratieff's investigation.
> 3. The regularity of long waves.
> 4. The hypothesis advanced by Kondratieff to explain the generation of the long cycles.[5]

And he adds his own assertions:

> Our analysis shows that the existence of long swings could not be proved by the production series studied by Kondratieff; that data for all major capitalistic countries and the two series with worldwide coverage pertain only to one cycle; that, consequently, neither the international character of the phenomenon nor its recurrence at regular time intervals can be ascertained from the material presented. The theory offered by

Kondratieff to explain the cyclical recurrence of long cycles has no empirical foundation. He did not show that investment of basic capital goods clustered around time points, by periods of from 48 to 60 years.

However, he did find and identify the long waves. He dated his waves trough to trough from 1789 to 1843, with a peak in 1814; 1843 through 1896, with a peak in 1864; 1896 to 1949, with a peak in 1920.

In his analysis Schumpeter identified major innovations and crises, noting the Industrial Revolution, the age of steam and steel, and the age of electricity, chemistry, and motors. For each Juglar (and some of the Kitchins) he identified the causal factors of upswings and declines.

Schumpeter's monumental work received mixed reviews. It was almost immediately eclipsed by the attention then being given to Keynes' general theory, which had been published a few years before in Britain and was rapidly becoming the accepted paradigm of the 1930s.

Edward Dewey And Edwin Dakin

In 1939 Edward Dewey and Edwin Dakin found that "the underlying 54-year rhythm in wholesale prices is on the decline. It turned in 1925; the pattern is due to reach bottom in 1952."[8]

Actual peaks in prices (which they relied on for definition) occurred in 1921.

This much deserves to be said: The resources of modern mathematics in the hands of our eminent mathematicians today are quite ample to demonstrate the possibility that random shock does account for our economic rhythms. But such a demonstration as to possibility is still far from final evidence that such shock, responded to with rhythm, is indeed the underlying cause of rhythmic economic fluctuations. There is no reason why it should not be accepted as a hypothesis by those who find it helpful. But in embracing it they should realize that, until we know considerably more than we do today, they are engaging in an act of faith.

Further, there are two characteristics of our economic rhythms that this theory apparently does not explain. First, it fails to tell us why, after a distortion, the rhythms snap back into phase with the old established pattern, as has been observed frequently. Second, it fails to account for the correspondence between so many of the economic and the "natural" rhythms.

Kondratieff too found that causes usually assumed for our rhythms reverse the causal connections, and take the consequence to be the cause, or see an accident where we really have to deal with a law governing the events. Sometimes improvements in technique have been alleged as a cause of a new Kondratieff; it would be a great error if one believed the inventions and intensity of those discoveries and inventions were merely accidental. . . . The development of technique itself is merely part of the long waves.

Edwin Frickey

Empirical research carried on by Edwin Frickey in 1942 on a grant from Harvard University carries the footnote:

> We must call attention (as we have several times previously) to the fact that the results so far obtained are at least consistent with the Kondratieff hypothesis.

The text notes:

> While our time period of analysis is (as we have previously indicated) too short to afford any decisive test of the Kondratieff long-wave hypothesis, we may nevertheless note in passing that the showing of the trend indication lines of Chart 27, and especially the behavior of these lines around the turn of the century, is at least consistent with this hypothesis. The upward movement of Kondratieff's third wave is scheduled as beginning around 1890–96 and the array of evidence upon this chart can be made to fit into his statistical scheme. In fact, if, in accordance with Kondratieff's practice of employing arithmetic-scale charts, we redraw the trend-indications of Chart 27 upon a new diagram, with arithmetic vertical scales—as in Chart 36—conformity to the general statistical scheme of Kondratieff appears. (Compare these graphic series with his curves in the *Review of Economic Statistics* for November 1935, pages 105–115). Since we have yet to develop evidence sufficiently cogent to justify our taking a stand, we are obliged (as we have earlier said) to assume an agnostic position with reference to the Kondratieff hypothesis. For the time being, we content ourselves with presenting such pertinent evidence as we may incidentally have obtained, and letting it speak for itself.

And again:

> Once more, it is necessary to say that with a more extended temporal and geographical basis of investigation the long-run tendencies might quite conceivably turn out to the manifestations of very long wave movements. Palpably, the long-run tendencies that we have observed—particularly the shift of mutual position in the link-relative chart just before the turn of the century—would fit into the Kondratieff system.[7]

Jay W. Forrester

Some economists saw the long wave in terms of overinvestment, which were similar to those of inventory cycles, overlooking the basic changes involved. Jay W. Forrester, Germeshausen Professor at the Alfred Sloan School of Management at the Massachusetts Institute of Technology, puts it this way:

> The long wave involves an overbuilding of the capital sectors in which they grow beyond the capital output rate needed for long-term

equilibrium. Capital plant throughout an economy is overbuilt beyond the level justified by the marginal productivity of capital. Finally, the over-expansion is ended by the hiatus of a great depression during which excess capital plant is physically worn out and is financially depreciated on the account books until the economic stage has been cleared for a new era of rebuilding.

Behavior of the long wave can be understood by recalling the last 50 years. During the depression of the 1930s and during World War II, there was very little new construction of capital plant. By 1945, physical capital at all levels had been depleted, in some countries by age alone, in other countries also by war damage. Consumers needed housing and durables. Industry needed school systems and highways. So a great rebuilding began. Capital sectors drew labor from consumer sectors, thereby producing a tight labor supply and still more incentive for consumer sectors to become capital intensive. Demand for capital was self-reinforcing; in order to expand, capital sectors themselves required new capital plant, thus creating further demand on capital sectors. A long, powerful regenerative process drove the expansion of the capital sectors.[8]

The Forrester approach is an application of the classic cyclical theory, holding that adjustments are created by oversupply and under-supply. The reality of the 1980s shows that the problems of mature industries like steel resulted from the failure to provide capital to encompass technological changes, and that in the automobile industry resulted from a reluctance to invest in new tooling to recreate a product competitive with those offered by Germany and Japan.

W. W. Rostow

"Most contemporary economists remember having run across this name [Kondratieff] and ideas in graduate school but have forgotten precisely what it was he said," W. W. Rostow writes.

He believed Kondratieff cycles were "caused primarily by periodic undershooting and overshooting of the dynamic optimum levels of capacity and output for food and raw materials in the world economy."[9]

In his own evaluation of four decades of commentary, he saw optimum levels attained "in a continuous dynamic equilibrium where capacity was smoothly adjusted to rates of increase in population and income." But deviations from optimum capacity he sees caused by a recognition lag in decision making, a gestation lag in establishing an infrastructure, and an exploitation lag in attaining efficient production and marketing. Rostow created a formal Kondratieff model of 16 equations of production function, input–output relation, factor availability, and income formation and disposal. He adapted the Kondratieff chronology of trough to peak to trough noted in Chapter 2, but holds that the cycles did not unfold smoothly because of wars.

In *Getting From Here to There*, Rostow examines the Kondratieff cycles principally in terms of the rise in world population and the relatively slower expansion of food supply. Written in 1978, soon after the Club of Rome's *Limits to Growth*, and the trauma of OPEC, it notes that "a pattern of economic and social progress which has persisted for almost a quarter century was broken" in the first half of the 1970s, and suggests a program for survival in a world falling into Malthusian disproportions during the fifth Kondratieff wave. He sees a relative imbalance in the prices of food and raw materials on one hand and industrial products on the other.

Gerhard Mensch

Gerhard Mensch, a leader in the Kondratieff revival in the early 1970s followed the Schumpeter line that credited innovation as the stimulus of a long-wave upswing. He sought to fill gaps in the massive Schumpeter analyses of what constituted an innovation. Mensch denied that the cyclical changes were a "deterministic recurrence of phase transition" and suggested that "the metamorphosis model of cycles of structure" changes through a series of intermittent innovative impulses that take the form of successive S-shaped cycles.[10] He distinguishes among innovations, accepting that they occur in clusters, creating new growth industries that stimulate economic growth. His metamorphosis model is the basic sigmoid curve or the product cycle.

Lloyd M. Valentine And Carl A. Dauten

Contemporary economists have been more reluctant to accept the long wave in recent years. Faced with empirical evidence they reason that the cycle in prices is not necessarily related to production. In a recent edition of *Business Cycles and Forecasting*, Lloyd M. Valentine and Carl A. Dauten comment:

> The theory of long waves has not been generally accepted by economists. Economic data expressed in money terms do show fluctuations that correspond in a general way to Kondratieff's long waves. This relationship is due to the inflation that occurs during major wars, but that does not mean that these were true waves in economic activity. There is no statistical evidence in production series in the United States of any long wave fluctuations of 50 to 60 years.
>
> A study of prices for the last 200 years shows wide fluctuations, which have at times been described as price cycles. To the extent that such cycles exist, they are primarily related to fluctuations in prices that have occurred as the result of inflationary policies during major wars. If wars are considered as political factors impinging upon the economy,

then these are not cycles in the same sense as other economic cycles. To those students of our economy, such as Karl Marx and N. D. Kondratieff, who believed that wars are an integral part of the capitalistic process, such cycles would, of course, be true economic cycles. These long-run price movements have also been influenced by major discoveries of gold as, for example, in the period after 1896. They may also have been influenced to some degree by increased demand resulting from major innovations, such as the railroads and the automobile.

In the United States prices rose to high levels during the Revolutionary War and then declined after the end of the war. They fluctuated more or less in harmony with the business cycle until the War of 1812, when the again reached high levels as a result of wartime inflationary finance.[11]

Arthur F. Burns And Wesley C. Mitchell

Arthur F. Burns and Wesley C. Mitchell make no evaluation. But they describe the Kondratieff approach in skeptical detail:

For many years, monetary writers have affirmed the existence of long waves in wholesale prices. The waves are supposed to last fifty to sixty years—a much longer period than is found in building construction, or in general economic activity according to Wardwell, Kuznets or Burns. The long waves in prices have usually been explained by accidental discoveries of gold deposits, improvements in gold refining, wars, and changes in the world's monetary systems. Kondratieff presents the more daring hypothesis that the long waves in wholesale prices are an organic part of a long cycle characteristic of capitalism. Kondratieff's statistical investigations cover the leading industrial countries of the world; they are based mainly on value series, but include also small samples of physical volume series.

Since 1799 there are only two complete long waves and an undetermined fraction of a third. Few series in our entire collection and none of the present sample go back so far. The longest series in our sample starts in 1857, while the monthly reference dates of business cycles in different countries start between 1854 and 1879. Under the circumstances it is impossible at present to come to serious grips with the problem whether business cycles tend to move in cycles within Kondratieff's periods.[12]

Burns at another point brushes off the Kondratieff approach: "Long waves of about fifty years—usually called Kondratieff cycles—have also been alleged to characterize aggregate economic activity of Western nations. The existence of these waves, while suggested by price movements, has not yet been established."[13]

Simon Kuznets

Later attacks on the Kondratieff wave were again based on: inadequate statistical evidence, inadequate explanation of causes, and the noncyclical nature of the changes.

A prime critic was Professor Simon Kuznets, whose 15- to 22-year investment cycles have been almost universally accepted in economic literature. He maintained that to establish the existence of cycles of a given type requires first a demonstration that fluctuations of the approximate duration recur with fair simultaneity, in the movements of various significant aspects of economic life (production and employment in various industries, prices of various groups of goods, interest rates, volumes of trade, flow of credit, etc.), and second, an indication of what external factors or peculiarities of the economic system properly account for such recurrent fluctuations. Unless the former basis is laid, the cyclical nature cannot be accepted as affecting economic life at large, although it may be specific to a limited part of the country's economic system. Unless the second theoretical basis is established there is no link that connects findings relating to empirical observations of a given type of cycle in a country over a particular period of time with the broader realm of already established knowledge. He found that neither of these bases had ever been satisfactorily laid for the Kondratieff cycles.

> Kondratieff's own statistical analysis refers largely to price indexes, interest rates, or volumes of activity in current prices—series necessarily dominated by the price peaks of the Napoleonic wars, the wars of the 1870s (not unconnected with the Civil War in this country), and the World War. The prevalence of such fifty-year cycles in volumes of production, either total or for important branches of activity, in employment, in physical volume of trade, has not been demonstrated; nor has the presumed existence of these cycles been reconciled with those of a duration from 18 to 25 years established for a number of production series in this and other countries. Nor has a satisfactory theory been advanced as to why these 50-year swings should recur: the explanations tend to emphasize external factors (inventions, wars, etc.) without demonstrating their cyclical character in their tendency to recur as a result of an underlying mechanism or as effects of another group of external factors of proven "cyclicity."[14]

Table 3.1. Kuznets Model Of Kondratieff Cycles

Prosperity	Recession	Depression	Revival
Industrial Revolution Kondratieff, 1787–1842: Cotton textiles, iron, steam power			
1787–1800	1801–1813	1814–1827	1828–1842
Bourgeois Kondratieff, 1842–1897: Railroadization			
1843–1858	1858–1869	1870–1884-5	1886–1897
Neo-mercantilist Kondratieff, 1897 to date: Electricity, automobile			
1898–1911	1912–1924-5		1925-6–1939

Nevertheless, Kuznets created a model of Kondratieff cycles (Table 3.1). Dates of the first and second cycle are based on events in Great Britain; the third is based on the U.S. experience. The specific dates for the three countries are somewhat different, but the differences are likely to be minor. Professor Schumpeter thought that the first Kondratieff cycle periodicity is not clearly shown in Germany.

Like other critics, Kuznets found that the concept that innovations come in clusters was a prime source of skepticism from its first announcement. The idea that obsolescence overtakes most capital about the same time, during the fiftieth year, appeared to be a distortion of the biblical Sabbatical Year. However, the idea that innovations enter the economy as a group had more logic, he thought, insofar as (1) the cost factors are more favorable in trough periods; (2) periods of prosperity are periods when ideas of "leave well enough alone" predominate; (3) periods of stress drive entrepreneurs to seek new sources of profit.

E. Rothbart

Another analyst, E. Rothbart, notes: "the decline of profits sharpens the wits of the old firms" (a major technological breakthrough suggests other avenues of change or improvement).[15] Thus the steam engine spawned a host of devices that could use it, the railroads opened new lands for development, automobiles changed the nature of spending, and electronics became the basis of many new industries.

Suggestions that cycles were to be regarded as self-generating were accepted with much misgiving by most other commentators.

Alvin H. Hansen

Alvin H. Hansen viewed the elements of economic progress as threefold: inventions, the opening of new territories and new resources, and the growth of population.[16] This led him to a pessimistic forecast. He felt that the dynamic of the long wave exists within itself and can be tied to its own and many other cyclical factors, including (but not exclusively) the cycle of birthrates, a cycle in tensions, the emergence of competition from new sources, the rise in expectations, and so on.

Dick Stoken

Other economists deal with the Kondratieff approach in less depth, relegating his work to a footnote. Dick Stoken comments:

We are victims of a 54-year cycle of economic activity which goes from bust to boom to bust again.

In a world that believes in reason and the inevitability of progress such explanations are seen as a throwback to more primitive times.

And the cycles that we do acknowledge, such as the traditional four-year business cycle, are taken to be an aberration that we have not yet learned to control.[17]

Paul Samuelson

Paul Samuelson, Nobel laureate economist, whose *Economics* is a basic text in contemporary teaching, reduces the four phases of the business cycle simply to recession and trough:

> Kuznets cycles should not be confused with alleged *very long waves*—the so-called Kondrateff cycles—whose complete cycle length is about half a century. Whether these long waves are simply historical accidents due to chance gold discoveries, inventions and political wars, it is still too soon to say. The reader may be referred to J. A. Schumpeter, *Business Cycles*, when long cycles are called Kondratieff's after their Russian discoverer.[18]

THE MACROECONOMIC APPROACH

A problem involved with the construction of models of the Kondratieff wave, basic to the utilization of macroeconomics, is that much data falls outside the confines of the standard models, which would increase the complexity and probability of error. In the complex ecology of today's economies, it is impossible to encompass the infinite variety of elements that affect it. Richard V. Clemence and Francis S. Doody put it this way:

> To the historian it must doubtless seem that the theorist is altogether too eager to force the facts into a mold, and too ready to throw away any that cannot be jammed in.[19]

The traditional restraints on investment and the traditional interest costs (which are lower during trough periods) plus the availability of capital (savings) are offset in modern times by the capacity of the Federal Reserve Board to create credit by manipulating money supply and thus the interest rate, and the rapid marketability of new products and processes.

Some concepts of innovations are limited to the term of the introduction of a new good; others to cost-lowering devices; some to inventions; and still others (including Schumpeter's) to all profit-motivated activities. All of these play a part in stimulating business activity (total spending).

Notwithstanding the criticisms, almost all the commentaries acknowledge that long waves exist in prices and other time series influenced by prices. They fail to find similar long waves in other series, and go on to discredit the wave theory. Some (notably Burns and Mitchell) contend that the price cycle is an "optical illusion," noting long periods (1825–1860) of stable prices and little fluctuation in other series not synchronous with any long wave.

T. S. Forrester

T. S. Forrester created large, long-term simulation models that take into consideration social and psychological factors.[20] His studies, including industrial, urban, and world dynamics, led to the Club of Rome report on *Limits of Growth*. His 15 industrial sector models are able to generate Konratieff cycles, sometimes with only consumer goods and capital goods elements.

James B. Schuman And David Rosenau

James B. Schuman and David Rosenau wrote a popular volume about the Kondratieff theory in 1972, making a prediction of a cyclical downturn in industry and the reversal of inflation (then seemingly a very remote possibility). They recite in broad terms the paths of three cycles since 1780 and predict the course of the economy for decades ahead.

It may seem that the long wave in prices has gone undetected. Actually, this is not the case. Proponents of the theory, however, have been ignored. But the facts pointing to the existence of the long wave are too consistent, the results too vivid to ignore. Professional economists have rejected the long-wave theory out of hand, probably because they have felt it is not scientific. Yet the accumulated evidence of more than 150 years, as the following chapters will prove, is too consistent to ignore.

In the ten years to come America will be a very different place than it has been for a long time: it will be in the middle of the one decade in five when there is high prosperity, full employment, no inflation, and peace and prosperity.[21]

They traced social, political, and economic patterns in cycles averaging 52 years. In a September 27, 1982 interview with Richard Widows of *Media General Financial Weekly*, they went on to predict a stock market crash by the end of the 1970s, followed by a depression in the early 1980s. The reporter compared their forcasts with those of Charles Hoskins, sometime editor of *Forbes*, writing in the 1930s: "The beginnings and ends of most important cycles in American business have been influenced by the major harmonics of 52 years." A few years later it appeared that they had been correct. But Keynesian devices intervened.

Julian Snyder

A small group of publishers of hard-money newsletters, as well as a number of chronic pessimists among the forecasters, have made much of the Kondratieff projections.

One enthusiast is Julian Snyder, who publishes *Money Line,* a newsletter tuned to cyclical trends, emphasizing money supply, gold, and silver prices. An associated firm published a translation of the Kondratieff papers in 1984 that is used in this study. In the introduction, Snyder notes:

Chronological calculation puts us on the plateau period of the long wave. This is a period when business is fundamentally tired, credit is over-extended and economic activity is sluggish. On the other hand, this underlying slowdown reduces the forces of inflation and makes it possible for a while for people to have their cake and eat it too, that is, to create purchasing power artificially without causing inflationary overheating. The phenomenon is similar to stepping on the gas in your automobile when the car is going down a hill; you get more speed without burning up quite as much energy. In economic terms, this slowing down provides an opportunity for financial liquidity to build up somewhat and pour into the few remaining healthy areas of the economy or into wild speculative ventures. Because the rate of inflation is declining, people begin to think that this problem has been solved and because they still have money in their pockets, they become suddenly optimistic and then finally euphoric. Maybe the scientists were right after all. Maybe the central bankers and economic planners have finally found the formula for defeating the cycles of nature and producing an endless prosperity. When this mood takes hold, as it did in 1929, the secondary depression of the long wave is not far off. However, it is the work of Forrester and his associates over the past couple of years which has removed some of the mystique from theories of the long wave and provided pragmatic proof of what is taking place. In simple terms, the economy of the world is like an old man searching for the fountain of youth. Overextended, and burned out, it no longer responds to the dominant theory of business cycles held by most governments and financial institutions.[22]

Eric von Baranov

Another Kondratieff devotee is Eric von Baranov, who published *K. Wave,* a "market-timing service based on the Kondratieff theory." His description is presented in this way:

He [Kondratieff] believed the interaction of current events produces a repetitive pattern over a long period of time. His theories interrelate economics and politics, taking into consideration such things as war, discoveries, public opinion, and weather as intergral parts of a long-term economic life cycle. Within a capitalistic society, Kondratieff proposed that economic trends tend to repeat themselves approximately every 54 years. This alternating of the "long wave" from prosperity to depression, complemented by many shorter cycles, leads a dynamic trend to the economy that to a large degree becomes predictable.

Kondratieff integrated the normal public reactions into the web of economic change, accepting social psychological force as part of the determinants of economic change. He held that people react differently during economic periods that are different, each pattern laying the groundwork for the pattern following. He sought and found changing environmental and demographic factors affecting the economic scene in a cyclical way, beyond merely a historical repetition.

At least one well-known market analyst, Robert R. Prechter, Jr., a Canadian accountant and attorney, bases his forecasts on the principles of the Kondratieff wave. He sees the long wave reflected in stock price movements of five irregular waves—three bull movements with two intervening bear movements.[23]

Most critics accept the more obvious 50- to 60-year cycle as it applies to wholesale prices, but strongly question a similar cycle applied to production or growth. The regularity of production cycles is obviously more difficult to sustain, in part because of the absence of a long and accurate system of measurement (most industries expire within half a century) and the difficulty of measuring total product. Wholesale prices, which are specific, and widely recorded over a long period of time, and essentially follow the pattern of the economy, provide a steadier measure, although they tend to lag or precede other time series in the cycle.

The Anatomy Of Four Waves

The Kondratieff hypothesis was based on empirical evidence rather than logical deduction. The causes of long waves, their regularity, even their existence was questioned (and still is) because no thread could be found that would satisfy the dominant paradigms of economics academia.

Kondratieff's discussions of causes were afterthoughts, a groping for forces that would satisfy the demands of his critics. The explanation that expansion and contraction of economies were the result of simultaneous innovation and obsolescence was open to question.

If we are to rely on empirical evidence, it is only logical that we examine more closely the anatomy of the four long waves in the United States history: the cycles, the expansions and contractions, the troughs and peaks, the euphorias and crises and panics, the declines and recoveries, and even more important, the analogies. We seek to find the threads common to each, the validity of past appraisals and contemporary forecasts, perhaps to illuminate the dynamics of the rise and fall of prosperity (Fig. 4.1).

For this reason, we provide this hindsight of the long waves and the short cycles that embroider them with their mitigating and accenting pressures. If hindsight can give us the perception necessary to replace dogma with new initiative, we can perhaps provide measures to avoid those dynamics that created the depressions of the past with their waste, their periods of misery, and apocalyptic effects.

Although the economic theories that preceded him were inherent in Kondratieff's thinking, the general theory and monetarism were not widely understood or accepted by contemporary analysts of economic cycles. Government budget deficits were sometimes utilized, but these were much deplored by statesmen and the public. Inflation on the scale we know it today was equated with bankruptcy (as in postwar Germany

Figure 4.1. Four Kondratieff Waves, Inflation Reflected

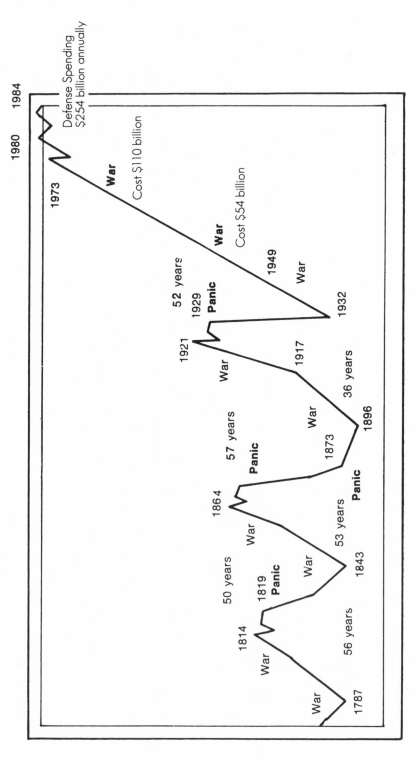

in 1921), but later economists thought a continuous expansion was possible, with a gradual inflation as the price to pay.

Kondratieff examined interest rates as an indicator of the cycles, and used it as one of the pillars on which his hypothesis stood. In this closer view we might conclude that monetary pressures were more likely to be causes, or at least stimulants, to expansions, and monetary retrenchment the cause of contractions. They were certainly the triggers that set panics in motion.

We examine here the anatomy of each cycle, evaluating those forces we can determine, including federal deficit spending, monetary expansion, investment, innovations, foreign influences, and the indentifiable Juglar and Kitchin cycles. We seek to avoid a tunnel approach to Kondratieff's conclusions (as he or his critics saw them) or as they fit into paradigms accepted before and after.

And we seek to find and record parallels of economic situations, the conditions that existed during each of these periods preceding, during, and after each trough, peak, and turning point. We hope thereby to better understand what really happened in each period, to illuminate the present, and to foretell the future.

A similar, even more detailed survey included in a classic text in 1939 (*Business Cycles* by Schumpeter) is a pre-Keynesian approach. Schumpeter identified not only the Kondratieff long waves, but also most of the intervening Juglar and Kitchin cycles, a pattern we have attempted to follow in part.

Half a century later, having seen the effects of applied Keynesian economics, macroeconomics, monetarism, supply-side economics, and the wisdom of economic advisors to presidents,* after several wars and an exponential explosion of technology, and with the understanding these events have provided, we take a new look (noting the factors involved in each philosphy) at four Kondratieff waves (trough and peak to trough): 1789–1814–1843, 1843–1864–1896, 1896–1920–1949, 1949–1973–2003 (?), or as they were adapted by some analysts.

We find that Kondratieff's approach had some elements of Keynes in that both appreciated that the essence of expansion of the economy was the stimulation of spending, and that spending was a key to expansion. Kondratieff found the motivation in innovation; Keynes in government deficit spending. Friedman found it in easy money.

In general, we have accepted the premise that the major expansions are ignited by diffusion of major innovations, not only inventions but also other changes that stimulate substantial increases in the spending pattern (particularly for investment in the production of new goods or

---

*Seven members of President Carter's cabinet of 13 held doctorates in economics.

Table 4.1. Purchasing Power Of The Dollar, 1800–1985

1800	.80	1916	.95	1957	.45
1810	.76	1917	.69	1958	52.1
1820	1.06	1918	.62	1960	51.7
1830	1.24	1919	.59	1965	45.6
1840	1.14	1920	.53	1967	45.0
1850	1.31	1925	.79	1970	38.7
1860	1.30	1930	.94	1975	27.9
1865	.62	1931	1.12	1976	26.4
1870	.94	1932	1.26	1977	24.9
1875	1.05	1933	1.24	1978	23.0
1880	1.25	1934	1.09	1979	20.7
1885	1.44	1935	1.02	1980	18.2
1890	1.45	1937	.94	1981	17.0
1895	1.67	1940	1.04	1982	15.91
1900	1.45	1941	.93	1983	15.34
1905	1.35	1945	.77	1984	14.91
1910	1.15	1950	.51	1985	14.31
1915	1.17	1955	.48		

Similar changes occurred in other nations.

Source: Research Council, American Bankers Association for Bureau of Labor Statistics.

services). The effect of wars and postwar adjustments on production, spending, and prosperity is duly noted. In terms of innovation, these may be seen as:

1789–1843   Use of steam power and the Industrial Revolution
1844–1896   The age of coal and steam
1897–1949   The age of electricity, chemicals, and motor vehicles
1949–1974   The age of plastics and electronics
1974–1984   The age of nuclear energy, aerospace, computers, and robots

We have tried particularly to identify the symptoms of the ending of an expansion. It is not difficult in hindsight to identify the innovations that created the expansion, the maturation plateau, and the dramatic drop when investment failed to continue the expansion. In most situations we found that a "ready" economy is pushed into a panic by some monetary contraction and a confidence crisis.

We have found, too, that forces from abroad have often affected the U.S. economy. These interacted particularly in creating monetary, military, demographic, and psychological pressures, influencing the economic scene in the United States and triggering marginal monetary forces.

We thus take a rapid telescopic view of cycles, short and long, in the U.S. economy over two centuries and four Kondratieff cycles to appraise these forces in detail as dynamics of the long wave and (not incidentally) examine them as a source of similarities to recent, present, and anticipated events in the economy. We always bear in mind, of course, George Santayana's aphorism, "Those who cannot remember the past are condemned to repeat it."

Because money values at different periods have little contemporary reality, we present a table to provide a basis by which to estimate values of the dollar of other times. (There was a time when a million dollars was a lot of money.) For most purposes, a million dollars in 1920 was the equivalent of a billion dollars in 1985 (Table 4.1).

The First Wave:
1789–1814–1843

The three decades from 1762 to 1789 decidedly were marked by recurrent and predominant economic depression—and they in turn mark what is probably the decisive turning point in the modern history of humanity.[1]

Andre Gunder Frank, *World Accumulation 1491–1789*

PRELUDE

Schumpeter, in providing his exhaustive analysis of the "long cycle or Kondratieff Cycles," notes that the first cycle analyzed "was not the first of its kind." Similar cycles have been traced to year 1250. He points out, however, that it was the first in the Americas and the first to provide a reasonably clear statistical description (Fig. 5.1).

This cycle was intimately tied to the Industrial Revolution. That phenomenon was not something that burst on the world unconnected to other events, nor was it a unique series of events that created a new economic or social order. For this reason it is not possible to say that the Industrial Revolution began in 1700 (Usher) or in 1770–1840 (Cunningham), nor in the second quarter of the nineteenth century (Tugen-Baranovskiy, Spielhof). Even prior to 1770 the seeds were laid, and the beginnings had emerged. The innovations that stimulated the cycles that began in the 1780s and the 1790s were long in preparation, although they did not exist in economic quantities sufficient to stimulate a major movement in prices until 1790.

U.S. economic history begins in 1775, when the nation was in an economic depression, blamed at the time on the mother country, particularly under the administration of George III.

Until 1750 British rule had imposed no real hardships on the American economy. It provided basic cost-free protection against powerful antagonistic French and Spanish forces on the new continent. The

Figure 5.1. The First Wave: 1789–1814–1843

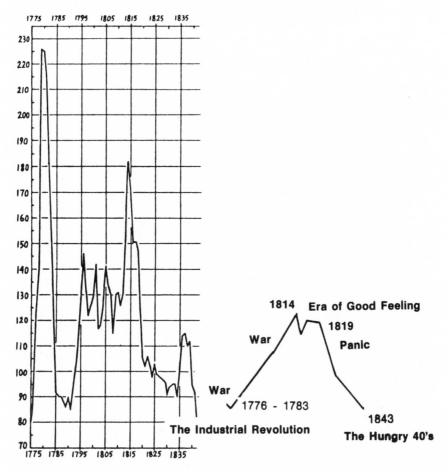

Warren and Pearson Wholesale Price Index for all commodities (1910–1914 = 100).

colonists were heard on trade regulation and other economic matters, and whatever laws were applied were enforced at the discretion of colonial judges. In addition, the colonies had free access to British markets, subject to few of the mercantile regulations that plagued the citizens of England themselves (Adam Smith recited most of them). Taxes were low and were used to support only colonial government operations. Actually Britain was subsidizing the colonies with more than £400,000 a year, equal to about one percent of the gross product of the colonies. In world trade the colonies were unimportant in themselves and even unimportant to the British merchants.

England's Seven Years War (the French and Indian War in America) ended in 1763, adding Canada to the British empire and eliminating a threat to the colonies from the French. The cost of men and material for the American War, in addition to the burden of the wars in Europe and Asia, left Britain with a large debt. It left many Americans the richer from the proceeds of having sold supplies to the British—and often to the French. Thus, after-tax incomes in the colonies remained higher than incomes in Britain. The logical adjustment was a tax on the colonists to relieve the British and to help reduce their national debt.

Although the end of the war had left the colonies free of the French and Spanish threats, colonial trade soon became encumbered by a British requirement that exports outside the empire (except, after 1770, fish, rice, and breadstuffs supplied south of a point in northwest Spain) had to be shipped via Britain. This was a costly and annoying stopover. The regulations were later modified and were enforced irregularly, but they remained a thorn in the side of colonists who depended substantially on trading. In addition, the British Parliament restricted issuance of money and banking activity in all of its colonies. Although these laws had small immediate economic effect, they did pose a threat to future trade. On the other hand, the British provided substantial military and diplomatic services for the colonies. A period of minor friction came to a climax in 1773.

The East India Company, in financial trouble, requested and was granted permission to ship tea directly from India to the colonies at a reduced tax. This reduced the cost of regularly imported tea to the colonies, which had been buying smuggled tea from Dutch sources. Although the consumers were beneficiaries, the merchants and smugglers were outraged. Tea ships met a hostile reception in American ports and often were forced to return to England without unloading their cargoes. The Boston Tea Party was a final affront that Britain found intolerable. The response was a series of laws, called by the Americans the "Intolerable Acts." Parliament closed Boston Harbor until the East India Company was reimbursed for the tea that had been destroyed.

It was in this climate that the American War of Independence erupted.

OVERVIEW

The beginnings of the first Kondratieff wave in the United States have been located in 1789, a few years after national independence, and are similar to those following 1848 and 1898.

The 54 years between 1789 and 1843 saw the U. S. economy through minor recessions leading to a postwar peak in 1814, five Juglar cycles, and a decline to a major depression in 1843. It was the worst period the nation had seen up to that time, and one of the three worst in U. S. history.

The economic expansion was the product of the steam engine and innovations created by the introduction of power machinery to replace

Table 5.1. Innovations Leading To The Industrial Revolution

Year	Innovation	Industry
1709	Coke-smelting process	Iron and steel
1733	Flying-shuttle	Textiles
1761	Manchester-Worsley Canal	Water transport
1764	Spinning-jenny	Textiles
1769	Steam engine	All industry
1769	Water-frame for spinning	Textiles
1776	Introduction of four-course rotation of crops	Agriculture
1776	Steam blast for smelting iron with coke	Iron and steel
1779	The spinning "mule"	Textiles
1784	Reverberatory furnace with "puddling process"	Iron and steel
1785	Power loom	Textiles

Source: Compiled by the author.

human and animal labor and by the Napoleonic wars. These basic inventions were followed by others, extending the use of steam power to other devices. A major factor was the relatively high cost of labor in a nation where people could go into the frontier to start a new, independent career with little capital. The diffusion of the new power inventions into industry occurred gradually as producers introduced new equipment to replace old, with progressive firms crowding out reluctant entrepreneurs or those who would not adapt. One listing of innovations that ushered in the Industrial Revolution in England is in Table 5.1.

The Beverly Cotton Manufactory was chartered in 1789 in a euphoria that culminated in the "cotton mania." Alexander Hamilton sponsored a huge project to take advantage of the falls in Passaic, NJ, creating, after many problems, a silk-weaving industry in Paterson. Following the Paterson experience, water power development grew, in Lowell, Lawrence, Manchester, Holyoke, Philadelphia, and Fall River. The investments in these projects took place during and after the War of 1812 and produced a Juglar cycle expansion after 1820. The Juglar cyclical downgrade was created by the movement of industry to the Middle West and to the water power regions of the South.

Additional innovations continued to stimulate new investment for several decades. The basic "pickers" and "willows" for the weaving industry were developed in 1807, and Lowell's loom made practical the use of power in 1814. These induced the formation and expansion of the textile industry.

The eighteenth century Industrial Revolution was not confined to the workplace. It changed radically the whole fabric of life and life styles. As it metamorphosed the simple way of life of the handicraft economy into a factory age, it forced women and children out of the home and changed the social structure.

Increases in money supply and inflation had little to do with the expansion that preceded 1812. For the most part sound money policies prevailed in the United States, and whatever expansion of business credit took place appears to have been a normal increase during a prosperous phase of the business cycle. This occurred in spite of strong inflation in England and some monetary disorders in Germany incident of the Napoleonic Wars.

The whole period was characterized by moderate unemployment, except for a few years before 1825. Although real wages rose without interruption, the labor market felt the strong influence of the replacement of men (many of whom were craftsmen) as workers by women and children. In addition, a large portion of industrial production was carried out in the homes of former workers as craft or cottage industries, even in the production of hard goods. Domestic furnaces even produced cannon. There was no reduction in total employment.

The steamboat, invented in 1807, started its commercial career in 1829. Railroad construction began about the same time: 490 miles were constructed by 1838. These were the major innovations during these periods. It is impossible to itemize the multitude of others suggested by each breakthrough or the multipliers and ripples that each of these set in motion, extending effects through the whole economy.

Similar stimulations as a result of the same inventions, were traceable in England and in Germany, but had much less impact. One explanation of the slowness in Europe rests on more conservative banking and the absence of speculative excesses. A boom in England followed peace with the colonies in 1783. The economic revival began in 1785, increasing in intensity until 1793. (A minor Kitchin depression occurred in 1788–1789.)

As the railroads did half a century later, investment in canals produced a wide impact on the economy. Canals opened new areas and brought prosperity to farmers by cutting transit costs and providing jobs. They led to construction of docks, roads, bridges, and made rural areas suitable for such industries as paper, woolens, and flour milling. Canals dramatically reduced the shipping cost per ton-mile to one-half to one-tenth of the former costs, as well as the shipping time for all products. Canal traffic reached its peak about 1840 when railroads (4000 miles by 1842) began to take over the movement of freight. Although major railroads started in 1830, it was not until 1835 that they were able to offer a major service.

In terms of contemporary investment, the period saw the concentration of investment in water power, the building of turnpikes and canals, iron production, machinery, shoes, leather and textiles, the invention and introduction of Whitney's cotton gin, and many minor inventions. Although the new devices had been invented years before, little use had yet been made of jennies, Arkwright frames and mules, the introduction which was a major influence in the second Kondratieff wave.

1784–1886

The period 1777–1781 was a time of hyperinflation in the new United States. The Continental Congress had financed the War of Independence with unsecured printing press money. "I don't give a Continental" indicated the low esteem in which this money was held. The nation ended the war in a depression.

The United States was recovering from a recession in 1784–86 caused primarily by its inability to export enough goods to pay for needed imports. The nation was then made up of 3.9 million people, of whom 700,000 were slaves; the people were divided almost equally between North and South. The urban population of 24 cities was 201,555; the rest of the nation was rural. Trade in a mercantilistic import-resistant world was limited. Britain, the nation's chief trading partner, took £1.2 million in trade, made up principally of tobacco, wheat and flour, rice, fish, and whale oil. Capital was scarce. Growth possiblities were evident only in the population. The birthrate was 55 per thousand.

1793

The first Juglar cycle peaked in 1793, stimulated by investment in shipbuilding, cotton production, and trade. It began with a speculative "cotton mania" during the French Revolution and during the following war between England and France. Between 1793 and 1803 the economy experienced a great spurt, principally due to exports and "canning." The exports were largely re-exports of products of tropical colonies, a trade that grew from $300,000 in 1790 to $59 million in 1807. The big export stimulus was created by the wars in Europe. Prices crashed in 1796.

A postwar revival in prosperity lasted until 1804, sustained by trade with Europe. It them subsided.

1804–1812

A second nine-year cycle, sparked by the Napoleonic War in Europe, peaked in 1807, when exports reached $108.3 million and imports $144.7 million, almost double the 1803 figures. But trouble in Europe caused a drop in exports to $22.4 million and in imports to $58.1 million in 1808. Inasmuch as foreign trade generated 25 percent of the U. S. gross national product, the impact of these declines devastated the economy. The chief export product was cotton, and U. S. prosperity depended very substantially on cotton trade and cotton prices. In the midst of a business recovery, the economy faced a monetary panic in 1807.

1807–1810

The Napoleonic Wars and the American War of 1812 gave the new country its first domestic wartime boom. Cotton exports rose from a very small figure in 1793 to £92 million in 1810, accounting for $14.2 million. Prosperity brought a rush to the cities. The urban population grew 50 percent between 1790 and 1810.

As Napoleon was the cause of new American wealth, his departure from the scene brought about its first cyclical decline. However, the decline of foreign markets led to a new emphasis on manufacturing at home and large investments. The 15 cotton mills grew to 102 in the two years 1808–1809. The number of spindles increased from 8000 in 1808 to 31,000 in 1809 and 80,000 in 1811.

1814

Following the war of 1812–1814, much of the investment, encouraged by wartime needs, became unprofitable. Although 1815 began with a spurt, 1816 produced the first postwar slump.

The crisis of 1815 bears a likeness to that of 1921 in ushering in postwar adjustments. Expansion had taken place in several U. S. industries in 1813 and 1814. These had existed before the war in a depressed state. The wartime boom had stimulated an unrealistic business euphoria, particularly in foreign trade. It lapsed for a few months during Napoleon's return from Elba, resumed after Waterloo, and collapsed in the fall of 1814. Without this excessive speculation, the following major Kondratieff recession might have been a minor one.

The 1814 peak was followed by a mild two-year recession and a five-year transition period during which the U. S. economy had to adjust from wartime spending to a peacetime economy. It saw a period of resumption of investment in innovations, with production to meet pent-up demand for consumer and business needs, the creation of new households, and a baby boom. It led to huge speculation that culminated in a collapse in prices and currency.

The recovery lasted five years. It was a period of postwar adjustment and prosperity known to history as "The Era of Good Feeling." In terms of the Kondratieff cycle it was the beginning of a plateau period following the high point (the equivalent of 1864, 1873, the 1920s, 1970s and, possibly, 1982–1985). The nation depended on shipping income to offset its chronic deficits in the balance of trade. In 1807 imports were $138 million, exports $108 million. By 1814 these figures had dropped to $13 million for imports and $7 million for exports.

The new nation also benefited from the investment boom in England.

1815–1818

Cotton prices were the key factor in the U. S. economy between 1815 and 1818 and again between 1832 and 1839. As new land was sold by the government, cleared, and prepared for cotton by two years of corn planting, the cotton supply increased steadily. It was the South that led economic expansion and contraction.

After the postwar resumption of specie payments in February 1817, the Second Bank of the United States expanded the amount of notes it issued, but in July 1818 the bank was forced into a period of currency contraction. A crisis occurred in September when the government retired $4.5 million in debt contracted for the Louisiana Purchase. In July 1819 cotton prices dropped to half the level of July 1818. The drop was steady, from 35𝒮 a pound in January 1818 to 8.5𝒮 in 1823. The result was a deflationary implosion.

1819

The resulting money panic brought about a two-year recession beginning in 1819. This was accompanied by an industrial crisis in Britain that reduced the demand for cotton and led to a call-back of British loans to the United States. This fell on a U. S. economy suffering because of a 1810 bumper wheat crop in Europe.

In 1819, a year of money panic, paper money was degraded. The nation, on a bimetallic money basis, and with few banks, which were all concentrated in cities (most of them in New England), faced its first depression in 1823.

1823

The economy expanded in production of machinery, iron, shoes, leather, and cotton and wool textiles. Canal building provided the medium for a speculative boom of the early 1820s. Some 125 million was invested in capital improvement between 1816 and 1840.

1825

In retrospect, both the 1825 crisis and the later 1837 panic were of monetary origin. Wildcat banking was the prime catalyst.

Bad loans (principally those made to Mexico and South America in 1824–1825), together with a stock exchange panic in May 1825, put the economy on edge. The period of recovery that followed was fed by credit expansion, which ended in a stock market crash in May 1835.

1830–1836

Although there was a money panic in 1837, there was no depression during the period 1830–1840, the railway age, when there was a huge development of railways and other infrastructure. The recovery was sustained by these two elements. Monetary factors had an important stimulating effect.

Major railroad expansion started in 1830 and provided much of the economic stimulation. By 1835 it had become a practical public service, and by 1842 there were 4000 miles of rails in the United States.

The Napoleonic Wars ended in 1830. The nation's population had increased dramatically from 13 million in 1830 to 15.5 million in 1836. There was a great increase in cotton trade despite the fact that shipments were stifled by blockades. Domestic manufacturing expanded rapidly, with gigantic schemes for internal improvement creating new need for labor and new markets for farmers.

In 1831 and again in 1832, President Jackson mentioned the "rare example of a great nation abounding in all means of happiness." The nation was prosperous, contented, even boastful.

The low point in this period was the monetary panic resulting from the Jackson controversy with the Bank of the United States.

During 1835 the economy seemed to be rolling again. The price of cotton rose from 11S a pound to 16S a pound. Sales of public land tripled. The United States treasury paid off its debt and piled up a surplus through the sale of public lands. New York real estate prices rose 150 percent in six years. During the seven years 1830 through 1836, 347 new banks were chartered; bank loans outstanding doubled from $28 million to $56 million; banking capital increased 1100 percent.

AGRICULTURE

The cyclical pattern in American agriculture was both a technical and a geographical movement. From 1815 to 1862 more Americans earned their living from agriculture than from any other occupation. Grain production moved from New England to Virginia and Maryland in colonial times, then to the South Atlantic states, then to Ohio and the Great Lakes area during the first part of the nineteenth century. From

1815 until the Civil War, the amount of land available to farmers increased greatly, and several technical advances increased their ability to produce. Each movement brought prosperity to the new areas but depression to the old.

1837

In 1837, President Jackson began to question the constitutionality and advisability of a national bank. Understandably, this step was vigorously opposed by Nicholas Biddle, one of the nation's leading bankers and spokesman for the banking community. Bank notes, the basic currency, were issued by the banks with little restriction. The year 1833 began with the nation in high prosperity. Private and business debts reached a historic peak. The nation was surfeited with paper wealth.

In the heat of expansion and high profits, rules were bent. Some banks made loans to stockholders before their capital had been paid in, to some immediately after the stock had been purchased, with the stock serving as collateral.

The banks issued their own currency, sometimes in an amount up to ten times the amount of the assets behind it, a few at 14 to 1, and one bank at 30 to 1. And much of the money was used for loans to the stockholders. The economy was ripe for a monetary crisis by 1837.

The Bank of the United States (the second bank with that name) had been granted a federal charter in 1816, the only federally chartered bank permitted to operate outside the District of Columbia. Conceived as an aid in financing the War of 1812, it was established too late for that purpose. One element that made it palatable to the federal government was the provision that stock sold to the public could be purchased with United States government bonds, a privilege that added to the popularity of government securities.

The original capital of the bank was $35 million, with one-fifth contributed by the federal government. Of the total, 75 percent of the capital was government bonds, and only 25 percent specie (silver or gold).

The bank was planned to be headquartered in Philadelphia with branches in other cities. It was authorized to receive government deposits and make government disbursements; to receive private deposits, make loans, permit checking accounts; and to issue currency. It was to be—and did become—the largest and most conservative bank in the nation, in effect the bank for other banks. But it remained a for-profit private institution.

After an unimpressive beginning under the new director, Norman Biddle, it began to assume the characteristics of a central bank, accumulating obligations of other banks and becoming the bank for redemption in specie of all bank notes as well as its own Bank of United States notes.

State banks, which were issuing their own notes (which served as currency), found that when these notes reached the Bank of the United States at some distant point, they were returned to their originators for redemption in either specie or for notes of the Bank of United States. This forced the state banks to increase their reserves and limited their capacity to circulate notes. (For a time the notes of these banks sold at varying discounts, up to 75 percent.) The Bank of United States soon became the source of all emerging funds for all banks. It bought and sold bonds for specie, and in effect manipulated the quality and quantity of money so as to provide and protect reserves for its own emergencies. However, the Bank of United States' effectiveness was limited because it had no voice in the reserve policy of state banks. Nevertheless, the system worked well until 1832.

In that year, President Jackson, who had a long-standing dislike and distrust of banks, refused to approve the renewal of the federal charter for the Bank of United States. The bank then obtained a Pennsylvania charter. But federal funds were withdrawn and placed in "pet banks" on a political basis.

In the period following 1815, the federal government had run up surpluses in almost every year, sums used to reduce the national debt. When, in 1837, the debt was completely retired, $28 million of a large federal surplus was distributed to the states, inspiring a great monetary euphoria. In effect the cash surplus was moved from the conservatively managed banks in the East to the banks in the West, providing the basis for expanded lending in that area.

Rapid expansion of the money supply had taken place from 1834 to 1836, from $172 million to $276 million (a 43 percent increase in 1835 alone), resulting in a 25 percent increase in prices.

The expansion of state bank notes helped to finance the purchase of western lands, which had been opened to homesteading. This in turn fired a huge speculation in land and a boom-time atmosphere in the whole economy. Bank loans doubled between 1830 and 1836. Land prices rose 30 percent in the West and in the cities. New York real estate prices rose 150 percent in six years.

Some contemporaries found reasons for uneasiness. In December 1836 a fire had destroyed $20 million in property in New York. Others saw problems in over-speculation, especially in land, which began in 1834.

A need to borrow abroad began with the pressure on Nicholas Biddle's United States Bank of Pennsylvania in July 1836, when the government removed its deposits. On July 11, 1836, a Specie Circular suspended payments in specie for outstanding paper money, and the government began using paper issued by the government for payment of purchases and debts. Immediately the banks assumed the same policy. The difficulty in obtaining specie set off the panic of 1837. Within weeks there were runs on the banks.

An added, possibly decisive factor arose from large foreign investment in the United States. High rates of interest in the United States had induced English bankers to send funds to the United States over a period of several years. Three English houses extended credits of nearly $19 million in the early 1830s, an enormous sum at the time. These credits were increased during 1836.

In the fall of 1836, credit retrenchment in Ireland resulted in difficulties for the Northern and Central Bank of England. Soon after, the troubles spread to a London bank. When called upon to help, the Bank of England insisted that credits to the United States be reduced. After a poor balance-of-trade year in 1836, Britain began to withdraw deposits. Gold and credit tightened. With British credit retrenchment and the shortage of specie to pay taxes and foreign debts, New York bills became uncollectable.

The price of specie rose dramatically. Loans that fell due were not renewed. A rash of investigations revealed irregularities and fraud. On May 10, 1837, New York banks suspended payments. Bank debtors were allowed to settle their accounts at 90 to 92 cents on the dollar. Business virtually stopped. Barges and towboats did not move; construction stopped in place. And of course, "when people do not work, we have unemployment."

Two currencies remained in circulation: depreciated paper, commonly used; and coin and specie, which soon disappeared from circulation. When relative normalcy arrived in 1838 with a new banking act, prices were substantially higher.

The year 1837 was payoff time for ventures that failed to meet expectations, and for excessive speculations, especially in land. Britain continued to tighten credit in the following years.

The Second Bank of United States, which had speculated unsuccessfully in cotton, closed its doors and set off a series of bank failures, collapsing highly mortgaged land investments based on the false hopes created. Banks continued to fail, eroding confidence, spending power, real estate prices, and indeed all capital values.

> The panic of 1837 was one of the most disastrous crises this nation has ever experienced. It was the culmination of a long train of events that extended back over a number of years. It marked the close of one epoch in our industrial history, and the beginning of a new era. It engulfed all classes and all phases of our economic life within its toils: and for seven long years the people of this land struggled to free themselves from its oppression.[2]

The trough was reached with the panic of 1843.

The Second Wave:
1843–1864–1896

OVERVIEW

The economy, which had reached high points in 1815 and 1837, continued at a low ebb until 1851, with some small recovery in 1847 and 1849 (Fig. 6.1).

The 64-month period that followed included the "Hungry Forties." It saw one of the worst depressions in the nation's history.

This second American long wave rode in on extension of power technology and renewal of investment. It was a period of extensive railroad expansion that began in 1849, bringing about the opening of huge areas of the West. By 1840 there were 30,000 miles of track in the United States built with $900 million, all borrowed in the 1850s. The lower cost of transportation brought all prices down. The opening of new land stimulated household formations and construction. It was the adoption of Cyrus McCormick's reaper, Howe's sewing machine, and machinery for working metals and wood, breaking stones, and setting type. Among the new processes developed during these years were the Solvay process for production of soda and phosphate fertilizers; sulfuric acid used in manufacturing on a large scale; new processes in the manufacture of glass, cement, paper, rubber, sugar refining, and tobacco processing.

But the largest investment sums spent during this period were for expansion of the railroads. Rails increased from 3000 miles in 1840 to 24,000 miles in 1857. This inspired foreign investment. Capital flowed in steadily from abroad—$14 million during the last third of the century alone. By 1897 the railroads represented a total investment of $9,168,072,000.

Even more important, the railroads changed the values of land, harvests, and money. It spawned a steel industry and coal and petroleum

Figure 6.1. The Second Wave, 1843–1864–1896

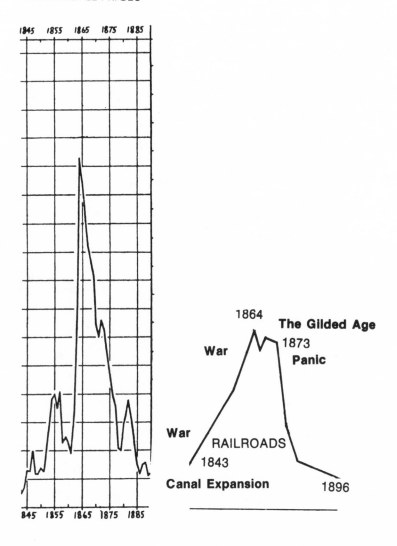

production. It also made obsolete the great investments of the 1820s in canals. And it offset the obsolescence and decline of clipper ships and the whaling industry. The peak of the wave came in 1864 with the huge expenditures for the Civil War, just 50 years after the peak of the previous cycle following the War of 1812.

During the 30 years following 1843, United States per capita product grew 30 percent from $96 to $128. The peak of consumption was reached in 1890. The crisis came in 1893, just 50 years after the 1843 panic, 56 years after 1837.

It was in this period that the steel industry was born. A new process invented by William Siemans, successful at Montucon in 1813, first failed in the United States, but in 1867 the Great Western Railroad ordered old iron rails to be converted at Sieman's steel stamp works at Birmingham. This work got under way in 1873.

The open hearth process, using scrap and alloys, scored its first success in the 1880s. It was especially useful for making moving parts in mines and elevators. Bethlehem and others developed high-speed cutting steel for use in machine shops, motor cars, railroads, and oil drills. These advances in metallurgy affected the machinery industry and electrical equipment for the next several decades.

The first commercially successful production of aluminum was begun in the 1880s by the Cowles brothers and Hérault-Hull. For a time two firms controlled the industry, the Pittsburgh Reductor (later American Aluminum Company) and Cowles Electric Smelting Company of Cleveland. By 1890 aluminum was selling at $1 a pound. It continued to drop in price until it could be used widely in motorcars, electrical appliances, the food industries, and for household use. At the same time the banking system expanded to meet monetary needs.

This was a period, too, of major social changes—the emergence of a bourgeois industrial and commercial class and the development of the limited liability company that made possible wide public participation in investments. Investment capital for this Kondratieff wave came principally from business profits, personal funds, and capital from abroad. The federal government was bound to a sound money policy and determined to repay the nation debt, a feat previously accomplished between 1832 and 1835. This did not deter some states from issuing business-stimulating additions to the money supply as well as a liberal amount of state bonds.

The beginning of the upturn in 1844 was unheralded and spurred by no discernible great change in the economy. The nation was sharply polarized between an agrarian South and an industrial North. The issues of the day were states' rights and free trade.

Prices of farm products rose steadily from 1843 through 1857 (the prosperity phase of the Kondratieff cycle), then fell continuously

(44 percent) until 1896, except for the Civil War period and its immediate aftermath (1861–1878).

The harsher personal effects of the 30-year-long decline of this wave and the preceding long wave problems of the 1830s were both somewhat mitigated by an escape valve of westward migration. Families by the tens of thousands abandoned their bankrupt farms and businesses in the East to move West to homestead free or almost free government land. These westward migrations occurred during each cyclical recession, in the 1830s and 1840s and again in the 1870s, 1880s, and 1890s.

1848–1853

The trough war of this period was fought with Mexico. The economic consequences were minor. Relatively little of the productive capacity of the nation was destroyed. The major trauma of the period was the peak "War between the States" 13 years later. The postwar reconstruction supplied the investment basis for a postwar boom, much like that following World War I, 54 years later.

It was during this period that the United States saw its first large wave of European immigrants. Some two million entered the nation between 1850 and 1855, accounting for more than half the total population increase during that period, increasingly the hungry from Ireland and Germany. They were in large measure young male adults with above-average skills, some education, and a great deal of ambition. They contributed a large and valuable human capital to the economy.

This period saw a huge influx of gold from California and Australia, resulting in sharp inflation everywhere. Bumper wheat and cotton crops sold at good prices in 1855, providing a lift to farm expansion and a relief for farm debt.

A wide area of investment including the railroads was evidently overextended and profits were not reaching expected levels. The demand for wheat created by the Crimean War came to an end, affecting farm prices and shipping.

France raised its interest rates, drawing off both United States and British funds.

1853–1855

Excessive speculation in the railroads and "gold fever" following 1849 discoveries led to a two-year crisis in 1853–1855.

1857

The crisis of 1857 was an international event, created in each country as a product of its own development. It came near the upper turning point of the long wave in the United States. (The Civil War extended that rise in prices.)

Farms were heavily mortgaged so that farmers could buy more land, which was mortgaged in turn. Railroads received 24 million acres of federal land grants from 1850 to 1857. The railroads disposed of half the land, much of it to speculators. By 1855 and 1856, $800 million had been invested in uncultivated land, three-quarters of it on credit. Southerners were buying to lessen their dependence on the North and to offset the increasing cost of slaves in labor-intensive cotton farming. Northerners and immigrants were moving West for better opportunities.

As in all such periods of prosperity there was extensive speculation. Brilliant promise existed in railroad stocks, sugar, and cotton. Europeans took part enthusiastically. This boom was fed by "easy money," largely the result of the gold discoveries in California. In France, Louis Napoleon provided an unusually good opportunity for investors to help build railroads. To finance these and other speculations, finance companies were formed, notably the Société Générale de Crédit Mobilier, formed in 1852. The promotors issued 600 million francs of stocks and bonds, secured by a 10 percent down payment, consisting largely of other securities. Shares immediately sold at a premium. The company then plunged into promotion of railways, steamship lines, and other ventures, and the stocks of other companies in France, Spain, Austria, and Germany. Dividends of 10 percent were paid in 1852, 13 percent in 1854, 50 percent in 1858 (much of it out of capital).

But things did not go well in 1856 and 1859. Cracks began to appear in the world credit structure as early as 1855.

A competing investment house, Crédit Foncier, made loans on French real estate, averaging 7 percent in dividends. It sold $10 million in bonds in small denominations (10 francs to 1000 francs) to reach a popular public market.

Such speculation overtaxed the banking system. Van Vleck, a historian of the period, puts it bluntly: "The discrepancy between means of payment and the quantity of payments which had to be made brought about the collapse of the boom."[1] The difficulties first appeared in British relationships with the Middle East and the Far East, where England had an unfavorable balance of trade, in part as a result of the Crimean War, wars in Persia and China, and exports of capital to India.

The difficulty of the situation was mitigated by some events abroad. Both England and France were in periods of prosperity fed by new gold from California. Increasingly bad wheat harvests in France in 1852 through 1856 forced France to import wheat from the United States and doubled the price of bread, which had been subsidized there for some years. A bad silk harvest in France in 1855 and 1856 added to the problem. Then in 1854 France undertook to finance its participation in the Crimean War by borrowing $300 million.

The French had made it national policy to retain a low interest rate to encourage investment. Because of a drain on their specie, investment fled to higher interest rate areas elsewhere. This forced Bank of France to raise its rates from 3 to 4 percent in 1854, then to 5 percent, then to 6 percent, the legal maximum. Short-term loans were limited to 75 days.

To maintain this low interest policy, Bank of France also bought gold in London, paying $2 million premium. The French drew out the gold surreptitiously by having the French House of Rothschild buy English commercial paper, present this for payment, then redeem the British bank notes for gold at the Bank of England.

With its own trade expanding, this placed an intolerable burden on the Bank of England. The French drain more than offset imports of gold from California, and forced money rates in London up to 7 and 8 percent. These increases in turn forced liquidation of British investments in America, creating a currency shortage and pushing down the values of stocks and bonds of the railroads and other companies. These securities were the chief underlying assets held by U. S. banks and insurance companies.

Although there was no marked recession in business, and although the public buying was brisk and optimistic, one summer day in 1857 U. S. bankers faced a world money market crisis.

On August 24 Charles Stetson of the New York branch of the Ohio Life Insurance Company announced that the company had suspended payments, brought about "in consequence of making loans here to parties who are unable to respond at this time." The company's crisis led to the discovery that the company cashier had embezzled virtually all the assets of the institution in spite of the supervision of its officers and directors.

The company had never done insurance business; it had served as a savings bank for individuals and brokers. The following day 55 New York banks, which had advanced money to Ohio, acknowledged their loss to the public and immediately began to contract their assets. All loan requirements were tightened. Four billion dollars in loans were called in within a week or were not renewed. Seven small banks, which had depended on the central city banks for their existence, were forced to close. Even the best credit risks found credit virtually impossible to arrange. Values of stocks given as collateral were reappraised downward, forcing many to find additional security or pay up.

Then the whole national credit structure began to collapse. When September 1 came, businessmen found themselves in desperate straits. Many could not meet their loan payments. Rumors of bankruptcies spread.

On September 9, Fitshugh and Littlejohn, a large transportation company in New York, failed. That was only the first of a string of ominous announcements. The panic spread to Philadelphia, and on September 25 to Chicago. With bank credit stifled, businesses could not pay bills, stocks plummeted, bank deposits were withdrawn. Banks closed. The whole monetary system crashed. Trade was paralyzed until December 14.

Railroads stopped construction. People bought only necessities. Prices dropped 33 to 50 percent. By June 30, 1858, the price of flour was down 34 percent, wool 16 percent, rice 13.5 percent, hay 20 percent, sugar 20 percent, and so on. The rich were ruined. Unemployment soared.

Confidence was restored when New York banks agreed to accept for payment the notes of all banks in the state, taking in $8 million in deposits. A continuing flow of gold from California and abroad helped. On December 14, the panic ended and the banks resumed specie payment.

After it was over, the crisis was blamed on the underlying lack of backing for banknote currency and the extreme reaction of banks to the Ohio Insurance failure.

Although the panic was over, it set in motion a recession that lasted through 1858, and in some areas through 1859. Real estate prices had collapsed, grain prices remained low. Chicago, revisited in 1858, was described by a *New York Times* correspondent as "proportionately like a retired country village."

Gradually business returned to normal.

1858–1860

The year 1858 witnessed falling prices, many failures, a continuing decline in construction, a better balance of trade, and the beginnings of a revival. A crunch came when prices fell dramatically (recovering only moderately in 1859) until the first quarter of 1861.

The period was marked by a shift in building activity from New England to the central Atlantic and middlewestern states.

Analysts see the Juglar cycle coming into a depression phase in 1857, intensified by trouble between the North and the South.

The period immediately preceding the Civil War was therefore one of great change and stress in the U. S. economy. The nation was shifting from agriculture to industry, while agriculture itself was passing from an occupation of self-sustaining households to one of crops for sale in a world market. Although half the population was still on the farm, manufactures increased from $1 billion in 1850 to $1.9 billion in 1860.

Exports played a major part in sustaining the economy. These were financed principally by London bankers (who were, in turn, dependent on the Bank of England) but also to some extent by banks in New York, Philadelphia, and New England.

1861

Before the Civil War the United States went through a price inflation even greater than that of 1834–1836 or 1968–1975. During the decade beginning in 1854 the wholesale price index rose from 31.3 to 70.4, an increase of 125 percent, an average of more than 20 percent per year for 6 years. The war added to the price inflation.

During the Civil War the Union government began to issue fiat United States notes (greenbacks) to finance its operations. These constituted two-thirds of the money in circulation in 1864. Although this money was universally accepted for bank deposits and was exchangeable for state bank notes, their addition to money in circulation tended to raise prices. Only gold coins were acceptable in payment for foreign goods. The result was a substantial (300 percent) inflation rate. The price of gold rose from $20.67 to $60 an ounce. But after the war the price dropped back to $30.

And the sharp increase in prices continued after the Civil War. This was not due to the infusion of new money. In fact, from a 1865 peak of $2.675 million, the federal debt continued to be reduced for 13 years until it reached $2.107 million in 1878. National banks held reserves of $211 million against $539 million in deposits. The pressure causing rising prices in 1865 was not supply of money but the scarcity of product, war-created "impediments to production," and trade, as well as speculative expectations.

1866–1872

It was this great availability of cash that permitted bank loans to jump from $500 to $900 million during the years 1866–1872, stimulating a 50 percent increase in output per capita in six years, with wages rising proportionately to sustain the demand.

1866–1872

The third Juglar cycle of this wave (1861–1869) was dominated by the war, distorting normal economic processes by deferring industrial developments, crowding them into the 1867–1872 period. Railroads began to expand again in 1871. They still competed for investment dollars with canals and turnpikes. All this changed the values in the areas through which they passed (or avoided), and their rates changed the competitive nature of products and the wealth of producers from all areas, just as new highways do today.

The postwar prosperity lasted seven years. It was fed by innovations which had been restrained from exploitation by the Civil War. This upswing was interrupted by a minor setback in 1869.

Kondratieff refers to these developments as products of the need for expansion.

> The opening up of new countries does not provoke the upsweep of a long wave. On the contrary, a new upsurge makes exploitation of new countries, new markets, and new sources of raw materials necessary and possible.

Of discoveries of gold, he says:

> Gold production, even though its increase can be a condition for an advance in commodity prices and for a general upswing in economic activity, is yet subordinate to the rhythm of the long waves and consequently cannot be regarded as a causal and random factor.

The land settlement policy following the Civil War, together with the bulding of the railroads, brought a large stream of immigrants. The railroad not only opened a region, but they also provided grain elevators, helped would-be farmers, even provided advice on what to raise and how to raise it. Product increased rapidly as the result of the increases in the amount of land under cultivation, but also because of a technological revolution in farming with the wider use of farm machinery. Problems arose because the greater product forced prices down. As a solution to this problem a system of tenant farming developed, resulting in major changes in the rural social system.

Steel production was established in the United States in 1867 with the development of innovations that revolutionized production. In that year, 1.6 thousand tons of steel were produced. By 1897 the product was being produced at the rate of 7.2 million tons a year.

The post–Civil War expansion had been ignited by the rush to the West and the railroad boom. Again there was a hectic pattern of speculative activity for right-of-way options, stocks, and trust equipment certificates.

Crédit Mobilier, the investment company created in France in 1852 that had helped construct the Union Pacific Railroad, was the focus of a huge scandal during the Grant administration, involving Grant's brother (for selling influence), cabinet members, senators and congressmen. Overcharges of 80 to 100 percent in construction costs were alleged.

The rise and decline of industrial centers as well as movement of industries played a part in the mechanism of the second cycle. Iron works from New England, New York, New Jersey, and Pennsylvania moved to central western states and the South. Thus idle furnaces continued to exist after 1866, even during periods of prosperity.

Old furnaces languished. Labor moved, changed to other work, or remained unemployed. The movement was spurred by technological obsolescence, which continued steadily during the three Juglar periods up to 1850, when the "drop bottom" made a radical change in production methods.

The Bessemer process, developed in the United States by W. Kelly in 1850, was not introduced into the U. S. industry until the pre-1873 prosperity, and then only eight firms had adopted it by 1875. Other improvements from Europe enabled modernizing firms to produce at lower prices from 1872 to 1897. The same delays occurred in the diffusion of the Thomas-Gilchrist process, adopted in 1881. The development of heavy armor plate and alloys (chrome and nickel steel) was completed in the 1870s and 1880s, but entered the economy only during the last Juglar period of this wave. These resulted in improved steel casting and brought scrap into use as raw material. A great nontechnical innovation in the steel industry came in 1891 with the founding of Carnegie Steel and the merger of productive capabilities of the major producers.

The peak year in prices (1864–65) followed a major inflation (100 percent), a result of the Civil War. It was followed by seven years of transition, the resumption of investment in innovations lying dormant because of the war, satisfaction of pent-up demand for goods, the creation of new households, and a baby boom. It led to speculation that culminated in the panic of 1873, and a six-year depression, 54 years after 1819.

No small factor in the postwar expansion was a huge ($700 million) government expenditure for bounties, pensions, and back pay distributed over a four-year period. (Similar bonus payments helped to mitigate but not to stop the depression of the 1930s.)

AGRICULTURE

At the same time the markets for food products were increasing dramatically all over the world. The U. S. acreage harvested increased from 15.4 to 38 million from 1866 to 1880.

In this situation, as farm production expanded, retail prices for food products remained stable but wholesale prices fell. For the highly mortgaged farmer (1 in 4) it was particularly devastating. Great hardships existed in many sectors of the economy, but the situation was ruinous in the agricultural sector. Wheat prices fell 50 percent between 1866 and 1870, cotton 50 percent within a six-month period. Between 1866 and 1880 prices fell an average of 4 percent a year.

1873

Then came Black Friday, which set in motion historic slides. Prices of everything fell, land and stock prices collapsed. Businesses failed in huge numbers. Imports decreased, exports increased. Banks suspended payments. The stock exchange closed. And unemployment became a serious problem.

A short postwar recession marked the end of the wartime expansion, culminating in a money panic in 1873 and a six-year depression. The trough was reached in 1876, four years after the turning point. However, it was six and a half years before the peak in production was reached. In the meantime the labor force and its productivity had increased considerably. On a personal economic basis, the trough-to-trough cycle was 11 years.

The trigger that signaled the downturn was a speculative maneuver that cornered the gold market in 1869.

As we noted, the Civil War had been financed in part by the printing of greenbacks, which were not redeemable in specie. This encouraged some gold traders to run down the price of paper to $241 for $100 in gold, driving the prices of wheat and cotton down 50 percent in terms specie. The postwar prosperity and growing public confidence brought the price of gold back to $131 by 1869.

At this point Jay Gould, who had accumulated a considerable larcenous fortune and controlled the treasury of the Erie Railroad, attempted the impossible, a corner of the gold market. Some $15 to $10 million constituted the entire floating supply in the United States. Picking up $7 million in gold on the market, he drove the price up to $140. Using the Erie Railroad funds, the funds of the Tammany Hall Bank, and funding of the Tenth National Bank (which he controlled), he and his associates bought all the floating supply of gold plus a substantial amount that had been sold short.

There was, however, a possible hitch. The United States Treasury held $75 to $80 million in gold. To avoid the hazard of the government entering the market, Gould enlisted U. S. Treasurer Abel R. Corbin, who in 1869 at the age of 64 had married the sister of President Grant.

Gould convinced Corbin that a higher price for gold created higher prices for farmers, better profits for the railroads, and greater prosperity for the nation, and that a policy of selling treasury gold would bring about a depression. This argument was reinforced with the purchase of $2 million in gold bonds for Corbin's account.

The combination of arguments was effective. The White House pressure on the Treasury secretary, George S. Boutwell, restrained the sale of government gold. Months later, when Major Dan Butterfield became assistant United States treasurer at New York, he found himself the owner, by gift, of $1.5 million in gold bonds which had been purchased by Gould on margin.

By August 1869 Gould, Jim Fiske, and a few associates owned twice the total floating supply of gold and they kept buying. On September 22 the price was $141.

But President Grant was becoming uneasy about the situation. Mrs. Grant wrote to Mrs. Corbin, telling her to stop speculating in gold. The next day Gould started selling gold at $144.25. At that price Beaufort sold out and wired to the secretary of the treasury details of the situation. The next day gold opened at $150, went to $160, and peaked at $164. President Grant then ordered that $5 million in government gold be sold immediately. Within 15 minutes the market broke 25 points as speculators unloaded. The date, September 24, became known as Black Friday.

Gould repudiated outstanding contracts to buy gold, barricaded himself and his associates in the Opera House, and obtained injunctions from Tammany Hall judges prohibiting collection on the gold contracts. There was panic in all the markets. According to General Butterfield, only the "gamblers" had lost.

The depression between 1873 and 1886 that followed matched the depression of 1929–1939.

1874–1879

The recovery from 1873 was much more difficult and prolonged than any before it. It lasted four years. It was, up to that time, the worst in personal terms for the people, and it was not exceeded until the Great Depression of the 1930s (which began 56 years later). One report notes three million tramps in the 1873–74 winter. The depression brought strikes, riots, agitation for easy money, and eventually agrarian reforms. Although this was a very severe depression, it was reversed by no special, immediately discernible stimulation or innovation.

1876

The tide began to turn in 1876 with a renewal of railroad expansion, a stock market revival in 1877, and a good (but low-priced) cotton crop in 1878. Economists date this fourth Juglar cycle at 1870 to 1879.

1882

There were 18 consecutive federal surpluses beginning in 1882, all on a declining leg of the long wave.

The fifth Juglar from March 1879 to March 1882 took place during the depression phase of the Kondratieff wave. It was characterized by a resumption of railroad construction from 1878 to 1881 to new peaks in 1885 and 1887. The first electric lights were installed in 1881 in New York City. Electricity became an important source of power in 1897, and a dominant one in 1900. And it became a major seminal factor in the diffusion of innovations during the third Kondratieff wave.

1883

By 1883 the Juglar had turned into a recession, which lasted through 1885, with a crisis in 1884, a stock exchange panic, bank failures, money market problems, and considerable unemployment. All this was not as severe as the 1873–1877 depression but possessed all of the discomfiture of bad times.

It was during this period that seeds were sown for an industry that added stimulus to the next Juglar period. Natural gas was first used in 1821 in Fredonia, PA. By 1843 gas meters made the sale of natural gas more practical. In 1873 it began to be used in Pennsylvania iron works.

The petroleum industry, born in 1857, began to contribute to the economy in the fourth Juglar cycle and made a major contribution in the fifth Juglar when Standard Oil Company was formed. This established centralized management for the industry.

1886–1892

The railroads continued to expand, but at a slower pace than during the 1878–1882 period. By 1892 the expansion began to fall off. A widening of the negative balance of payments resulted in shipments of gold abroad, a lowering of bank reserves, and a tightening of credit.

1893

In February 1893, the market crashed and the bank panic began.

The contest between easy money (silver) and sound money (gold) was the cause of underlying monetary problems. These currency problems were responsible for triggering the depression in 1893 and a catastrophic panic in 1896.

Under pressure of silver mining interests, the Treasury had been required by law to buy silver in specified amounts, to be paid for in treasury notes. These were redeemable in gold or silver, at the option of the Treasury. Gold was soon driven out of circulation. That law was repealed in 1893.

1894–1897

The sixth Juglar of this second wave occurred during the period 1889 through 1897. It continued to be stimulated by railroad expansion, but this was the last period so affected. Thereafter the growth ceased to be stimulant to the economy but rather became part of the established structure. Nevertheless the crisis of 1893, more than any of the previous crises, did involve railroad expansion, which had by itself sustained an expanding economy. Electric light and telephone companies were also large factors in the economic expansion of this period.

The last three decades of the nineteenth century saw a gradual long-term drop in prices (29 percent) attributed to a retardation in the growth of money supply, with a commitment to return to the gold standard. No silver was coined from 1873 to 1878. Federal policy contributed to the deflation as the Federal debt was reduced. Taxes remained high. The decline was not uniform in all products, creating imbalances in the costs of land, labor, and the values of investments.

It was the decline in rail earnings in 1894 in the face of decreasing traffic, and in construction which fell to 1852 levels, that pointed up the declining trend in the economy. It was at least in part a case of eliminating the nutrient effect of an expanding industry. (A revival of construction a few years later fed the new prosperity in the following decade.)

The lack of a national banking system so increased the likelihood of disruption of the stock exchange and the monetary system that financial panics occurred about once a decade. These triggered recessions and associated disorders as conflicting interests tried to adjust to changes in business and technology and the changeover from an agricultural to an industrial economy.

The depression of 1893–1897 was, up to that point in history, rivaled only by those of the 1840s and the 1870s. It was a depression with two bottoms in 1894 and 1897, during which plants operated at 75 percent of capacity. A recovery appeared to be in the making in 1892, but monetary problems involving bimetallism undermined business confidence.

One factor was the failure of the Philadelphia & Reading Railroad. While the economy grew from $22.480 billion in 1880 (1929 dollars) to $40.450 billion in 1890, agriculture grew from $5.53 billion to $7.4 billion.

Panic hit the stock market on May 3, 1893, when the market fell 15 points in a day, the sharpest drop since 1884. On May 4 National Cordage Company went into receivership and three brokerage houses failed.

Until August the market continued to decline with momentum sustained by reports of suspensions and bank failures. Gold was hoarded or exported. Unemployment spread.

The panic is described in retrospect by some historians as similar to that of 1929. In a single year, 158 national banks failed (153 of them in the South and West). Altogether 568 banks failed; 125 railroads went into receivership.

One contemporary historian, Charles Hoffman, reports: "All records in this regard . . . even those of 1873 were broken by the panic of 1893." A reviewer commented, "The business year 1893 promises to go into history with heavier net losses in financial, commerical and industrial circles throughout the United States than in the more severe among other panics in the past 80 years."[2]

Again the long wave cycle ended in a depression. Hoffman reports:

The depression . . . may be viewed as a profound economic dislocation arising from forces which were transforming an agricultural-industrial economy into an industrial-manufacturing economy with continuing large scale agriculture.[3]

The depression of the 1890s was worldwide. In England it was epitomized by the failure of the Baring Company. In Germany and France the depression lasted from January 1890 to February 1899. Hoffman continued:

It was one of long duration and wide amplitude, with a trough period of up to 10 years. In Britain production fell to 10 percent of potential capacity. The 1890 declines in Europe had minor impact in the United States until 1892. The 1890–1893 period was salvaged by a poor crop (famine in 1891) in Europe and a bumper harvest in the United States.[4]

IN ENGLAND

The second Kondratieff wave in England was largely the product of an emerging cotton textile industry using raw cotton from the Middle

East. This supply entered a market that for 200 years previously had been supported by Germany and Switzerland. That trade had progressed through several stages: (1) the use of Indian fabrics as a new consumer good brought in by the East India Company, supplanting markets for the woolen and silk industries. (2) This competition brought about protective measures in 1721, such as the prohibition of the sale or wearing of printed, painted, or dyed calicoes. (3) Another innovation grew silently as cotton was increasingly used as a weft with a linen warp. This required special legislation in 1736, increasing the demand for cotton yarn. (4) In 1774 it again became legal to produce cotton fabrics, a third innovation in the cyclical stimulus that bore fruit in the 1780s.

During these years production technology improved with the invention of the flying shuttle, the jenny, Barker's loom, the waterframe, and other cost-cutting equipment. But many of these devices did not affect production until after the cyclical peak.

Europe's long wave was complicated by the war between Germany and France. The French indemnity paid in 1870 (4,999 million francs) stimulated excesses of prosperity in Germany, which made the crash of 1873 even more violent there than for other nations and more lenient for France.

7

The Third Wave:
1896–1920–1949

OVERVIEW

The beginning of the twentieth century was widely recognized as a new economic age. In part this was the result of the centennial; people were talking about "changes." The new century ushered in a wave of liberalism in the United States and England. In Germany it was a period of high taxation for expenditure on armaments.

As an economic revolution analogous in many respects to the Industrial Revolution, it was recorded by historians as the end of an era. It was, of course, the beginning of another in which industrial and commercial interests dominated the power structure, replacing agriculture as the prime source of economic activity, a period during which natural gas, petroleum, and electricity replaced steam power, already past its production peak of 2,278,000 kilowatt-hours.

Schumpeter dates the third wave from 1913. As he put it:

The processes of every cycle are contributed to by the completion and the working of the inheritance of preceding evolution, even as they hand over their own contribution to the next cycles.[1]

From 1880 to 1910 the nation's wealth increased by 250 percent and its output by 220 percent. The third wave (Fig. 7.1) was seeded by earlier developments in the chemical industry, rubber processing, the combustion engine, and turbines (which were later to make the steam railroads obsolete). Earlier development of coal tar dyes (1846) and ammonia azo dyes (1863) were the basis of other new burgeoning industries. Discovery of potassium deposits begot industries that produced sulfur, sulfuric acid, sodium chloride, benzol (from 1849), fertilizers, safety matches (from 1855), wood pulp, explosives, and oleomargarine (1868).

Electricity had been discovered in 1831, but its first applications to industry did not affect the economy until 1895. Thereafter its impact

Figure 7.1. The Third Wave: 1896–1920–1949

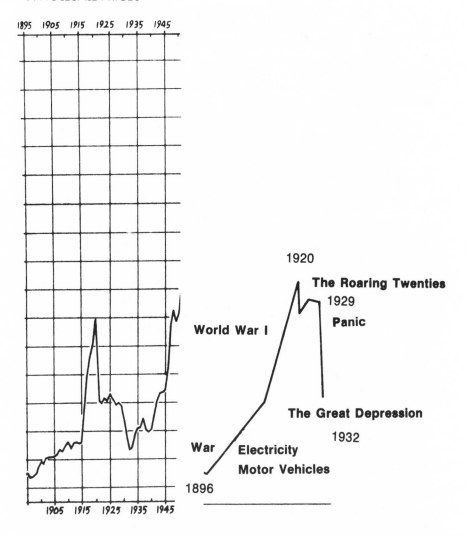

WHOLESALE PRICES

extended in many directions. Electrochemical technology gave birth to dyes, pharmacological products, metallurgical technologies, and so on. Production of electric power rose from 3.15 million kilowatt-hours in 1899 to 19.652 kilowatt-hours in 1914.

The beginning of the twentieth century saw major investments in long-distance transmission, hydroelectric generators, great electrical power stations (which had started in 1895 at Niagara Falls), the substitution of electrical power in textile manufacture, paper, metallurgy, and chemical industries, local trams, and underground railways. These were small industries in 1897. The electric industry employed 28,000 workers at the time of the 1890 census.

The automobile was first produced in 1893 and entered the economic scene in 1903 when Henry Ford incorporated with $100,000 capital, of which $28,000 was paid up. As with all new industries, mortality among pioneers was high; 322 companies began operations between 1902 and 1907. By the end of that year, 8,423 cars were sold, gross revenues was $5.5 million, net revenue $1 million. Ford changed the industry product with a cheap 4-cylinder car in 1908. By 1914, with 415 firms in the field, he produced about half the total number of vehicles.

Vulcanization of rubber had been the innovation contributing most to the first Juglar cycle of the second Kondratieff wave (about 1842). The motorcar provided a new expanding market beginning in 1908.

Cleveland advocated a deflationary gold standard policy as opposed to the Sherman Silver (16 to 1) Act, which was later repealed to halt the depletion of gold. To avert a money panic, Cleveland borrowed from J. P. Morgan and August Belmont to buy 3.5 million ounces of gold for a reserve, but he was soon forced to draw on this.

The monetarist views of the depressions of the 1890s are described in a study by Charles Hoffman:

> The money market tightened just prior to the downturn in 1893 and 1896, due to a complex of factors in which currency policy played a role. Tighter credit conditions contributed to economic contraction but could not be blamed for the downturn and depression. The money forms in use contracted though not sharply, during the depression. There was less money and it was used less as economic activity contracted. The increased issue of Treasury notes under the Sherman Silver Act did not lead to a marked increase in money though it did postpone credit contraction by augmenting bank reserves as gold flowed out of the economy. Insofar as Treasury deficits were not funded, they complicated the monetary picture. Their inflationary or expansionary impact must be recognized but as a relatively minor factor.[2]

The trigger that precipitated the decline of 1896–1897 was a threatening message from President Cleveland to Great Britain on December 17,

1895, invoking the Monroe Doctrine in a dispute with Venezuela on its boundary with British Guyana. Within four days the stock market had fallen dramatically. There was a rash of bank failures, twice as many in 1896 as in 1895. Business failures increased by 16 percent. Only action by the clearing house in issuing script averted the worst effects. "Coxey's Army" marched from Ohio to Washington to petition for unemployment relief.

The contraction in the United States coincided with an expansion in Europe, resulting in a favorable balance of payments. A bumper crop in 1897, sold at good prices, turned the corner (Table 7.1).

The manufacturing production index of 100 in 1899 rose to 214 by 1919. Acreage increased from 4.6 billion to 6.5 billion, and farm labor increased from 9.9 million to 11.4 million. The tractor, introduced in 1910, replaced laborers with 258,000 units. Growth was the result of an annual reinvestment of 20 percent of output during this period. From 1910 to 1930 investment increased at a rate of 5 percent per year. By 1918 the United States, which had been a debtor nation (to the extent of $3.7 billion in 1914), became a $7 billion creditor nation.

The fits and starts of this period were substantially influenced by an inelastic credit system dependent on policies of individual banks. No central bank existed. The major sources of leverage were government budgets which contracted the economy with surpluses and expanded currency with deficits. Robber barons, the high debt ratio of corporations, a slow increase of wages during periods of increasing productivity, and much muckraking in the press, contributed complications.

In 1900 the motorcar gave new direction to a gasoline industry, although kerosene remained 57.7 percent of the petroleum market. Refined petroleum use rose from 21 million to 71 million gallons between 1899 and 1914, and crude production from 60 million barrels to 250 million.

Although railroad expansion had slowed almost to a stop, railroad earnings rose sharply in 1897 and reached new peaks in 1904, 1907, and 1910, with 70,000 miles added and $9 billion in new capital in 1897, $15.3 billion in 1913. The rails reached their maturity as a stimulant to the economy early in the twentieth century.

Agriculture had conquered the far West by the end of the nineteenth century, using improved threshers, combines, gas engines, and (after 1900) light tractors. Horsepower used rose 32 percent from 1888 to 1909. Acreage increased one-third in 20 years. Food problems in Europe helped the recovery from 1897: there were floods in Austria, the Balkans, and Russia and a drought in France.

Introduction of the tank furnace in 1898 revolutionized glass making. Semi-automatic (then the completely automatic) machines eliminated the occupation of the glass blower, and a cylinder machine mechanized the production of window glass.

Table 7.1. Tentative Reference Dates Of Business Cycles In The United States, 1897–1937

Initial Trough	Peak	By Months Terminal Trough	Expansion	Contraction	Total
June 1897	June 1899	December 1900	24	18	42
December 1900	September 1902	August 1904	21	23	44
August 1904	May 1907	June 1908	33	13	46
June 1908	January 1910	January 1912	19	24	43
January 1912	January 1913	December 1914	12	23	35
December 1914	August 1918	April 1919	44	8	52
April 1919	January 1920	September 1921	9	20	29
September 1921	May 1923	July 1924	20	14	34
July 1924	October 1926	December 1927	27	14	41
December 1927	June 1929	March 1933	18	45	63
March 1933	May 1937	May 1938	50	12	62

By Calendar Years			
Trough	Peak	Trough	Peak
1896	1899	1914	1918
1900	1903	1919	1920
1904	1907	1921	1923
1908	1910	1924	1926
1911	1913	1927	1929
		1932	1937
		1938	

Source: Wesley C. Mitchell and Arthur F. Burns, *Measuring Business Cycles* (New York: National Bureau of Economic Research, 1946).

Industrial reorganizations increased productivity, provided for new types of plant and equipment, new types of division of labor, new locations, and the implementation of new technology.

After 1896 the financial community suffered a typical liquidation which lasted until May 1899. Call money rates ran up to 86 percent on December 18 of that year, due largely to financial problems in England.

A wave of bankruptcies in the railroads cleared the way for needed repairs and new construction, averaging 3400 miles a year from 1897 to 1902. This stimulated the demand for steel, materials for locomotives and cars, and opened new geographic areas for exploitation. The need for labor encouraged immigration, which averaged a million a year for the period. The cities flourished with new populations, stimulating construction activity. The Spanish-American War created additional demand for steel, munitions, and ships.

Throughout this period a favorable trade balance brought in shipments of gold, increased by gold strikes in Alaska and South

Africa. In due course speculation was encouraged. The short panic of 1903 was a rich man's panic.

1898–1900

The limited "trough war" of 1898 (50 years after the "limited" Mexican War of 1848) sparked an upswing of the long wave that lasted (with incidental financial crises in 1903 and 1907) past World War I. The expansion was accompanied by a slow, steady (2–3 percent) inflation. But the course was not without minefields.

1901–1903

In April 1901 the U. S. economy was at a new peak. Industrial production was up 100 percent from 1876. The news from Washington and Europe echoed calm and stability. New issues of securities were offered every day and mergers were equally in the news: the United States Steel Company, United Fruit, Borden Condensed Milk, Eastman Kodak, Corn Products, United Gypsum, National Distillers. Investment bankers were buying up small companies to create huge institutions.

United States Steel was an assemblage of 170 independent firms whose owners quickly became paper millionaires. All was well with the world. The stock market churned at a rate 35 percent faster than it had at any other time (35 percent faster than in 1928), with as much as 5 percent of all stocks traded.

In this milieu, E. H. Harriman decided to revenge a financial defeat of the previous year and to consummate an ambition of long standing—to obtain control of a major transcontinental railroad line.

The Union Pacific was his first objective. It had gone bankrupt in 1893 and had passed into the hands of Kuhn, Leob & Co., headed by Jacob Schiff. Reorganization of the line was going smoothly until hurdles created by Harriman made progress too costly and he was able to force the bankers to give him control.

However, the Union Pacific had no access to Chicago, a basic requirement for the necessary tie to the East. Chicago, Burlington & Quincy had the required terminus as well as an excellent system of feeder lines.

James Hill, another railroad giant, had similar ambitions. His bankers were J. P. Morgan & Co., who had helped finance his acquisition of the Northern Pacific and other properties.

Both Harriman and Hill began acquiring the stock of Chicago, Burlington & Quincy in the spring of 1900, seeking the 200,000 shares needed for control. Kuhn-Loeb, acting for Harriman, accumulated 80,300 shares before the market supply ran dry. At this point, Morgan induced the Chicago, Burlington & Quincy directors to merge with Hill interests. Harriman accepted defeat, sold his holdings (at a good profit), and the merger with Northern Pacific took place. Harriman was left with a great deal of cash but not the attainment of his ambition.

That summer Morgan left for a trip to Europe; Hill went off to the far West. And Harriman conceived a daring plan—to get control of the 800,000 outstanding shares of Northern Pacific, and thus of the CB & Q. Kohn-Loeb began buying. The stock's range in 1900 was $45\frac{3}{4}$–$86\frac{1}{2}$. It was $77\frac{1}{2}$ during the first quarter of 1901, and gained $7\frac{5}{6}$ points in the following week. By April 16 it had reached $107\frac{3}{4}$. Financial analysts suggested the buying was in anticipation of higher profits.

That was the weekend during which the Exchange moved into new quarters. When the Exchange reopened on Monday, the whole market moved up strongly. Northern Pacific rose $10\frac{1}{4}$ points. On May 1 the price was 115.

In Seattle, James Hill was suspicious and disturbed. A special railroad track was cleared for him as he rushed back to Wall Street and confronted Jacob Schiff of Kuhn-Loeb.

While this was going on, a similar attempt by persons unknown (possibly J. P. Morgan or William K. Vanderbilt) had been accumulating the stock of Harriman's railroad, the Union Pacific, which had 959,993 shares outstanding. Prices had moved up from 82 to 120 in the same period.

On Friday, May 3, the market began to feel the strain. Northern Pacific dropped $5\frac{1}{2}$ points, Union Pacific 6 points. Schiff assured Harriman that he already controlled Northern Pacific with 370,000 shares of the 800,000 total, as well as 420,000 shares of voting preferred stock.

However, Harriman found on Sunday that he lacked a majority of the stock. Hill had enlisted the help of James Keene, "the silver fox of Wall Street." On Monday morning two forces were set up on the floor of the stock exchange, the Morgan (Hill) group and the Schiff (Harriman) group, each buying blocks of 1000 shares of Northern Pacific. In a dwindling supply of stocks, 363,400 shares were traded, much of it made up of short sales of stock borrowed from brokers who had no knowledge of what was going on, but who considered a price of $125 totally unrealistic. Northern Pacific closed up $17\frac{1}{2}$ points at $127\frac{1}{2}$. The contest continued on Tuesday, with some of those who had sold short on Monday rushing to cover. But others, less cautious, were still selling short. The price reached $149\frac{3}{4}$, closing at $143\frac{1}{2}$.

At the end of the day, both Hill and Harriman believed they owned a majority of the Northern Pacific stock, of both common and preferred shares. Much of the stock each held had come from short sales, much of which could never be delivered.

On Wednesday, shorts tried to cover themselves, bidding for a nonexistent supply of stock. Brokers sold other share holdings to pay for covering the short sales of Northern Pacific stock, which rose 23 points to 160. That night Wall Street learned that Northern Pacific stock had been cornered. On Thursday the market panicked; every stock except Northern Pacific fell precipitously. At noon Northern Pacific was bid at 1000.

To avoid an even greater panic that could destroy their other interests, Morgan and Kuhn-Loeb announced that they would not demand immediate delivery of borrowed stock that had been sold short during the prevous weeks.

In the end, Hill and Harriman, Morgan and Kuhn-Loeb came to an accommodation and the market returned to normal. But the incident left its mark and many investors were poorer.

The year 1903 marked "the rich man's panic," the aftermath of the attempt to corner the stock of Northern Pacific Railroad. It laid the groundwork for the panic of 1907.

1907

The crisis of 1907 was entirely in the financial sector. It was of short duration and had a worldwide effect. In the United States it was precipitated by the failure of the Knickerbocker Trust on October 22. The panic and the year are not recognized by most historians as part of Kondratieff wave dynamics.

The nation was at another peak of prosperity in October 1907, at the end of 10 years of rapid growth. Money in circulation had grown from $91.5 million in 1896 to $2.7 billion. Bank deposits were at $4.3 billion, compared with $1.6 billion in 1897. Financial institutions had assets of $21 billion, versus $9.1 billion a decade earlier.

The salubrious economic picture was similar around the world. Security prices moved apace. The Dow Jones average moved from the 20s in 1904 to 75 in 1907.

And interest rates were moving up. The London market was paying $2\frac{1}{2}$ to $2\frac{3}{4}$ percent in 1903. The rate was moved up from 4 to 5 percent on October 22, 1906, to 6 percent on October 19, close to the top level in 100 years. Money flowed from industry and commerce to stocks and bonds. In January 1906 Jacob Schiff predicted, "If the currency conditions of this country are not changed materially you will have such a panic in this country as will make all previous panics look like child's play." Hill suggested that the nation needed $1 billion a year in new capital to avoid commercial paralysis.

Early in 1907 the crunch began to be felt. Short-term money commanded 5 to 7 percent, but long-term funds were not available even for blue-chip companies. Without any hard bad news, the psychological climate was changing.

The stock market broke on March 13 while corporate earnings were being reported at new highs. Leading the way down were rail and copper stocks. Margin calls, increasing bankruptcies, failing brokers, fed a spiraling decline. Blue-chip stock prices dropped 25 percent in a few weeks, other stocks 30 percent.

During the first week in April it appeared that the decline was over. In mid-April the prices on the Alexandria Stock Exchange in Egypt took a bad tumble and London was forced to send $3 million in gold to save the situation. That started a run on the pound. In late April a plummeting of stocks on the Tokyo Exchange led to a wave of bank failures in Japan. Then things calmed down. But jittery bankers and investors began to hoard gold.

Paris began cashing in U. S. securities and dollars. It repatriated $3.3 million in gold early in June and continued with shipments of $1 million on June 6, $3.6 million on June 8, $2 million on June 14, $2.5 million on June 19, $4.625 million on June 22.

London began to follow suit on June 19 with a $1.1 million shipment and another $1 million on June 22.

There was a jittery feeling in New York but no panic. A $50 million Russian gold bond was being sold, and this was suggested as an explanation.

The economic climate was edgy. In 1907 President Roosevelt extended his antitrust campaign against Standard Oil of New Jersey with 529 counts of illegal rebates, and won a $1,623,900 judgment against a subsidiary.

When Boston offered a $4 million bond issue on August 9, only $200,000 in bids were received. On August 12 New York City tried to borrow $15 million at 4 percent but could get only $2.3 million in takers. There was just no cash available for long-term loans.

Business expansion stopped for lack of funding. When its bonds could not be sold, a leading iron manufacturing company filed for bankruptcy. Westinghouse could sell only one-third of 100,000 shares offered at $50.

The stock market was only mildly bearish.

But in the background a personal feud was going on between the Standard Oil owners (principally William Rockefeller, H. H. Rogers, and James Stillman) and Augustus Heinze. The controversy had its origins in Montana in 1897 when Heinze, a small copper producer, fought and bested Rockefeller interests by having the miners disrupt operations, forcing a $10.5 million settlement for himself.

With this cash and a new partner, Charles W. Morse, Heinze came to Wall Street and gained control of the Bank of North America. He used this bank's assets to gain control of the Mercantile National Bank, and pyramided its cash to gain control of Knickerbocker Trust, the third largest bank in New York. The pyramiding process was repeated until a network of many small- to medium-sized banks were under their wing.

With these assets available, Heinze and his partners established United Copper as a holding company to be used as a speculating medium. United sold and bought shares and options with the various bank funds available to them.

H. H. Rogers, one of the Standard Oil personalities, had vowed to destroy Heinze. When copper stocks began to fall sharply on October 10, the price of United Copper held firm. Heinze and Morse had a virtual corner on the United stock in anticipation of making a killing. Much of the stock had been sold short, and the price was driven from $37\frac{1}{2}$ to 60 on October 14. Brokers were instructed to demand delivery.

For some reason the calls were "bungled" and not sent out. In the meantime other copper stocks were falling sharply and other holders of United, frightened by the bear market, began to sell. Some newspapers, possibly at the suggestion of interested brokers, reported rumors of irregularities. Banks began to call in loans made to the Heinze-Morse group and suggested to customers that United Copper stock be unloaded.

United Copper began to fall, from 60 on October 14 to 36 on October 15 and 16. Then a run began on the weakest bank of the combination, the Mercantile. On Friday, October 18, Heinze and Morse were forced to resign their positions at the bank to qualify for help from other banks.

This should have ended the series of events, but it did not. The panic spread to other Morse interests. On Monday, October 21, Morse-controlled American Ice stock fell from 16 to $9\frac{7}{8}$. Knickerbocker Ice stock fell from $51\frac{1}{2}$ to 20. Other stocks fell a few points.

Panics are not easily stopped. Westinghouse, already in trouble, fell from 102 to $79\frac{7}{8}$ and was suspended from trading. The next day it was selling over the counter at 35. Many speculators and some brokers were wiped out. Runs began on banks not controlled by Morse and Heinze. On Monday the Knickerbocker Trust closed. On Wednesday Lincoln Trust lost $14 million of its depostis, and insiders learned that other trust companies would be closing, notably the Trust Company of North America, which had loaned $175,000 to Knickerbocker. While bankers were debating whether to save the Trust Company of North America, its assets dwindled because of a run on the bank, from $60 million to $180,000 at 2:15 on Wednesday. At this point, the decision was made to save the situation, and J. P. Morgan advanced $35 million to New York banks, which in turn loaned the money to the Trust Company of North America.

That did not stop the runs on other banks. Stock fell, margin calls went out, stocks were dumped, the Exchange demanded cash. Morgan arranged another loan of $27 million to save the Exchange. When cash was no longer available, Morgan "ordered" the clearing house to print script for emergency money, an order obeyed only because of his immense prestige.

On Friday the situation was still tense; panic was widespread. The city's trust companies refused to pool their assets in spite of Morgan pressure. Even J. P. Morgan was scraping the bottom of his resources barrel. On Saturday optimistic comments were issued instead of cash. A story (false) was circulated that Morgan had obtained $3 million from his London offices to meet the crisis.

On Sunday night another problem was added. While the Morgan staff was meeting to determine what was to be done on Monday to sedate the panic, New York's Mayor George McClellan called on Morgan with his problem. Because the city had not been able to sell its bond issue, some $30 million in cash was needed immediately to meet New York's payroll and other obligations.

The banking community was already in desperate straits. The money market in Europe was also overburdened.

The solution was to have the New York Clearing House buy New York City bonds in exchange for script. There was no time to get approvals from the clearing house or from the banks that they would accept the script. Morgan announced the transaction on Monday morning as "done." And so it was accepted under the stress of the emergency.

Meanwhile, prices of U. S. securities continued to fall in Europe. Gold shipments to the United States stopped. Runs continued on the banks. For two days it was touch and go, with Morgan delivering "bags of money" to the banks in very obvious ways.

By November the money panic had subsided. The economy suffered only a year of contraction.

1908

The years after 1907 saw a number of minor recessions, in 1910, 1913, 1918, 1923, and 1926, and a major depression (beginning in 1920) before the 1929 crash.

The economy moved up with relative steadiness from 1908 to 1912. Major investments were being made in the development of electric power, steel, chemicals, automobile, and petroleum industries. In 1910 the 10 largest industries were machinery, lumber, printing and publishing, iron and steel, malt liquors, men's clothing, cotton goods, tobacco, railroad cars, and boots and shoes. New products, fuels, and methods were introduced at a steady pace and were readily accepted by consumers. The overall market was increasing rapidly through immigration and a high birth rate. And competition kept prices low—metal goods cost little more in 1910 than they had in 1865.

Other changes in the economy were created by the movement of industry. The textile industry, established in New England, had moved 400 of its spindles to the South by 1910. When the economic momentum appeared to be slowing down in 1913, a huge market was being created as Europe went to war.

1914

Gross national product fell 4.3 percent in 1914, 8 percent in 1915, and 7.9 percent in 1916. Most analysts saw a recession (a Juglar recession) impending or in progress in 1914. The stock market underwent a sharp drop.

The following period of wartime stimulation covered a substantial part of the third Kondratieff wave, including two incompleted Juglar waves, the third and the fourth of the period.

The root of the 1914 problem was a poor grain crop in 1913 with a consequent lag in exports, while imports rose steadily. The United States was still substantially an agricultural nation with crops as its largest export. Thus the size of the crop was most important to its economy. The balance of payments for 1914 was the worst since 1895, and gold shipments to adjust the balance of payments reached a seven-year record.

In 1914 the United States was still a debtor nation* and vulnerable to demand for return of investments. Europeans owned some $6 billion in U. S. securities. British investments of $3.5 billion, German investments of $1 billion, and French investments made up the bulk of this. War in Europe could lead to a quick conversion of these investments to gold and need for shipment home to meet domestic needs. The result could create panic on the American scene as it had in the past. There were additional fears of a blockade of the European market, dwindling exports, and a long-term destruction of the European market.

The news of early July gave no warning of a serious crisis, but on Monday, July 27, gold rose slightly and stocks dropped sharply. Thirteen million dollars in gold left for Europe that week. On Tuesday, when Austria declared war on Serbia, stocks dropped again in increasing volume.

As good news alternated with bad, stock prices moved up and down, but gold continued to move out. Exchanges closed in Berlin,

---

*As it became again in 1984.

Vienna, Budapest, Brussels, Antwerp, and Rome. On Thursday, July 30, all European exchanges were closed. In New York, stock prices dropped 20 to 30 percent. On Friday, the New York Stock Exchange decided to close. Deliveries of securities were suspended. For the two weeks previous there had been a slow run on the nation's banks with $80 million withdrawn, $73 million of it in gold.

That day Germany declared war on Russia.

Again the clearing house issued script to fill the need for currency, $211 million worth in August and September. For a while investors fled from the dollar to the pound, raising its value from $4.89 to $7, but as the situation in Britain deteriorated, the currency shortage alleviated. A law permitting the secretary of the treasury to issue emergency money based on assets of banks was passed, as it had been during the 1907 crisis. Together with clearing house certificates, this provided enough currency to avoid panic.

To meet the anticipated demand of foreign creditors, a pool of $108 million in gold was raised by U. S. bankers, but European bankers apparently decided that during a prolonged war gold was safer in the United States.

With the Stock Exchange closed, brokers soon established their own over-the-counter markets to handle stock trading. On August 12 the Exchange reopened.

1915

By 1915 the economy began to prosper as a result of the wartime requirements of Europe. The first reimbursements came from the sale of Europe's investments in the United States. Later they were paid for from U. S. government loans to the Allies.

1920–1921

The cyclical peak of 1920 followed the major inflation brought about by World War I.

In the first years after the war, retail sales had increased faster than production. Prices continued their wartime rise. At the same time the government reduced its debt by $1.2 billion in fiscal 1919–1920. Gold imports of $750 million added to the deflationary pressure. The combined effect of retrenchment in government spending for war and for debt reduction deflated the economy to a point where wages and prices of commodities and stocks dropped precipitously.

There was substantial diffusion of innovations during these years. The radio became part of the American scene. There was expansion in the automobile industry, in aeronautics, and in chemicals because of the assumption of some German patents. A pent-up demand for housing had begun to be felt, but new housing dropped 6 percent as money became tight. The electric industry, railroads, and even the automobile industry had stopped expanding. But there was a great surge in captial formation, with investment concentrated in producer durable goods and construction. Auto production rose from 485,000 units in 1913 to 1,934,000 in 1919, 4,180,000 in 1923, and 5,622,000 in 1929. Overall production increased from an index of 100 in 1921 to 188 in 1929.

Productivity per worker-hour in manufacturing improved by some 70 percent in the 1919–1929 decade, due largely to greater mass production and use of automatization. Wages rose, but not as rapidly as productivity.

Toward the end of 1920 readjustments and government fears of runaway speculation and inflation led to more retrenchment. The military payroll was substantially smaller. War contract payments were no longer paid. The Emergency Fleet Corporation was out of business. The Federal Reserve System attempted to curb what it saw as an inventory bubble: it ordered banks under its regulation to stop making loans for "speculative" inventory accumulations. The resulting contraction set a downward spiral in motion.

Although it was short, the 1920–21 depression was serious enough to create sufficient panic in the relatively new Federal Reserve System (which had been established in 1914) to force adoption of an aggressive easy money policy. The depression ran for 23 months. It was short but was the sharpest up to that time.

Long-term interest rates for high-grade corporate bonds dropped from the 1920 peak areas of 6 or $6\frac{1}{2}$ percent to $4\frac{1}{2}$ percent. However, long-term rates remained more or less flat in the $4\frac{1}{4}$–$4\frac{3}{4}$ percent area for the remainder of the 1920s and into the early 1930s, before beginning the final slide to 2 percent in the trough years of the late 1940s.

Wholesale prices peaked at an index of 86.2 in May 1920, then dropped to a low of 47.1 in January 1922, a 45 percent decline in 20 months. Consumer prices dropped 10.9 percent. (An almost identical commodities "crash" had occurred following the 1864 peak, 56 years earlier.)

Between March 1920 and 1922, the Federal Reserve contracted money supply by 8 to 9 percent in an attempt to check or reverse the inflation of 1915–1920.

At the same time armed forces demobilization was taking place in a totally disorganized manner, sending thousands looking for jobs in an economy not prepared for them.

Stock prices, measured by the Dow Jones Industrial Average, fell 46 percent from a 1919 high of 119.62 to a 1921 low of 63.90.

Unemployment rose from 1.4 percent in 1919 to 5.2 percent in 1920 and 11.7 percent in 1921.

The escape valve of westward migration, which had mitigated the negative effect of the first two Kondratieff cycles, was no longer available. Americans by the tens of thousands had in the past abandoned bankrupt farms and businesses in the hard-hit commercial and industrial East and moved westward to free government homestead land. These westward migrations occurred in the 1830s and 1840s and again in the 1870s, 1880s, and 1890s, the decades of decline of the first and second long cycles. Europe, in turn, exported its surplus populations to the United States during these periods. But this type of movement was no longer an economic panacea.

The end of the boom, and the inflation of the third long cycle that occurred during and immediately after World War I were experiences almost identical to those following the Civil War. However, whereas the actual peak of 1864 was concurrent with the height of the war, the 1920 peak followed some 18 months after the end of hostilities. The lag may have been the result of government attempts to control prices through legislation and rationing during World War I. This delayed but did not prevent the final climax in 1920. Double-digit inflation occurred from 1915 through 1920.

Industrial production fell sharply. Farm mortgage debt, which had increased 30 percent in two years, caused farm foreclosures to triple between 1920 and 1922 (from 3.8 per 1000 farms to 11.2 per thousand), a trend that continued through 1926 (7 per thousand farms). Bank failures followed.

By mid-November 1922, the great stock break was over, and the market, stimulated by artificial credit, began to move upward again.

1922

Although the 1920–21 depression had been sufficiently serious to cause widespread bankruptcies and high unemployment, recovery was well under way by mid-1922. It was followed by seven years of economic adjustment, monetary and credit re-expansion, resumption of heavy investment, satisfaction of pent-up wartime demand, a boom in the creation of new households, an immigration boom, and a baby boom.

Treasury currency, created in the form of silver certificates, played a major role in the inflation of 1921–1923. Congress authorized the treasury to buy silver at $1 an ounce under the Pitman Act of 1918 to replace silver sold to Britain. This was designed as a subsidy to silver production.

Credits offered to farmers by the Fed in July 1921 added up to cheap money. Low interest rates encouraged further borrowing. But monetary factors played no obvious role in the early 1920s boom. Credit was ample till 1927. It was during this period that the Federal Reserve Bank developed open-market operations as an instrument of monetary policy.

1923–1926

By 1923 the economy had readjusted. In February unemployment was virtually invisible. Steel was booming again (19 new furnaces); electric power expanded (4 new plants) to meet demand; coal and cotton production was pushing new records. However, this was a period of prolonged agricultural depression, culminating in a giant farm product surplus in 1924 and early 1925 and a consequent sharp drop in prices for agricultural products. This was later seen as an underlying force in the decline of 1927–1929.

Real estate development was strong. A report by Robert Gordon notes that office buildings, apartment houses, homes and hotels

> were built with almost reckless abandon under the spur of promoters' profits and the ease with which securities could be sold to finance the cost of construction. Banks loaned heavily on bonds and mortgages, without adequate safeguard as to amortization and later found themselves with "frozen assets" whose value had to be scaled down drastically.[3]

The fourth Juglar in this wave was created by a great boom in power financing, and the real estate investment that started in the second decade matured in the 1920s. Consumers led the upswing by buying new electrical appliances, challenging the producers of electricity to keep up with the demand. The number of radios increased from a quarter-million to seven million in the first postwar decade. Refrigerators increased from 315,000 to 1,680,000. Passenger cars (which led every upswing and downswing), an infant product in 1902, had 23,121,589 vehicles registered in 1929 (and even in 1933 accounted for $4,831,800,000 in product). Highways tried to keep pace.

The seizure of German patents and later tariff protection stimulated large new industries in the manufacture of coal tar derivatives and other chemicals.

The attitude of the 1920s was well described by Ortega y Gasset:

> What did life appear to offer to the masses of humanity which the nineteenth century was producing in ever greater numbers? Above all, it promised general material well-being. Never had the average man been able

to solve his economic problems with such facility. While large concentrations of wealth were declining in relative terms and life was becoming more difficult for the industrial worker, the economic horizon for the average man was continually widening. He became accustomed to enjoying more and more luxuries in his daily life, and his position became increasingly secure and independent of outsiders' demands. What before would have been considered a stroke of luck to be accepted with humble gratitude, was now viewed as a right to be insisted upon.[4]

The following years witnessed a great production boom to service the war-recovering world.

Loan and investments from the United States helped in the postwar reconstruction of Europe, with much of the money used to pay for exported goods and services. According to Charles Kindelberger,

Many of the American loans were unwisely made. American investment bankers, inexperienced in the international field, encouraged foreign firms and governments to borrow more than they could productively use. Germany was the largest borrower. The ease with which foreign loans could be secured led to unwise public expenditures, particularly by local German governments; impaired Germany's ability to export by inflating her costs and prices; ... Similar overborrowing, though on a smaller scale, took place in some of the Latin American countries.[5]

During the 1923–1929 period, unemployment averaged 3.3 percent.

There had been an almost unnoticed dip in 1924 and 1925. Total product, which amounted to $724.5 million in 1912–1913, was up to $3.9 billion in 1925. By 1925 expenses had caught up. Corporate profits were disappointing.

1924

In hindsight we can see how the seeds of 1929 were laid. In May 1921 the adjusted reparations to be paid by Germany were fixed at 132 billion gold marks, an amount John Maynard Keynes estimated was three times the maximum Germany could pay. The debt bore interest and amortization at 6 percent. An initial German bond of 50 billion in gold marks was floated. Wartime attitudes, not postwar morals, were pervasive.

On the domestic scene, the "easy money" that existed in the United States during the 1920s was, at least in part, the result of British pride and British–American friendship.

Winston Churchill had resolved to have Britain return to the gold standard with the pound at $4.865, a rate 10 to 20 percent higher than the then current exchange rate. This would necessitate either a reduction in British prices to become competitive in world markets, an essential for that nation, or expectation of a negative balance of payments and export of gold.

The realities made a reduction in prices impossible. Credit was not allowed to contract, in the fear of increasing unemployment. Instead, Britain increased its money supply. To offset its loss of gold it appealed to the United States to inflate its currency to avoid adjusting the value of the pound.

The United States responded by making a $200 million shipment of gold. Additional credits were created by J. P. Morgan. At a meeting in 1927 (and at several subsequent meetings) Montagu Norman, head of the Bank of England, Hjalmar Schlacht, governor of Germany's Reichsbank, and Benjamin Strong, governor of the Federal Reserve Bank of New York set up a cooperating inflationary policy for the United States.

1927

The year of 1927 displayed a mixed bag of economic disappointment.

Suddenly there was widespread publicity about unsound business practices in many fields. Retail and wholesale trade fell off. Business failures spurted. Henry Ford shut down his plant for retooling. There was a bad Mississippi flood. Construction dropped 12 percent in the year.

But some major innovations appeared. Kraft paper was developed to create a new industry in the South. New diesel-powered locomotives were adopted. New gas pipelines were built.

Specialists in comparisons point to the similarity to the economic configuration of 1873. Until May, business was running at a high level. Then a decline set in. Schumpeter identifies this as a Kitchin depression relieved by a Juglar upswing wave. The market collapse in September was not taken seriously because business was so good. Steel production was at a record high in April. Construction and automobile sales hit new highs in June. But unemployment moved up and the demand for luxuries dropped sharply. In commodities it was a buyers market.

The most affected sector in the decline in investment spending from 1925 onward was residential and nonresidential construction. The decline was from a pace set for catching up with the backlog of demand in housing which had been created during World War I. Another adjustment was necessary because of a slowing of the population growth after the postwar boom from 17 million a year in the 1920s to 5 million in the 1930s. Higher money costs were another element; mortgages had to compete for cash with the demand of speculators. Farm incomes stopped moving upward after 1925.

Similarly, consumer needs for cars, radios, and electrical appliances stopped growing. Farm incomes stopped rising in 1925 as world supplies pushed prices down. Auto production provided an early indication of a slowdown. It dropped from 622,000 vehicles in March to 46,000 in September. The monthly industrial production index fell from the August rate of 20 percent to $7\frac{1}{2}$ percent, and then to 5 percent.

In November construction fell off even more substantially. When auto sales dropped, orders for steel were reduced. Then prices began to drop in earnest for commodities and other products: pig iron, aircraft, radios, refrigerators, cigarettes. And the Fed decided to raise its discount rate from $5\frac{1}{2}$ percent to 6 percent.

Signs of the declining production also appeared in Australia, Germany, Canada, and Argentina in 1927, and virtually all commodity prices began to fall in the second half of 1928.

1928

Interest rates began a steady rise in the United States in 1928, keeping funds at home and discouraging loans abroad. No help could be found in the British money market. And of course, after October 1929, no funds were available for old borrowers. Commodity control schemes, designed to hold prices stable, collapsed. Primary producer countries put restrictions on imports, spreading the depression in industrial countries.

Excess capacity was developing in a number of lines, and this meant a decline in demand for capital goods.

The land boom in Florida from 1925 to 1928 reflected the fever of the period. Farmland 15 miles from the ocean was sold as "waterfront" lots (some at 23 lots to an acre) for $15,000 to $20,000 a lot. The sales were made at a 10 percent down, 20 years to pay basis. (One of the "developers" was Charles Ponzi.) That bubble burst in 1928—and remained a symbol of the 1920s.

The period, like the postwar prosperity following the War of 1812 and the Civil War, was marked by a carnival atmosphere, a loosening of moral restraints, heavy drinking, and a mania for gambling and stock speculation, as celebrated by Mark Twain in his book on the post–Civil War era, The Gilded Age. It created the economic climate for Jay Gould, Jim Fiske, Cornelius Vanderbilt, Danial Drew, and the other "robber barons." These were the "Roaring Twenties," providing the opportunity for the same type of financial pirates, speculators, and stock swindlers. Like the preceding postwar era, the 1920s "plateau" period was one long party.

Politically both periods saw a swing to the right, with conservative administrations reversing the "liberal" policies carried on during the early rising phase of the cycle. As Lincoln was followed by Grant and Hayes, Wilson was followed by Harding, Coolidge, and Hoover. Both replacement administrations were ineffective and were marred by scandal and corruption.

WORLD MONETARY FORCES

Following World War I, the United States emerged as the world's principal creditor, and Europe as its largest borrower. Germany was the big debtor, borrowing 4 billion marks from 1924 to 1929, to partly offset reparations. Other large borrowers were Austria, Bulgaria, Czechoslovakia, Hungary, Poland, and Rumania. Beyond Europe, Argentina and Australia, originally exporters of capital, began to borrow heavily in the 1920s. So did the Union of South Africa. Unlike pre–World War I lending, which went to nations that supplied foodstuffs and raw materials, postwar loans went to nations, particularly in Europe, that were competitive with U. S. industry. This postwar pattern of loans served to maintain an equitable international balance of payment.

The spirit of mercantilism made a resurgence in the 1920s. The gold exchange standard induced countries to build up reserves of convertible currencies. Many countries accomplished this by short-term borrowing, a system vulnerable to changes in confidence. In addition, these countries kept sterling and dollars as reserves, forcing New York and London to hold large stocks of gold. London did not have such reserves. And London, consistent with its world position as a center of finance, could not place a ban on capital exports.

Another complicating element was the desire of some countries to hold gold as a matter of prestige. In 1928 France decided to accept nothing but gold in settlement of its debts and capital repatriation. Britain and the United States adopted a policy of "sterilizing" their gold holdings, offsetting domestic effects of gold inflows and outflows by reducing holdings of government securities—in effect reducing the currency in circulation.

There were weaknesses in this course of action. The problem became particularly acute as the amount of U. S. imports began to decline at the time that primary producers were facing declining prices. In part it was the loans that financed expansion of output that created the decline in prices. So it happened that payments of interest and dividends (including reparations) from abroad rose from $1.4 billion in about 1920 to $2.5 billion in 1928.

The distribution among nations was not even. Payments by Australia and Argentina rose between 50 percent and 100 percent; those from central and eastern Europe were even larger. One analyst remarked:

> The effect on a country's balance of payments of these developments could be concealed only as long as creditor countries were prepared to fill the gap with new loans and thus give at least an appearance of equilibrium to a situation frought with instability and danger.[6]

Further complicating this situation was the volatile inward flow of French foreign short-term investments after 1924, funds that were reloaned at long term by British and U. S. bankers.

There were contractions in business activity from May 1923 to July 1924 and from October 1926 to November 1927, in what might be called Kitchin cycles. But these were both mild and short (the industrial index fell 6 percent).

1928

In 1928 the Federal Reserve System began to contract credit in an attempt to curb speculation. Rediscount rates were raised in $\frac{1}{2}$ percent steps from $3\frac{1}{2}$ percent in January 1928 to 5 percent in July, and the System sold more government securities than it bought. But banks continued to lend for the purchase of securities and most analysts feel in retrospect that the Fed could have done little more to curb speculation.

In the 1927–1929 period, $31.2 billion in new issues was placed on the market, $10.4 billion in corporate stocks and $7.6 billion in corporate bonds. Much (perhaps most) of these funds went into the creation of financial superstructures of holding companies, to the great profit of promoters. But Milton Friedman saw it differently:

> The expansion of 1927–1929 is unusual for its deflation not inflationary character. The quantity of money, including commercial bank time deposits (M2) grew less during that expansion than in any other cyclical expansion since 1869; currency plus demand deposits (M2) showed practically no increase at all.[7]

In 1928–1929 expansion in industrial product was sharp and fast, with substantial expansion in durable goods production.

THE 1929 CRASH

About 30 percent of those alive today remember the crash and the Great Depression of 1930–1932. They remember that the Dow Jones Industrial Average dropped 89 percent from the 1929 high. (It had gone up 1800 percent in the previous 32 years.) An "intermediate cycle" depression in 1919–1921 caused a drop of 64 percent, and the later 1973–1974 "adjustment" created a 48 percent drop.

On September 3, 1929, the New York Stock Exchange prices hit a historic high of close to 400. American Telephone stock sold for $304; U. S. Steel at $216; Radio Corporation at $505; General Electric at $256.

When, on October 24, the stock market turned, many brushed off the decline as an "adjustment." Business was too good, profit reports too optimistic to warrant any substantial liquidation.

But most brokerage accounts were on margin and cash was tight. A spiraling liquidation began, throwing more and more securities onto the market place.

The whole population was involved in speculation, from shoeshine boys to professionals. And most of them "owned" their "investments" on 40 percent margins. In 1926, call loans, used to finance stockholdings, totaled $2 billion. On December 31, 1928, the total was $3.885 billion. On October 4, 1929, the figure was $6.640 billion.

Investment trusts provided an exponential type of leverage to which the public responded with enthusiasm. The new investment trust corporations purchased stock, which in turn provided collateral for their loans. The shares purchased by the public were, in turn, the collateral for margin loans. When prices began to fall in 1929, the investment trusts attempted to sustain the market price of their own shares by buying in the open market. But as the prices of underlying shares dropped, the publicly held investment trust shares were being sold and the trusts were swamped in their own shares.

The confidence, even euphoria, of 1929, is hard to conjure up. In June Bernard Baruch told Bruce Barton in an interview for *American Magazine* that "the economic condition of the world seems on the verge of a great forward movement." Professor Irving Fisher of Yale estimated that "stock prices have reached what looks like a permanently high plateau."

The stock market dominated the news, conversations, the entire culture. There were 1,548,707 customers listed by Wall Street brokers, about 600,000 of them margin traders.

The stock market boom of the 1920s had begun in 1924. The *New York Times* Index was 106 in May, and went up to 135 in December 1925. There was a setback in February and March of 1925 that dropped the Index from 172 to 143, but in 1927 the market was bullish for 10 of the 12 months. When the Index of Industrial Production dropped (while Henry Ford was retooling to change Model T to Model A), there was some talk of a depression, but it passed. There was another big drop on March 12, 1928, when the *New York Times* reported; "Wall Street's bull market collapsed yesterday with a detonation heard around the world." But by December 1928, the Index of Industrial Stock was up 86 points to 331.

Brokers' loans, an indicator of speculative involvement, reached an incredible sum of $3,480,780,000 in 1927; $4 billion by June 1928; $5 billion in November; and almost $6 billion by the end of December. Interest rates on call loans, which were collateralized by securities, were earning 12 percent by the end of the year, in a market where commercial loans ran at 5 percent.

On September 5, the *New York Times* Industrials fell 10 points in increasing volume (5,565,280 shares). One trigger was a speech by Roger Babson at the annual National Business Conference: "Sooner or later a crash is coming, and it may be terrific."

On October 6, the decline was laid to brokers' loans. A leading banker, Charles E. Mitchell, said he saw no signs of a predicted slump. Irving Fisher predicted the rise would be permanent, based on realized and perspective earnings, which justificed current prices. Banking and business leaders kept up a barrage of reassuring comments. John D. Rockefeller claimed current business status did not warrant severe declines and that he and his sons were buying heavily.

On October 20 the decline of 5 to 20 points was attributed to the "hammering" of a group of bears led by James L. Livermore. (He immediately denied the existence of such a group.) Others compared the drop in prices with 1920, 1907, 1903, and 1901. Then on October 26, the market returned to normal.

Pessimism climaxed on "Black Thursday," October 24, when a huge backlog of selling orders had accumulated.

At noon that day leading financial figures gathered at the J. P. Morgan offices across the street from the Stock Exchange: Thomas W. Lamont, senior partner of J. P. Morgan, Albert H. Wiggin, chairman of Chase National Bank, Charles E. Mitchell, chairman of the Board of National City Bank, William C. Potter of the Guaranty Trust Co., and Sewell Prosser, chairman of Bankers Trust Company. They agreed to support the market with a sum of money, variously reported to be $30 million to $240 million. In minutes, Richard Whitney was moving along the floor placing orders for 1000 shares of leading stocks.

The decline for the day was stopped at 8 points, as an almost unprecedented 12,894,650 shares changed hands. Lamont announced that "there has been a little distress selling in the Stock Exchange due to a technical condition of the market," and that the bankers had decided to take matters in hand.

But as margin calls could not be met, the declines continued.

There were just no buyers at any price. One bright young man, reputedly a messenger, entered a bid for a block of stock at a dollar a share and got it.[9] The *Times* industrial average dropped 43 points in a day. Inasmuch as the ticker tape was hours behind, small investors were sold out without knowing it. Paper millionaires were wiped out in minutes.

Prices steadied for two days, but then again the market continued to fall. Each day people felt reassured that the price drop had been a catharsis and prices were so low they could not drop further. But they did.

Reassurances came from everyone: bankers, economists, politicians. President Hoover announced that "The fundamental business of the country, that is, production and distribution of commodities, is on a sound and prosperous basis." But he would not say more or do more.

The public was not reassured. Over the weekend, a mountain of selling decisions was made. On Monday, October 28, they piled in with a volume of 9.5 million shares. And there was nothing of the customary rally at the end of a day of severe selling. Tuesday was even worse: 16,410,030 shares were sold that day. The *Times* Industrial Index dropped another 43 points. Sixteen leading issues lost $2.9 billion, bringing their loss to $10 billion for the month.

Then the funds that had been accumulated from around the country to provide call loans at 12 percent, began to be called back, forcing more margin calls. The Fed tried to help by cutting margin requirements to 25 percent.

The price drop continued on Monday, November 2, with six million shares traded, and with a 21-point loss on the index. On Wednesday (the market was closed for Election Day), six million more shares were traded for a 37-point loss. This continued on November 11, 12, and 13. By the end of November the market had dropped 33 percent, representing a loss of $26 billion. The *Times* Index of 50 leading stocks dropped from 311.90 to 164.43, its Industrial Stock Index from 469 to 220.95.

The crash hurt, but almost no one expected it to be a prelude to a great depression. The crash did not produce the depression and it was not the cause of the severity of the depression. It did, however, affect monetary policy, which helped create the catastrophe.

An epidemic of bank failures started in November 1929. Nevada declared a bank holiday November 1. The holiday idea gained momentum in January and February, and spread to Michigan, Indiana, Maryland, Arkansas and Ohio. On March 9, immediately after his inauguration, Franklin Roosevelt obtained emergency legislation to close all banks. A main cause suggested by analysts was the farm failures of the Midwest and the West.

The spiral thus set into motion created a new dimension for the depression. Pressures created by huge losses exposed huge areas of malfeasance as well as bad judgment. In subsequent investigations, executives of Chase, National City Bank, the New York Stock Exchange, and scores of huge corporations were exposed and pilloried for illegal or questionable practices. Reputations for wisdom, good sense, even honesty were shattered. The journalist Edward Angly compiled an anthology of reassurances dating from 1928 through 1931 and had them published in 1932 by Viking Press under the title, *Oh Yeah!*

There will always be a chicken-or-the-egg argument in economics. Did the fall in stock prices cause the crash in corporate profits or did it forecast the fall of corporate earnings? The record shows that price earnings ratios did not change very much. The Standard and Poor composite at the year's end was 17.64 in 1928, 13.32 in 1929, 15.81 in 1930, 13.31 in 1931, and 16.80 in 1932. Thus the treatment of the "crash" as an exogenous factor is open to much question.

What were the conditions in 1928 that might have provided a warning? There was a plentitude of new stock issues and mergers. the investment company was born (186 were organized in 1928), but initially these were not listed on the Stock Exchange. Margins were at 45 percent to 50 percent.

Although the Great Depression began early in 1929, popular perception of a change in the economic trend was not awakened until the market crash on the climactic day in October.

THE GREAT DEPRESSION

Industrial production began to fall early in the year, but the change was hardly noticed. However, the speed and size of the drop in industrial production was soon reflected in the panic on the Exchange. The index fell from 110 in October to 105 in November and 100 in December. A large factor was the drop in automobile sales and auto production—from 440,000 units in August to 319,000 in October, 169,500 in November, and 92,500 in December.

Americans remember the depression of the 1930s for its misery, its length, and for its resistance to recovery. In figures it showed a 45 percent drop in product (30 percent in real terms), an 85 percent drop in real investment, and a 20 percent drop in real consumer expenditures. Unemployment went from 3.2 percent to 24.9 percent. (The 1937 "recovery" figure was 14.3 percent.) The wholesale price index fell from 98 to 59.8. Farm produce prices fell from 107.6 (1935–1939 = 100) to 40. And stock prices hit a low with the Dow Jones averages at 40, a 90 percent drop.

Capital increases resulted from retained profits and new investments.

During the 1920s, underwriters found lucrative income from arranging generous loans to foreign governments, especially to Germany and South America. Competition to make the loans was keen, and both bribes and bonuses figured in the deals to make them (much as the situation was in the 1960s and 1970s). Inasmuch as much of the world was under the domination of dictators, substantial amounts ended in Swiss bank accounts. Cuba's dictator, Machado, had a personal line of credit which reached $200,000.

Activity flattened for a period in 1926 due to a leveling of almost all types of business. The rise in 1927 was substantial but not spectacular. However, construction reached levels in 1929 that could not be sustained.

By 1929 debts reached highly abnormal levels for stock purchases, residential building, and consumer credit, the last an important factor for the first time.

Agriculture did not share in the 1920s boom to the same degree as industry. However, the wartime disruption in Europe led to a strong demand. More land was bought, planted, and mortgaged, creating a huge farm debt. When Europe began to replant (a process more rapid than replacing industry), prices fell, leaving farmers with large interest payments. Nevertheless farmers prospered from 1921 to 1925. In that year several international commodity control schemes broke down and prices began to fall. Although the impact on the 1929 economy was not crucial, the farm problem contributed to the severity of the problems of the 1930s.

Money supply fell 30 percent between August 1929 and March 1933. But after runs on banks became common in the fall of 1930, currency in circulation increased 50 percent.

The dominant government posture was laissez-faire. At a conference called to discuss unemployment, President Harding indicated his attitude:

There has been vast unemployment before and there will be again. There will be depression and inflation just as surely as the tides ebb and flow. I would have little enthusiasm for any proposed remedy which seeks either palliation or tonic from the Public Treasury.

Secretary of Commerce Herbert Hoover echoed:

independence and ability of action amongst our own people . . . saves our Government from that ultimate paternalism that will undermine our whole political life.

Gross production had fallen more than 10 percent in the United States only twice, in 1893–1894 (14 percent) and in 1907–1908 (17 percent).

In 1929-30 it fell from $104.4 billion to $95.1 billion. The following year it fell from $89.5 billion, then to $76.5 billion, and $74.1 billion in 1933 or 19 percent.

Real consumption fell from $79 billion to $64.6 billion; unemployment rose from 3.2 percent to 24.9 percent; and gross investment, the element that was most needed, fell from $16.2 billion to $3 billion. The investment that was made was principally in construction (Table 7.2). Like the panic of 1873, 56 years earlier, the 1929 crash ushered in a long and difficult era.

Notwithstanding the poignant experience of this period, and in spite of all the study and commentary, economists have not found a satisfying explanation of the length or severity of the depression, nor the method of avoiding recessions. Some failings were evident.

Monetarists Milton Friedman and Anna Schwartz held that rigid exchange rates of the gold standard were a major source of problems, but the 1970s discredited control of money supply as the ultimate solution.[9] Arthur Lewis holds that farm price supports would have avoided the debacle. Another reason was given: there was no concerted expansionary macroeconomic policy between 1929 and 1933—neither a monetary policy nor a fiscal policy.

As a nonsignificant illustration of the effects of cyclical dynamics, Schumpeter noted, "The 1929 period is widely seen as the result of coincident cycles."[10] After taking an admittedly absurd assumption of strict periodicity of the three Kondratieff cycles (that all are of equal duration), Schumpeter computed a conjuncture from the fall of 1925, which became most severe from July 1930 to mid-November 1932. This would be followed by a Juglar recovery in a Kondratieff recession to

Table 7.2. Proportion Of The Change In Investment In Various Components In Three Periods

Component	1920–21	1920–30	1937–38
Construction	.06	.42	.10
Equipment	.19	.22	.28
Inventories	.75	.36	.62
	1919–21	1928–30	1936–38
Construction	−.09	.82	−.33
Equipment	.20	.18	.28
Inventories	.89	0	1.06

Source: Swanson, Joseph and Williamson, Samuel, "Estimate of National Product and Income for the United States Economy." Economic History 10, No. 1 (Fall 1972): 55.

March 1935. This, in turn, would include three phases of a Kitchin cycle, with a depression phase in mid-April 1931, a revival in January 1932, and prosperity in mid-November 1932, slowing the rates of decrease.

Kindelberger blames the malfunctioning of the economic system, a system distorted by World War I. He suggests that difficulties might have been lessened by an open market for distress goods, long-term loans, and a system of discounting in crisis. Leadership for such a course was provided by Britain before 1913. The United States did not cooperate.

The Keynes view reinforced the spending scenario:

> The boom of 1928–1929 and the slump of 1929–1930 in the United States correspond respectively to an excess and deficiency of investment. . . .
>
> I attribute the slump of 1930 to the deterrent effects on investment of the long period of dear money which preceded the stock market collapse and only secondarily to the collapse itself. But the collapse having occurred, it greatly aggravated matters, especially in the United States by causing a disinvestment in working capital.[11]

Describing the 1928 setting, in 1939 Schumpeter charges the accumulation of debt:

> The American debt situation and the American bank epidemics—there were three of them—are in a class by themselves. Given the way in which both firms and households had run into debt during the twenties, it is clear that the accumulated load—in many cases, though not in all, very sensitive to a fall in price level—was instrumental in precipitating the depression. In particular, it set into motion a vicious spiral within which everybody's efforts to reduce that load for a time only availed to increase it. There is thus no objection to the debt-inflation theory of the American crisis, provided it does not mean more than this.[12]

Professor Irving Fisher added "that over-indebtedness and deflation were strong and indeed dominating factors" in impairing the debtor's ability to pay.[13]

FOREIGN INFLUENCES

One of the most dramatic elements of the 1930s was the breakdown of the international banking and monetary systems. Although banking collapses appeared as a sudden phenomenon, they resulted from deflation and interaction of many forces all over the world.

Some historians trace the Great Depression of the 1930s as beginning in Germany in April 1929, in the United States in June, in Great Britain in July, and in other Western countries within the following few months. In Europe, the economic catastrophe set in motion the political changes that led to World War II.

But the chronology can be traced with equal justification from Poland in early 1929 to Canada, Argentina, the United States in the third quarter, and then to Belgium, Italy and so on.

Whatever the sequence of the financial problems, the depression took strong hold in the United States among the first, and by early 1930 most of the Western world was on the same slide, although for most countries it was neither as deep nor as long.

The United States was most widely held to be responsible. As the richest nation, with the largest supply of monetary gold, as the world's biggest lender, and the largest purchaser of goods, it constituted a logical choice.

Specifically, the restrictions of credit in late 1928 and 1929 were seen as the triggering cause. This retrenchment in the flow of U. S. lending and higher interest rates attracted foreign funds to the United States, tightening credit conditions in many other countries. It led eventually to the shock of the stock market crash, to the subsequent decrease of U. S. demand for imports, and to the virtual cessation of American foreign lending after mid-1930.

However, it must have been obvious that runaway speculation had to be restrained at some point. Call money rates of 20 percent were syphoning cash from industry. And security prices were apparently beyond reason.

President Hoover parried the blame by pointing to the "new disturbances originating in other countries, in the greatest war in history, the inheritances from it... the fears and panics and dreadful economic catastrophes which developed from these causes in foreign countries."

THE MONETARIST VIEW, 1930

Two other views have been offered: that autonomous spending restraints caused the depression, and that money restraints were the chief cause. In a sense these were so intertwined that they were the same force. Income and prices fell because spending fell. This led to a decrease in the demand for money. Interest rates, the price of money, fell. If the supply of money had remained static, an inflationary climate might have been created. But as interest rates fell, the supply of money and credit fell, creating panic among the banks.

During this period, M1, the narrowest definition of money, fell 27 percent (from \$36.4 billion to \$29.4 billion), and M2 fell 33 percent (from \$46.2 billion to \$30.8 billion). Wholesale prices fell 31 percent. As the depression worsened, consumers continued to decrease their spending, keeping the spiral moving downward. In dollar terms, the value of goods and services dropped by almost half in the period.

By the end of 1929, the Fed had lowered the discount rate, its basis for short-term loans to banks, from 6 percent to 2.5 percent. The stock market responded in 1930 when production appeared to pick up slightly.

But a new wave of bad news soon came. Debt had accumulated in all sectors of the economy. As lenders became more cautious, lending policies tightened and declined. Bankruptcies rose as profits disappeared. Loan renewals became more difficult. Agricultural prices, which had been declining through the 1920s, fell precipitously in 1930. Adjustments in purchasing policies led to further decline in all prices. By mid-1930 it was apparent that the recovery was not yet to be.

The depression of the 1930s was deepened by a continuous re-contagion of the lack-of-liquidity disease. The primary producing nations had been dependent on American lending from the early 1920s. In addition to the loss of the depressed American market, they suffered from tight money policies, contributing to the decline of Europe. The 1930 tariff isolated their exports further. Europe was forced to put up its own tariff walls. As the European economy declined, the markets for American exports were exhausted. And ultimately the primary producing countries were driven to depression, economic isolation, and bankruptcy.

The government tried to keep the economy moving. It generated a \$900 million deficit largely due to a fall in revenue, but also by generating \$251 million in expenditures. The Federal Reserve System bought \$560 million in government securities to put more currency in circulation, although this had not worked in 1924 and 1927.

During the difficult years the Fed adopted a "passive, defensive, hesitant policy," according to Milton Friedman and Anna A. Schwartz.[14] But it did try to provide liquidity for New York banks through discounting loans and other measures. This fiscal policy (then not considered an instrument of economic policy) provided no help. Budgets were designed to be balanced or show a surplus. Proposals for public works projects were summarily dismissed by President Hoover. Some help came only from Congress, which passed, over the president's veto, a billion-dollar veterans' bonus. With depression cutting revenues, this turned the surplus into a deficit.

The total federal expenditures remained in a narrow range: \$2.6 billion in 1929, \$2.8 billion in 1930, \$4.2 billion in 1931, and \$3.2 billion in 1932.

There followed a broad range of measures designed to relieve individual hardships for the unemployed, farmers, industry, and financial institutions.

THE PERSONAL DEPRESSION

Before the 1930s only the hungry 1840s and the 1890s exhibited such severe conditions, but neither reached the 25 percent unemployment and 25 percent drop in prices of that period. The shock of a crashing nominal wealth undoubtedly upset the spending pattern for the million and a half who had held securities and had for a few years considered themselves rich. Many types of conspicuous wealth were dumped on the market. But the drop in industrial production, which began before the market crash, was dramatic in itself, from 127 in June to 99 in December. The drop in the postwar pent-up demand for housing began to be felt in 1920–1921 (16 percent drop), but in 1929–1930 the drop was 42 percent, and in 1937–1938, 10 percent. Construction fell by $2 billion between 1926 and 1929, and by $2.3 billion from 1929 to 1930.

The depression of the 1930s was substantially a depression in agriculture as well as in industry, each independent of, but reinforcing the other. In fact the event was also a conjuncture of overproduction in the cycles of rubber, coffee, sugar, silver, zinc, and to some extent cotton, an inventory crisis created by high prices, many created in turn by speculators.

By the spring of 1932, breadlines were part of the New York scene. Unemployment increased from 1.5 million to 13 million, one of four in the labor force. By October the number of families on relief had tripled. In Philadelphia children starved. The number of homeless men and families was a major problem. Squatters began to build cardboard and tin huts along the Hudson River waterfront.

The situation of the farms, as Schumpeter saw it, was even worse:

> Compared with the plight of a large part of the agrarian sector, all that was done during those two years was surprisingly inadequate. Since 1929 the index of farm products at the farm had fallen over 60%. (Goods bought by farmers fell 30%). . . . The nationwide indices of land values—as of March 1, was 115 in 1930, 106 in 1931, 89 in 1932 (1912 to 1914 = 100), a maximum of 170 occurring in 1920. . . . For a minority, but a negligible one, net income must have been negative and for a considerable minority net worth of the farm must have been zero or less. Foreclosures increased rapidly and so did the proportion of forced sales that were due to tax delinquency.[15]

Moreover, in the 1930s there was no new frontier for Americans or for Europeans. Immigration laws restricted Europeans to Europe and Asians to Asia.

A side effect of turning the corner from prosperity to decline is a hardening of isolationism and resulting problems. One apparent fast response to unemployment is protectionism. In the 1930s this brought about the Fordney-Macomber Tariff, and then the even more restrictive Smoot-Hawley Tariff. Both urged policies of expanding exports and restricting imports, leading to measures protecting home producers. In the United States, the Smoot-Hawley Act of June 1930 was the more damaging, particularly toward products of Germany and the rest of Europe.

The world braced itself for another recession, which was expected to last for a year or two.

1931

In 1929 forecasters foresaw a recession no worse and no longer than that of 1921. During the first half of 1930 stock prices rallied, money was easy (off 2 percent in August), and improvement seemed under way. It was during the second half of the year that the picture changed dramatically. Contraction quickened. But new corporate issues continued to appear ($5.473 billion more than in 1920, but 55 percent of the 1929 figure). Emerging statistics brought more bad news. But there was no feeling of panic until the privately owned Bank of United States failed in December. Retail prices fell another 10 percent, wholesale prices 20 percent below the January average.

The economic climate of the world had improved in 1930 as interest rates were lowered. The rediscount rate was lowered in 1/2 percent steps, from 6 percent in August 1929 to 2 1/2 percent in June 1930. But indebtedness continued to drop. No open market operations were undertaken to increase money in circulation. Milton Friedman and Anna Schwartz argue that increasing the stock of money would have been effective where low interest rates, in the absence of investment opportunities, were fruitless. Nevertheless, the continuing fall of commodity prices aborted whatever recovery trend existed.

FOREIGN INFLUENCES

United States lending abroad was minimal during the years preceding 1924. During the next three years, the total averaged $725 million a year and made possible the purchase of $400 million in gold for the United States. Short-term credits were established while substantial U.S. net exports continued.

This easy lending of dollars stopped suddenly when the Federal Reserve Board abandoned its easy money policy during the second half of 1928, a restriction that was aimed at restraining the use of credit for stock market speculation.

The Federal Reserve Board cut back the money supply by selling government securities in the open market, and raising the discount rate, thus raising the entire interest rate structure. Short-term rates, especially brokers' call rates, rose most of all, to over 20 percent.

Immediately the demand for new issues of foreign securities dropped, precipitously, from $2.120 million during the first half of 1928 to $898 million during the second half, $1.417 million for all of 1929, $72 million in 1931, and $72 million in 1932.

There was one encouraging interlude during 1930; $2.180 million was loaned abroad, a reversal of policy that followed the deflation of security prices. This permitted $100 million in gold to flow from the United States to foreign banks and provided a short respite in Europe. The United States, which exported about $725 million in capital funds to Europe each year from 1924 to 1927, became a net importer of funds in 1931.

The banking system prior to 1929 was largely a collection of small, relatively weak units with little staying power in a crisis. Three waves of bank failures kept the economy reeling. In 1931, just as the economy showed signs of turning, a wave of bankruptcies in Europe forced the Federal Reserve System to raise the rediscount rate to stop the gold outflow.

The 1931 banking crisis halted an incipient recovery, led to the demise of the gold standard, and eventually exacerbated a very severe depression around the world. It began with the failure of Kreditanstalt in Vienna, an important bank, in May 1931 in response to the French opposition to a Hungarian credit union. This failure quickly shook world confidence in all Austrian banks and in the ability of the Austrian government to maintain a gold backing for its currency. As a result, foreigners (and some Austrians) began to withdraw short-term funds from other Austrian banks.

The national central banks of Europe and the United States and the Bank for International Settlements provided immediate assistance, about $14 million, of which more than $7 million came from the Federal Reserve Bank. But this was not sufficient to stop the run, and Austria refused to impose strict currency controls, a measure that would have stifled trade and capital movements in this small nation, which was very much dependent on business intercourse with the rest of Europe.

The contagion of panic spread to Hungary within two months. Again foreign aid was too little and too late. Germany, already badly hurt by losses in Austria (itself with a depressed economy) and a huge short-term debt to foreigners, was the next to face a run. Withdrawals between May and July were almost $700 million. Again aid was offered by foreign bankers, this time about $700 million.

The no-confidence tide ran stronger in spite of President Hoover's proposal for a one-year moratorium.

In June the German banks were faced with a run. It was well known that Germany owed a huge short-term debt to foreigners and had large investments in Austria. This time the foreign central banks raised $100 million ($25 million from the Federal Reserve). But the runs continued.

The crisis arrived in due course in London, where conditions appeared to be improving, with gold reserves up $125 million in 1931. The immediate reasons are somewhat obscure. One possibility was the release of the Macmillan Report showing that Britain's short-term liabilities were larger than had been known previously. But the climate had been created by loss of confidence in all currencies that followed the collapse of central banks in Austria, Hungary, and Germany.

The run on the pound began in July while the discount rate was 2 1/2 percent. The Federal Reserve Bank and the Bank of France offered a credit of $125 million, and private sources provided another $400 million. The discount rates were raised to 4 1/2 percent. But by September 2, $1 billion had been withdrawn. The discount rate had been raised to 6 percent. Britain went off the gold standard.

It was a signal for all the world to follow. Before the end of 1932, only the United States, France, Belgium, Switzerland, South Africa, and the Netherlands remained with currency redeemable in gold. The world entered a period of great deflation, and matching money depreciation started later, during one month in February 1933 when the gold dollar collapsed.

1932

Almost everywhere in the world the cyclical trough occurred in mid-1932. (Japan, ready for industrialization, was an exception.) Canada's trough came the following February. Runs on foreign banks began. The banks rushed to convert their holdings of U.S. exchange to gold; $722 million in gold was exported or earmarked for foreign banks within a month.

By the end of 1932, most of the world had suspended all gold payments: Britain and all its territories, Scandinavia, Portugal, Egypt, Latvia, most of Latin America, and Japan. The United States still had

$2 billion in gold left. To stop the drain, while remaining on the gold standard, the Fed had to adopt a savage deflationary policy in spite of the depression. On April 20, 1933, the gold standard was suspended for all time, and no means for flexible international payments remained.

THE RECOVERY, 1933–1937

Let us look more closely at the anatomy of the recovery from the Great Depression. Many analysts suggest that only the stimulation of Lend Lease and World War II created the major expansion period for the United States. GNP did not reach the 1929 level until 1937, and it then fell in 1938. The unemployment rate was over 14.3 percent until 1941, when it fell to 9.9 percent. Franklin D. Roosevelt assumed the presidency March 4, 1933.

The time was one for new appraisals, with real output 30 percent below 1929 levels, employment at 35 percent below full levels, 25 percent of the labor force unemployed, national income at 50 percent of 1928 levels, and prices down 25 percent and agricultural prices even lower. Mortgage credit was virtually impossible to get, and credit for business was stifled. If financial statements had been published citing current values, virtually every bank would have appeared insolvent. State and local governments faced huge tax delinquencies and extra relief costs. The rest of the world was in virtually the same situation.

The cycle of national income, based on an 1928 index, ran:

1929	−100	1935	−69	1939	−87
1932	−56	1936	−79	1940	−117
1933	−53	1937	−87		
1934	−62	1938	−81		

Unemployment rate was:

1919	− .32	1935	−20.1	1939	−17.2
1932	−23.6	1936	−16.9	1940	−14.5
1933	−24.9	1937	−14.3	1941	− 9.9
1934	−21.7	1938	−19.0		

Money was made easy but there were few takers. Corporate profits remained low. But real wages were significantly higher in the mid-1930s than in 1929.

Capital expenditures were being made only to replace old equipment. Investment in new directions was at a standstill. Industries that led the expansion of the 1920s (public utilities, automotive vehicles) were static. At this point, government deficits began to help fill the gap.

The New Deal measures were motivated by a need to relieve acute distress rather than to stimulate the economy. These led to federal deficits, which provided some business stimulation, but deficit spending was not yet accepted as an established stimulation technique.

Throughout this 1930–1938 period, balancing the budget remained an administration objective. After that it was ignored in creating the World War II defense program.

Federal Budget Deficits

Year	Billions of dollars
1933	1.315
1934	2.853
1935	2.571
1936	3.629
1937	1.8
1938	2.129
1939	2.209

On another level, government spending was extended when the Unemployment Relief Act of March 31, 1933 enrolled men for jobs in forestation, soil erosion prevention, and so on. An Emergency Relief Act in May 12, 1933 amended the Reconstruction Finance Corporation concept to provide money for industrial development. The creation of the Federal Relief Administration and the National Recovery Act in June provided funds for state programs. The multiplier effect of these efforts is indicated by the effect on consumers. National income increased $8.6 billion in 1934, $5.2 billion in 1935, and $8.8 billion in 1938. The effect in the private sector was felt in expanding operations, repayment of bank loans, and added employment restoration of consumer credit, all of which set in motion other positive elements and raised confidence levels.

But total federal expenditures played a small role in the economy during this period. Total budgets ran less than 6 percent of gross national product (versus 26 percent in the 1980s). They rose from $58 billion in 1932 to $90.5 billion in 1939. States' local spending ran at $8.2 billion at that time. The 1936 veteran bonus gave some energy to the economy. In that conservative year the federal deficit was reduced from $3.9 billion (1936) to $1.8 billion (1937), accented in part by new social security taxes. In creating fiscal policy during the 1930s, government sights were always on spending. Tax reductions were not considered at all. On every occasion taxes were actually increased.

Anticipation of rising prices provided a peg for renewed confidence in 1933 and 1934. There was a sharp rise in output and employment beginning in the second quarter of 1933, and a small, short speculative boom in 1934.

1936

In the spring of 1936 prices, wages, and other costs began to move up again slowly, and glimmers of speculation were seen.

Suddenly, in September, the stock market started to plummet. The Standard Statistics industrial index dropped from 141 to 125 during the last two weeks of summer, to 113 by the end of August, and then on October 19 (Black Thursday) it fell to 102.

Industrial production fell from an average 116 (100 for 1923–25) average to 83 in December. The textile index fell from 143 to 81. Farm product prices fell 24 percent in nine months. Looking for reasons, analysts could only assume a misinterpretation of earlier statistics. The reassessment brought about a wider acceptance of the Keynesian approach to regulating the economy.

The automotive industry revived to some extent, with production rising to 4 million units in 1935, 5 million in 1937. Industry was stimulated by some innovations: the diesel engine, air conditioning ($35 million in 1935, $85 million in 1937), and aviation. Some major underlying stimulants to the upturn were developments in chemicals (coatings), steel (improved quality), armaments, and construction (prefabricated and mobile homes).

The largest sums contributing to spending for this cycle came from special government construction projects: power development at Boulder Dam, Bonneville, Grand Coulee, Fort Pech, and Muscle Shoals.

The period 1936–1937 was notable for another pressure. CIO organizing drives led to sharp increases in strikes, wages, and subsequently prices. During the eight months of this short recovery, industrial production actually fell 30 percent. Overall the cause lay in a deficiency in long-term investment in the face of short-term expectations and the slow accumulation of inventories. Monetary and fiscal policy helped raise the balance.

1937

As could be seen, the U.S. economy was recovering from the 1930s depression reluctantly. In 1937 there was a shuddering threat of a new recession, a "submerged peak," with a sharp 40 percent stock market drop in February. It was only the stimulus of Lend Lease and World War II that avoided a major drop in overall production. The rest of the world helped pull itself and the United States out of the depression by its "defense spending."

Many have held that the world depression of the 1930s was cured only by giant expansion of spending for armaments, first in Germany, then in Italy and Japan. These nations, with the greatest density of population, hard hit by the depression, turned to policies of violence, much as the United States erupted after 1843 with a Mexican adventure and at the end of the 1897 depression with an armed trip to the Caribbean and the Pacific. But in 1937 the economy had not really recovered from 1932.

Business was stable in mid-1937. Some prices (cotton, grains) fell because of bumper crops. Business activity was good, but was sustained largely by inventory accumulation. This halted in May 1937, with a sharp decline beginning in September and lasting till June 1938. This could be charged to an increase in bank reserve requirements in August and again in March and May 1937, in total effecting a doubling of reserve requirements. This reduced excess bank reserves from $3 billion to $1 billion. Gold imports were "sterilized" under the same policy. Banks were then forced to sell bond holdings. Although these measures had relatively little effect on commercial loans, they did help create a psychology of restraint.

By 1937 the gross national product had returned to $90.4 billion compared with $103.1 billion in 1929. It dropped to $84.7 billion in 1938 and recovered to $90.5 billion the following year.

Investment in producer durables, $5.6 billion in 1929, had dropped to $1.5 billion in 1933. It returned to $4 billion in 1936, $4.9 billion in 1937. After a drop to $3.5 billion in 1938, it returned to $4 billion in 1939. There was no indication of a massive recovery expansion.

1938–1946

From June 1938 to December 1941, production increased rapidly. Spending for World War II dominated the next years. A drop in government expenditures in the third quarter of 1943, in spite of the continuing war, did not adversely affect demand because of the large reservoir of savings and unsatisfied demand.

Consumers had been spending 75 percent of their income during the war years. By the fourth quarter of 1945, the ratio went up to 87 percent in spite of rising prices. Substantial mustering out pay fed the demand. But these increases offset only 40 percent of the decline in government expenditures. Sustaining elements in maintaining production were a rise in exports and an increase in inventory accumulation spurred by rising prices.

The difference in total demand was felt in reduced production activity, elimination of overtime, and speeded retirements. By the first quarter of 1946, the economy had leveled off. It was a very mild recession. Unemployment stayed at about 3 million, refuting forecasts of a postwar unemployment of 8 million.

1946–1948

The postwar years were affected by the emergence of a number of new industries whose youthful growth, already begun in the 1930s, had been interrupted by the war. This was a typical postwar boom. In its new confidence, Congress decided to "outlaw" depressions, based on Keynes' philosophy. It passed the Employment Act of 1946, committing the nation to the pursuit of "maximum employment, production, and purchasing power." It created a Council of Economic Advisors to help reach this end. Economic growth jumped to a 3.5 percent annual rate, three times the rate of 1929–1940. But the cost was a 33 percent rise in consumer prices and a 50 percent rise in wholesale prices.

The demand, pent up during the war years, fed by an expansion in money supply, was being felt, and was offset only in part by federal surpluses. There was a boom in investment. American exports were in demand all over the reconstructing world, created in part and paid for by the Marshall Plan.

But for the most part the "recovery" was brought about by inflation. President Truman freed wage rates from wartime controls (so long as they did not require a rise in prices), suggesting 15 percent in manufacturing industries for 1946, and an additional 10 percent in 1947. Later the increase in cost of living from 1941 levels was defined as 33 percent, and the Wage Stabilization Board automatically approved increases up to this amount.

A series of strikes (in autos, steel, and coal) cost 4 percent of the nation's working time in 1946.

Prices rose as much in five months as they had in three years. Mild controls were reinstated but they were enforced less than diligently. By October 14, 1946 all consumer cost controls except rent were eliminated. In 1947 wholesale prices rose 15 percent, then leveled off by mid-1948. The 2½ year rise was 60 percent.

1948–1949

The inventory accumulated during the previous two years began to be liquidated in 1947. As a result wholesale prices dropped 10 percent beginning in late 1947. The effect was felt most poignantly in housing and durable goods, especially in producers' durables.

The 1949 depression has usually been compared with the postwar depression of 1921 following World War I, which was much more severe. Inventory liquidation at that time was 7 percent, versus 3 percent in 1948–1949, with the difference due to a lesser amount of speculation. In addition, greater support was obtained from government expenditures, up 20 percent in 1948–1949, compared with no increase from 1920 to 1921.

It was the end of another 54-year cycle—the first terminus in 180 years that did not produce a catastrophic depression. The earlier 1932 era marked the trough of the wave, and some analysts close the cycle at that point.

Indeed, the new devices of Keynesian strategy for government investment, monetarism, and the techniques of macroeconomics had produced a promise—a formula that appeared to have banished the great depression from the world's ills. But at a price.

8

The Fourth Wave:
1949–1973–2003

OVERVIEW

The contemporary Kondratieff wave is generally regarded as having begun in 1949, when the U.S. economy returned to a normal postwar pace, although the trough of the third wave occurred in 1932 (Fig. 8.1). There was no major expansion following the Great Depression; only the stimulation of the demands of the war revived production.

The economic milieu from 1945 to 1949 followed a typical postwar pattern, with an initial recession followed by a long period of expansion of 25 years.

The intervening wars in Korea and Vietnam helped sustain this expansion. They occurred almost as if ordained: Korea, a limited war, occurred 52 years after 1898; Vietnam, conceived as a limited but absolute war, was 48 years after 1917.

The new economics of government, created demand and monetary manipulation, were overtly adopted in 1974 when the stagnation of major sectors of industry became apparent. Federal deficit spending took a giant leap forward during the Carter administration. The wartime deficits of $14.8 billion in 1973 and $4.7 billion in 1974 jumped to $45.2 billion in 1975 and $66.4 billion in 1976. The effect was some stimulation, but it was not a sufficient remedy. The national economy reacted to more spending and increases in money supply with stagflation. Following the 1979 depression, federal deficits ran to $59.6 billion in 1980 and $57.9 billion in 1980.

But this was not enough. The Reagan administration's new dimension, with deficits that run into the $200 billion range, and substantial increases in defense spending, is supported by annual increases in money supply that run to 7 to 15 percent.

Six mild recessions are noted in this period, with troughs in 1953 (1.3 percent); 1957 (1.4 percent); 1961 (6 percent); 1970 (0.2 percent);

Figure 8.1. The Fourth Wave (1949–1973–?)

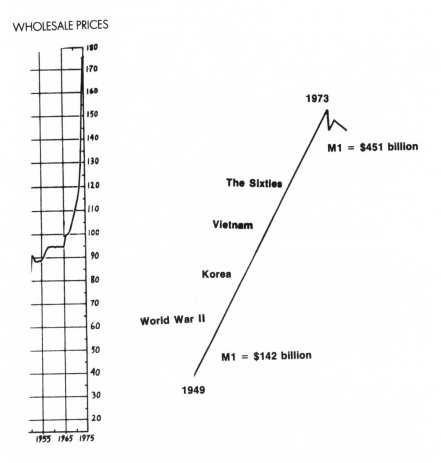

WHOLESALE PRICES

1973

M1 = $451 billion

The Sixties

Vietnam

Korea

World War II

M1 = $142 billion

1949

1973 (0.6 percent); 1974 (1.2 percent); and 1980 (0.4 percent), but each setback was recouped within two years. In spite of these, real per capita income grew during the 14-year expansion phase, 19 percent in the 1950s, 32 percent in the 1960s, and 26 percent in the 1970s. By 1949 the new cyclical movement was evident. The labor force retreated to 60.97 million, of which 3.9 percent were unemployed. It took six years and the Korean War to restore the labor force to its 1945 level, but the unemployment rate continued at around 3 percent.

1949

The recession of early 1949 was hardly noticed in an economy that was operating in a relatively high gear. Inflationary pressures continued, so prices did not fall; they leveled off at 71.4 to 72.1 percent of the 1967 level. Unemployment rose 1.4 million from 2.276 million in 1948. Stock prices, which had dropped 12 percent from an all-time high level (S & P 17.08 in 1946) remained steady (15.17 in 1947, 15.55 in 1948, 15.23 in 1949), then moved up sharply when the Korean War came into focus (to 18.40 in 1950). The gross national product was static in 1949, but by mid-1950 it had jumped to 9.6 percent growth.

1950

Government spending of about $55 billion to sustain the Korean War resulted in some inflation, but this subsided. (In 1964 consumer prices were only 17 percent higher than in 1952.)

Demobilization and the entrance of more women, farmers, and blacks into the urban labor force, stimulated by World War II needs, increased its size rapidly in the postwar years. In 1940 the labor force was measured at 56.18 million, with unemployment at 14.6 percent. By 1945 the total had expanded to 65.29 million with only 1.9 percent unemployed.

1949–1951

Industrial production was at a low in July 1949, but by May 1950 defense spending for Korea had returned it to 1948 levels.

Again inventory replenishment was the chief stimulant. In the last quarter of 1949 and the first two quarters of 1950 it returned to 1948 levels. Residential housing increased similarly. A decline in Marshall Plan payments cut back the federal budget, producing a surplus. This was offset in the economy by increased consumer spending, much of it scare buying in anticipation of rising prices.

Before the end of 1950, government participation in the economy resumed its upward course. Taxes rose in 1950 and 1951, so that government continued its surplus. Korean War spending that began in 1950 brought about a 20 percent rise in wholesale prices before March 1951. Price controls in 1950 leveled off consumer credit.

1951–1952

The Korean War now led to an immediate surge in federal spending, an 8 percent rise in consumer prices in a year, and an inflationary surge that continued without end through 1984. Money supply (M1) grew from $114.1 billion to $125.2 billion in two years. Unemployment fell to 1.221 million, less than 3 percent of the labor force. Each setback was recouped, at least in substantial part, during the following year. Europe had mild setbacks in 1953 and 1958.

The underlying stimulant throughout the period was an almost continuous flow of federal funds for defense, grants, subsidies, loans, and loan guarantees that together created a euphoric inflationary atmosphere around the economy. Most business errors were buried in the upward swing of prices. Steady inflation made it possible to borrow hard money and repay with cheaper money. Government guarantees eliminated the traumas associated with mortgages or the fear of bank failures.

1953–1954

A 13-month postwar adjustment recession from July 1953 to August 1954 brought a 1.3 percent decline in GNP and a rise in unemployment from 2.5 percent to 6 percent. Prices did not change noticeably, and wages continued to rise, although more slowly. It is apparent that two elements were factors in the decline, a drop in federal spending (from $81.9 billion rate in the second quarter of 1954) and a drop in inventories. (The drop in federal spending, of course, came as a result of the Korean truce in January 1954.)

The level of retail sales had shot upward following a steel strike in July 1952. The flattening of sales resulted in the inventory adjustment, in spite of a $4.5 billion increase in total consumption expenditures. This change was accompanied by a shift from goods to services, which increased $5.1 billion in the period.

Money supply kept increasing, at about the rate of product growth, creating inevitable inflation (see table).

The prosperity of the 1950–1969 period was the product of a new type of spending stimulation created by guaranteed loans. Trillions of dollars of mortgages were guaranteed by federal agencies to make possible the construction and often the purchase of homes, public housing, hospitals, utilities, and virtually any project for the public good. By 1983 this contingent federal liability exceeded $3 trillion.

Year	Currency in circulation (in billions of dollars)	Gross national product (in billions of dollars)	Wholesale prices index (1967 = 100)
1950	25.05	284.8	81.8
1955	27.63	398.0	87.8
1960	28.99	503.7	94.9
1965	35.26	684.9	96.6
1970	47.69	977.1	110.4

1954–1956

A boom in residential building, stimulated by easy credit, accompanied a steady expansion of consumer spending. There was a lag in plant and equipment expenditure until 1955. In that year a boom began, concentrated in durable goods; much of the demand accumulated during the Korean War. In spite of considerable investment in equipment, labor productivity growth was quite small in 1956 and 1957. Inflation continued, with wages rising faster than product or prices. Unemployment remained over 4 percent. Plants were operating at close to capacity (90 percent).

At this point the money supply was tightened; it rose much less rapidly than GNP. Interest rates hit a 20-year high as both government and business competed for available funds. By 1957 deflationary forces were dominant. New orders for durable goods began to fall.

There followed a sharp, but short (nine-month) recession from August 1957 to April 1958, which was felt in several nations. Uncharacteristically, although retail sales fell off, prices continued to rise. Expenditures for plant and equipment fell rapidly and inventory liquidation was substantial.

Increased federal spending, better farm incomes, homebuilding, and rising state and local government expenditures contributed to a turnaround in March 1958.

Over the four-year period consumption expenditures increased from $234.6 billion to $284.5 billion; gross national product increased from $360.4 million to $424.7 million.

1958–1961

The period 1953 through 1960 was dominated by an Eisenhower government policy designed to achieve growth and price stability, with full employment as a secondary consideration. Five percent unemployment was thought to be acceptable. A Keynesian approach to money supply was accepted and adopted, but its implementation was too late to help in the 1957 decline and much too restrictive in 1959. This, combined with a federal surplus in 1959, held back economic expansion and contributed to a recession in 1961. The unemployment rate was 5.5 percent or more from 1957 through January 1961.

1961–1963

The Kennedy years began the longest unbroken cyclical upswing in recent economic history. It reflected the use of federal fiscal policy to restore full employment. Spending rather than tax cuts was favored. The accepted "normal" rate of 4 percent unemployment was achieved in 1965, exhibiting a triumph of "New Economics." This was capped by a tax reduction in 1964. But business investment, in constant dollars, lagged. The 1962 figure was less than that in 1957.

1964–1967

Theory fell by the wayside with the Vietnam War. In Kondratieff terms this was designed as a limited war at a time in the expansion cycle when an absolute war might have been expected, 55 years after the absolute World War II. The baby boom that followed World War II was entering the labor force. Defense spending rose 15 percent. Unemployment rates, at 3.5 percent in December 1969, rose to 6.1 percent a year later and peaked at 7.1 percent in May 1962. The immediate cost of the Vietnam War was $110 billion; the ultimate cost was $352 billion.

Almost 19 million young people entered the labor force in seven years (1963–70), compared with a level of one million a year before the war. The war absorbed much of the bulge in the 18 to 22 age group (which was ready to enter the labor market) not only by the draft, but also by encouragement toward advanced education for draft avoidance and by employment in defense industries.

The progress and price stability of the first half of the 1960s was affected by a rise in labor productivity, which increased faster than wages. This in turn was achieved through an "incomes policy," including a set of guidelines promulgated by the Kennedy administration. These were tied to long-run growth rates in productivity, which were later targeted at 3.2 percent per year. Prices rose moderately, slightly slower than wages. Sales increased, and profits increased even faster.

Nevertheless, the deficit spending escalated inflation into a major problem. The extra spending for Vietnam was offset in part by a drop in residential building (due to a credit crunch) and a decline in automobile sales.

After seven years of price stability the big surge of inflation began in 1965, and did not stop for 19 years. Early in 1966, in an attempt to restrain inflation, the Fed began to restrain increases in money supply and credit. Bank reserves requirements were increased. Money supply expansion was halted. Interest rates rose quickly. By August 1966 the restrictions had reached crisis proportions.

As a result, inventories contracted at a $15 billion rate during a six-month period. Although there was some increase in defense spending and residential building, a mini-recession was felt in 1967 with a $1.5 billion decline in product during the first quarter. Recovery resumed by the third quarter of the year.

A new surge in the economy was created by private fixed investment and a resurgence in residential building. Much of this demand had been retarded by the uncertainties and economic climate associated with the Vietnam War.

Eventually overall government spending stopped rising; nondefense spending was cut back while defense spending continued to rise until mid-1969. The increases in government spending helped create a billion dollar federal deficit between 1961 and 1968, raising the United States government debt from less than $1 billion in 1962 to $60.5 billion at the end of eight years. State and local debt doubled from $77 billion in 1961 to $144.8 billion in 1970. Federal deficits ran at $3.4 billion in 1961, $7.1 billion in 1962, $4.8 billion in 1963, $5.9 billion in 1964, $1.6 billion in 1965, $3.8 billion in 1966, $8.7 billion in 1967, and $25.2 billion in 1968. This helped keep the economy in high gear. The consumer price index ran parallel to this, up from 91.7 (1967 = 100) in 1963 to 116.3 in 1971.

The euphoria of the 1960s was expressed as a "we're on our way to the moon" public attitude. Writers were forecasting an average personal income of $20,000 (in 1960 prices). The Keynesian paradigm of the time dictated: stimulate expansion despite the cost of inflation. It duplicated the euphoria of the Era of Good Feeling, the Reconstruction period, The Gilded Age, and the Roaring Twenties.

The impact of the policies of the 1960s, which kept interest rates high, were felt in tottering mature industries with large plant, debt, and overhead (construction, autos, steel and business equipment) where sales and operating costs were highly dependent on the cost and availability of long-term credit. Ultimately the inflationary excesses during the 1960s were paid for by losses in industrial activity during the ensuing recessionary periods.

Inflation seemed to have some salubrious effects on the economy. It made people feel good. They saved less and borrowed more in anticipation of paying debt with cheaper dollars.

While demand for most products remained strong, industrial concentration in order to achieve more mass production and economies of scale produced more failures of smaller firms and resulted in increased unemployment.

1968–1970

The depression in the "smokestack industries," those maturing manufactures that had sustained the expansion of the economy for half a century or more in their own expansion, began following the boom of 1966–1967. Increasingly, large sectors of former growth industries, as well as the industries that supported them, began to decline. Investment for modernization and expansion declined. The trickle of innovations to offset this trend was resisted because of the poor outlook for the industries as a whole and the temptation to avoid calamity by diversifying investment. Profit-motivated policies indicated that closing factories and retrenchment were preferable to such modernizations as were available.

The trend was synergistic. As the automotive industry contracted, its effects were felt in steel, rubber, glass, textiles, and petroleum.

1971

A "New Economic Policy" presented by President Nixon in August 1971 attempted to control inflation with a wage and price freeze, and tax incentives to stimulate investment spending (faster depreciation, investment tax credits, etc.). Business investment began to speed up. Unemployment dropped to 4 percent.

This was an era of partnership between fiscal policy and monetary policy in an effort to revive and stabilize the economy. Money supply was expanded moderately, credit was made easier, and government regulations were made more sensitive to unemployment. But cheap money tended to flow abroad, causing balance-of-payment problems.

It was a high point in the era of Keynes and macroeconomics; someone termed it "the golden age of economics."

1971–1973

The world began to lose its euphoria in 1970. In the United States, gross national product declined slightly (0.2 percent in 1970). The downward trend resumed again in 1973 (– 0.6 percent) and in 1974 (– 1.2 percent).

What was remarkable was the fact that these declines occurred in spite of large government deficits resulting from the Vietnam conflict and its aftermath: $2.3 billion in 1971, $23.4 billion in 1972, $14.8 billion in 1973, $4.7 billion in 1974, $45.2 billion in 1975, $66.4 billion in 1976, $44.9 billion in 1977, and $48.8 billion in 1979.

After 40 years of continuous growth, the economy had hit a stone wall, the kind of resistance predicted by Kondratieff in 1926.

Analyzing the recession, economists could see a slowdown in innovations and technical changes. Research and development expenditures dropped from 2.9 percent of gross national product in the 1960s to 2.2 percent in 1978. New patents fell from 56,000 in 1971 to 37,000 in 1980.

The trigger for industrial decline , runaway inflation, and economic change was the OPEC cartel and its oil price explosion in 1973. This reversed the rise in use of energy from 1.92 percent a year to a decline of 1.87 percent a year. Investment stalled. The overall increase in the ratio of capital to labor slowed down and declined.

The cyclical maturity was accented where foreign producers were able to enter the American market with the type of durable goods manufactures in which the United States had long led the world. Appeals for protection (by tariff, quota, or procedural regulations) resulted in measures that helped sustain some basic industries, but a reckoning fell in 1973–1974 with what appeared to be the peak—the turning point of the fourth cycle.

A decline in United States productivity started between 1965 and 1968. From 1950 to 1965 the average increase was 3 percent a year; from 1965 to 1973 it dropped to 2.13 percent a year; and from 1973 to 1981 it averaged 0.64 percent annually. Measured in terms of "multifactor productivity" (real output divided by input of labor and capital), productivity growth from 1973 to 1982 was less than zero (0.06 percent). In its normal growth expectation, without this drop in productivity, national product would have increased by 20 percent.

In spite of the Vietnam War, 1973 was the watershed year, much like 1928.

1973–1974

The turn begat an increase in money supply and other measures urged by economists in residence. The result was an inflationary recession. The monetary base expanded at a rate of 4.7 percent a year for M1 and 9.1 percent for M2. During the years 1972, 1973 and 1974, the consumer price index moved up at a rate of 6.2 percent, 11 percent, and 9.1 percent respectively.

Some economists find a similarity between 1966–1973 activity and that of 1920–1929 that is typical of long-wave recessions. Both expansions were created by scarcities resulting from wartime restraints on production. Economic growth and higher prices were taken for granted. Consumer durables were produced in great volume to satisfy pent-up demand for products and services, such as radios, telephones, television sets, refrigerators, and automobiles (as were automobiles and radios during the 1920s).

Both periods saw a large increase in mergers and acquisitions, some for the sake of technology, many for the sake of diversification. (In the 1920s acquiring management was a major factor.)

Both saw a downturn in the building (Kuznets) cycle (1927 and 1972).

By 1973 inflation was already a problem of eight years' standing and a concern all over the world. Only in the United States, of the Western nations, were wages increasing at less than 10 percent a year.

The period 1971–1975 "saw a bunching of unfortunate disturbances unlikely to be repeated on the same scale, the impact of which was compounded by some avoidable errors in economic policy," according to the Office of Economic Development report for 1977. The world was in a period described as a "malaise" by President Carter.

The economic cycles of all the Western nations synchronized in a decline, all triggered by the crisis created by the Organization of Petroleum Exporting Countries (OPEC). Productivity declines were the worst seen by industrial nations in three decades.

The same malaise was seen in the Common Market by Edgar Salin, who wrote in 1973:

The light of the new circumstances we face, I do not say merely "apparently" but maintain that in fact we are in a condition which would be termed a coma if one were referring to human illnesses; a coma from which it is possible to return to full consciousness but which could also conceivably lead to a peaceful death.

1974–1977

The growth rate during the 1966–1977 Juglar cycle was lower than the rate in 1948–1957 and 1957–1966. There was already a marked movement of employment from goods to services. Profit rates began to decline in the mid-1960s.

Crop failures drove food prices up. The years 1974 and 1975 saw major stagflation. The explanation is to be found in supply of goods and in the persistent inflationary expectations that held the inflation rate up in spite of a low level of aggregate demand.

Some questions remain about this decline. To what degree were the economic problems of the 1970s purely cyclical, how much were they the result of the OPEC 400 percent oil price increase? How much was due to Vietnam peace adjustments? Certainly the recession and maladjustment that followed were the most serious encountered by the West since 1943. There was a weak recovery in 1975–1979, but there was also a doubling in oil prices in 1979–1980 (to $34 a barrel from the $2 level of 1971, $3 in 1973). This increase in the cost of oil imports represented 1 to 3 percent of the gross national product of all importing nations.

The recovery after 1975 was slow and fitful. Oil price increases reduced the growth rate in the West only 0.15 percent, but increased the inflation rate by 0.6 percent.

During the highly profitable mature years (the early 1970s) United States chemical makers, seeing no end to the growth of demand, eagerly added new capacity. This eagerness to expand came back to haunt the industry, however, when world demand fell short of expectations. Developing countries (Mexico, Saudi Arabia, and Kuwait) and Canada built large, efficient petrochemical operations to exploit their inexpensive and ample supply of raw material. These additions raised worldwide capacity by almost 10 percent, and helped push down the capacity utilization rate of some United States petrochemical operations to less than 70 percent.

The retrenchment of the petrochemical industry provided part of the cyclical pressure that contributed to the decline of other industries.

On the financial scene, the symptoms of a peak's end were registered in several ways. In March there was the Oklahoma Bank debacle; in June 1970 Penn Central abandoned a major issue of bonds and filed for bankruptcy. In 1975 New York City faced a fiscal crisis.

The maturation of the U.S. motor vehicle industry was the inevitable result of a self-satisfied oligopoly that produced 4000-pound passenger vehicles with 400 cc, 400 horsepower engines (this is power sufficient to propel a truck carrying 20 tons of freight). The idea of smaller, lighter vehicles was derided with the statement that the saving in steel was relatively minor—until OPEC. Thereafter, it was German and Japanese competition that forced the issue. The new compacts cut back the industry by 25 percent. New production efficiencies and declining sales reduced its payrolls by an equal portion, eliminating 100,000 jobs from 500,000. The ripple effect was felt by steel, plastics, textiles, glass, rubber, and so on, bringing a slowdown in those industries. The same retrenchment was evident in energy consumption, a substantial result of smaller motor vehicles.

The production curve in steel, long renewed and sustained by new cost-reducing technologies, flattened and turned downward with the substitution of plastics, the reduction in the needs of smaller motor vehicles, and modernized foreign competition. The decline in major producers was forecast by the development of sheet steel production methods that made the huge, high-fixed asset plants unnecessary. Steel mini-plants could produce body materials for the 15 percent of the market composed of motor vehicles.

During this trying period, Federal government intervention (unthinkable in earlier periods) averted the calamity that might have been triggered by any one of half a dozen crises. New York City bankruptcy would have devastated the bond market. Lockheed, then Chrysler, if left to fend for themselves, would have triggered a chain of bankruptcies.

Notwithstanding these interventions, the personal effect on economy reflected in the Misery Index, or the Discomfort Index (the combination of unemployment rate and inflation rate) were traumatic.

Misery Index

Year	Inflation Rate (consumer price index)	Unemployment Rate
1973	6.2	4.9
1974	11.0	5.6
1975	9.1	8.5
1976	5.8	7.7
1977	6.5	7.0
1978	7.7	6.0
1979	11.3	5.8
1980	13.5	7.1
1981	10.4	8.3
1982	7.1	10.4
1983	3.3	7.6
1984	4.1	7.6

THE END OF THE FOURTH-WAVE EXPANSION

A decade after 1974 it is evident that the fourth Kondratieff wave had peaked in that year for basic manufacturing industries just as it had in 1920. Industrial growth stopped rather abruptly in four decades, with a contagious stagnation among most of the industries that had sustained economic expansion. Total national product declined 0.6 percent in 1973–74, 0.9% in 1974. On a per capita basis the decline was even more dramatic, –1.5 percent and –1.9% for the two fiscal years. Nowhere else in the world, not even in Canada, was the drop so substantial.

Gross private domestic investment, which had been running at 12.2 percent and 11.5 percent of national product during the two previous years, dropped to a rate of – 10.1 percent and – 20.8 percent.

While some wholesale prices began to fall, the overall rate of price increases dropped from 7.7 percent in 1983 to 4.0 percent in 1984. Then in July, wholesale prices began to fall for the first time since 1952. They had moved up for 32 years of expansion.

If the economy were to imitate the course of previous Kondratieff waves, it would thus be facing a primary postwar plateau preceding a recession similar to that of 1920–1923. That plateau would have started at the end of 1973. The initial drop in 1972–1974 could be equated with 1920. The 1980 recession would have been part of this pattern.

Although nominally in the 1350 range in 1985, the real level in 1972 dollars remained near this level in 1972 dollars through 1984. If the stock market is to be taken as an indicator, it is notable that the Dow Jones industrial average in constant dollars stopped its 17-year rise in 1965 at a wall of 1000, slumping below 600 (1972 dollars) in 1974.

1974

After five years of little or no growth, with inflation continuing (at 11 percent in 1974, 9.1 percent in 1975, 5.8 percent in 1976, 6.5 percent in 1977, and 7.7 percent in 1978), signs of recovery appeared. But they were not sustained.

Unemployment continued to rise from a growth rate of 5.1 percent in 1970 to 5.6 percent in 1974.

Employment growth rate	Year	Employment growth rate	Year
5.1	1975	7.6	1981
7.7	1976	9.5	1982
7.1	1977	9.6	1983
6.1	1978	7.6	1984
5.8	1979	7.3	1985
7.1	1980		

And inflation continued.

A temporary change in direction of industrial production growth was the first signal of a turning in August 1927 (Table 8.1). Such a signal was evident in 1981, but the economy recovered briefly in 1982. Industrial production, which grew at about 9 percent a year between 1949 and 1979, rose 1.5 percent a year between 1979 and 1985 in spite of steadily increasing volumes of defense orders, and it dropped to 1.2 percent in 1985.

Table 8.1. Industrial Production Indexes: Manufacturing

Third Wave		Fourth Wave		
1914	13	1960	65	
1919	15	1965	90	
1920	15	1970	106	
1921	12	1972	119	
1922	15	1973	130	
1923	18	1974	129*	
1924	17	1975	116*	
1925	19	1976	130	
1926	20	1977	138	
1927	20*	1978	147	
1928	21	1979	154	
1929	23	1980	147*	
1930	19	1981	138	
1931	15	1982	138.6	
1932	12	1983	147.6	
1933	14	1984	161	(est.)
1934	15			
1936	18			

1967 = 100.
*Signals.

The 1974 peak in the automotive industries was reflected in a similar peak in the steel industry. During the following decade, some of the leading companies filed for bankruptcy: McLoud Steel in 1981; Phoenix Steel in 1983; Weirton Steel in 1984; Bethlehem; Bar, Rod & Wire; Seattle Steel, and Wheeling Pittsburgh in 1985. These represented 10 percent of the nation's steel production. All were able to remain in business with deep wage cuts (20 to 25 percent) and substantial layoffs.

The nation's investor-owned utilities slashed their capital appropriations in the first quarter of 1984 to a ten-year low. New capital appropriations by the utilities tumbled to $5.3 billion (seasonally adjusted) in the first quarter, down 26 percent from the final quarter of 1983. They reached only $4.34 billion in the first quarter of 1984, a 25 percent drop from the previous quarter and the lowest total since 1972. Actual capital spending by the electric utilities totaled $7.88 billion in current dollars in the first quarter of 1984, up 6 percent from the fourth quarter of 1983 but 6 percent below the record $8.42 billion spent in the second quarter of the previous year. Appropriations by the gas utilities amounted to $1 billion in the first quarter, falling 30 percent from the high $1.43 billion figure registered in the last quarter of 1983.

The stagnating capital investment outlook for the electric utilities reflected both lowered demand expectations and the loss of anticipated revenues from halted nuclear power projects. Unless the utilities could complete these projects, their capital investment was likely to remain in the doldrums.

In addition, the upswing of the 1960s saw the mature sectors of U.S. industry struggling to compete with national economies it had itself financed in South Korea, Brazil, Japan, Taiwan, and West Germany. In 1950 the United States produced 46.6 percent of the world's steel. In 1960 the figure was 26 percent; in 1980 it was 14.1 percent. In cyclical terms, the United States was suffering from the classic upswing maladies, high wages, counterproductive work rules, inefficient and outmoded plants, an education system neglecting mathematics and science, government regulations pushing up the costs of doing business and inhibiting new development, and a new educational and labor mix created by affirmative action designed to bring a wider spectrum of minorities into the labor force.

If the cycle were to follow the pattern of previous long waves, the economy could expect a gradual decline in wholesale (producer) prices. The decline of the inflationary pressure would help bring down interest rates. A decline in needs for expansion would relieve the demand for funds, accelerating this process.

Debts, already at a high level, would continue to grow. The declining inflation rate would cause problems in the payments of these debts when prices and values failed to meet the expectations of borrowers and values of land and inventories became out of balance. Loan renewals would become more difficult and bad debts and foreclosures would increase. More banks would fail, particularly among the small banks in farm areas whose loans were extended to farmers at relatively high interest.

At some point the economy would suffer a shocking event—an unsalvageable bank situation, a default by one of the major foreign debtors (which would domino to others), a sudden, sharp drop in stock prices, or perhaps even a major natural disaster. As debts accumulate the economy because more vulnerable and the all-important confidence level more fragile. In the past each plateau had met such a trigger, what used to be called a panic.

The trend was evident even during the late 1960s, when investment expenses began to contract (48.5 percent of GNP for the decade), and in the early 1970s (Table 8.2). But in terms of physical capital per hour worked, which is basic to increasing productivity, it dropped 4.3 percent between 1975 and 1979. And there was still a pressing need to absorb the last of the huge bulge in working-age population of the post–World War II baby boom, which lasted until the early 1980s.

Table 8.2. Gross Private Domestic Investment

Year	In 1972 Dollars (billions)	Change (%)	
1970	159	+ 10.4	(2-year average)
1972	195	+ 21.4)	(3-year average)
1973	218	+ 1.5)	
1974	196	– 10.1)	The drop
1975	155	– 20.8)	
1976	185	+ 19.4	
1977	214	+ 15.7	
1978	230	+ 7.6	
1979	233	+ 1.3	
1980	204	– 12.4	

1978

The economic wall was hit again in October 1978, a phenomenon that developed when the economy stopped generating new earned money from production of goods and services for the previous five years.

The situation was hard to accept. Nothing like "the wall" had ever happened in the prior 200 years of American economic history. Growth stopped in all the basic industries. Steel production (150.8 million tons), motor vehicles (11.2 million vehicles, large-sized), and electric generating plants (2319 billion kwh capacity) peaked in the early 1970s. Production declined, and there appeared no real hope for its revival. A few years later, Steven Greenhouse noted in the New York Times the "growing pains" in chemicals:

> It happened in steel, it happened in copper and now it is starting to happen in basic petrochemicals.
>
> A once-thriving U.S. industry reaches maturity while still young. Then producers in developing countries, which often have lower costs for raw materials and labor, build new plants. That floods the world with excess capacity and forces many manufacturers in the developed nations to close their high cost operation.[1]

Greenhouse pointed out that the same pattern existed in the petrochemical industries, resulting in a shakeout among producers of basics like methane and ethylene, the building blocks of more sophisticated chemical products. One response to the advantaged competition is a movement toward more sophisticated chemicals with specific uses and designed for specific users.

Commenting along the same line, Charles H. Kline, the chief of a chemical consulting firm, puts it bluntly: "The bloom is off the rose in petrochemicals. . . . It's the classic old shakeout when an industry matures." In that shakeout, Cities Service moved out of petrochemicals and Monsanto cut back its line.

The phenomenon was described by Peter F. Drucker, writing in the *Wall Street Journal* in January 1985:

> Primary producing economies—such as the American and the Canadian farm belts; sugar producers, whether in Hawaii, South America or in the Caribbean; the growers of coffee and cocoa; the copper miners in the American Southwest, in Southeast Africa and in Chile; the tin producers in Malaysia—have all been in a severe depression for almost five years now. And measured against the prices of manufactured goods and major services, such as finance, insurance, communications and transportation, the prices of primary products are now in the sub-sub-sub-basement, and in many cases as low as they were in 1932. Indeed, the primary-producing economies show all the traits of the "Great Depression" of the classical 50-year cycle.

The economic problems of the 1970s involved multiple causes, not the least of which was the coming to maturity of the remaining millions of baby boomers who kept teenage unemployment figures in the range of 20 to 30 percent.

1980

In 1980 recession may be charged to the second oil price rise after the fall of the Shah of Iran in 1979. It depressed the economy of the entire world. It also triggered the decline of the continuing smokestack industries, which exerted downward pressure on prices of metals and other commodities.

The economic problems of the 1970s involved multiple causes, not the least of which was the influx of 17 million baby boomers into the labor market, inflation, and high oil prices. But tired technology was also a major factor. In spite of a 47.1 percent rise in fixed capital in the decade and 48.5 percent in the 1960s, U.S. industry fell behind. Years of reliance on quantitative growth to attain economies of scale added to historic resistance to innovations. The high unemployment rate was a product of a slow growth rate, the bulge in the working population, and the entry of large numbers of women into the labor force.

The Keynesian and monetary pressures applied are reflected in the record (Table 8.3) of efforts to direct the economy in that decade.

Table 8.3. Government Action in the Economy

Year	Increases In Federal Budget (%)	Budget Deficits (billion dollars)	Increases In Money Supply (% Change) M1-B
1973	6.5	– 14.8	5.5
1974	9.1	– 4.7	4.4
1975	21.0	– 45.2	5.0
1976	12.3	– 66.4	6.6
1977	9.9	– 44.9	8.1
1978	11.9	– 48.8	8.3
1979	9.5	– 27.7	7.2
1980	17.1	– 59.6	6.4
1981	13.0	– 54.9	5.4

Although interest rates did not register a continuous decline, they did drop 40 percent from a 16.38 percent federal fund rate in 1981 to 9.5 percent in 1984, and went through a further drop to 8.5 percent in 1985.

According to the consensus of Keynesian and monetary wisdom, the huge federal deficits and the sustained increases in money supply of the Reagan years should have had obvious effects, which many economists predicted and deplored: higher interest rates, a higher rate of inflation, a retrenchment in investment, and higher unemployment. These trends, also predictable from a historical view of the Kondratieff wave, would have evolved into a decline in prices and a decline in interest rates.

The two substantial elements, a high defense budget (in the $200 billion range) and easy money, changed the course of the economy in 1982. They led to a large increase in defense spending ($1 trillion, 6 percent of GNP, in four years) and investment spending (twice the rate during any of the previous postwar recoveries) in new technologies, creating the new inventions noted by Kondratieff from previous expansion phases of the long wave, and attributed to depression-associated factors.

Even without the stimulus of low interest rates and a surplus of unused savings, real capital spending rose from 12.6 percent of GNP in 1983 to 17.1 percent during the first two quarters of 1984, and plans indicated an even sharper rise in 1985. The motivation came from the "swarm" of new high-technology developments that grew out of the microchip and microbiology, the laser, and new ceramics. The fuel for financing this expansion came largely from increases in the money supply and a torrent of foreign capital.

The decline in the basic industries that fed the expansion of the fourth Kondratieff wave was evident early in the 1970s both in the United States and in Europe. As the basic industries that fed the post–World War II expansion matured, their investment spending declined. Some major companies changed direction and "diversified." The decline in demand for steel led U.S. Steel to change its product mix from 73.1 percent steel in 1979 to 32 percent in 1984. At that time oil and gas constituted 53 percent of its product.

At the same time new competition entered the various fields from other products and materials (plastics), and because of taste changes and foreign competition. This happened to all the smokestack industries (motor vehicles, steel, chemicals, rubber, textiles, glass). Some companies adapted or diversified.

The expansion of motor vehicles and electricity production stopped abruptly. The U.S. auto industry faced more foreign competition, and utilities fell into the quagmire of nuclear energy expansion and new developments with fuel cells. The pattern is one predicted by the commentators on the Kondratieff wave.

THE PLATEAU

After a recovery in 1974–1978, typical of the Kondratieff pattern, a recession of 1980–1982 appeared to forecast the declining plateau similar to the periods from 1820 to 1823, 1870 to 1873, and 1921 to 1927.

However, the problems of inflation and unemployment in the U.S. economy underwent a sharp reversal in 1982. In two years the inflation rate dropped 61.6 percent from the rate at the beginning of that year.

A new economic policy, utilizing even larger federal budgets, larger budget deficits, and larger increases in money supply, was able to reverse the Misery Index. The growth rate became positive, the inflation rate dropped to 4 percent, and unemployment dropped to 7.1 percent.

But underlying forces continued to push basic (smokestack) industries into decline. Commodity prices, particularly metals (but even energy prices and food prices), moved downward; these were indicators of a declining economy.

1982–1985

As the smokestack industries, the industrial base on which American power had been built, turned downward, a new economy was forming around new technologies: the computer and robotics, biotechnology and genetics, nuclear energy, and a host of services. Of the new investments in the United States in 1984, computers absorbed 38 percent, electronics 13 percent, and health services 5 percent. The new directions were labeled "information services."

But these new directions were filled with pitfalls. The year 1985 saw a shakeout in new computer companies. As quickly as new technology was developed, it was adapted, met, or improved in Japan or pirated elsewhere. The nation continued to hover on a plateau supported principally by federal deficit spending.

9

Causes And Consequences I: Innovation, Investment, And Maturation

It is apparent from the historical record that fiscal and monetary policies had a substantial effect on the cyclical pattern. However, in light of the pressures seen in the long wave, the effect of these measures appears almost superficial, except that they could, and did, trigger the panics that initiated long and difficult depressions.

Endemic to each of the major expansions were the diffusion of a major, seminal innovation that induced massive investment in its own development and stimulated other corollary industries; and spending for defense, wars, and rehabilitation from wars. In the nature of capitalism, these stimuli caused overexpansion, overinvestment, and adjustments noticeable as short-term cycles. But the long waves were made of sterner stuff.

Kondratieff and Schumpeter (as well as van Gelderen[1] in 1915 and Lescure[2] in 1913) believed that innovations were the chief igniting factor. Other economists, notably DeWolff in 1924 and Clark in 1944, extended the explanation to the investments involved in promoting these inventions.[3,4] Keynes gave more credit to government spending for stimulation. Kitchin in 1923, Woytinski in 1931, Cassel in 1932, Warren and Pearson in 1935, and Friedman in 1936 attributed the greatest importance to money supply factors.[5-9] A few others, notably Sirol, saw the market for food products as a vital force.[10] All, of course, recognized that low costs of money, labor, raw materials, and rent were an underlying factor.

In a cycle each cause is a consequence of preceding forces and each consequence is the cause of following dynamics. From the beginning, Kondratieff acknowledged the difficulty in distinguishing between causes and consequences, asserting that the causes usually assumed for our rhythms "reverse the causal connections and take the consequences to be the cause, or see an accident where we really have to deal with a law governing the events." It appears that cause and consequence interact to reinforce the long-wave spirals.

Sometimes improvements in technique have been alleged to be a cause of a Kondratieff wave. Kondratieff noted that it would be a great error

> if one believes the change, action, and intensity of those discoveries and inventions were merely accidental . . . . The development of technique itself is part of the long waves.

Kondratieff held that the long waves were inherent in the nature of capitalism, a product of capital accumulation. He saw changes in production, wars, the postwar depressions, the opening of new markets, the rush of innovations all as integral parts of a dynamic long-wave rhythm. His distinction between cause and consequence was different from (often the reverse of) today's conventional wisdom. Expansion into new markets, he held, did not stimulate an upswing; rather, the expansion created the need for new markets. In the same way, he saw the decline in the economy leading to the exploitation of existing discoveries, bringing about the next expansion. Inventions remained unexploited during the Kondratieff upswings.

A difficulty in eliciting causes lies in the complicated mechanism of the whole economy, which responds erratically, or perhaps with an incomprehensible logic, to stimulation.

The thought was to be carried further. DeWolff in 1929 and Clark in 1944 accented the spending element involved. This was the essence of Keynes' general theory.

The strongest support was elicited by Schumpeter, who believed that the volume of innovations was heavily dependent on the stage of the business cycle, and held that low costs and availability of capital were the dominant stimulants to investment.

Using the analogy of a motor vehicle we have used before, an innovation is seen as a spark plug; investment spending provides the ignition; available capital, materials, and labor provide varieties of fuel; the market is the road; and expectation of profits is the destination. All these factors must be in gear to create momentum. Deficiencies in any of the elements tend to speed or stop the movement.

SPENDING

The volatile factor most effective in stimulating the economy is spending— the demand for goods and services. In effect, national product is the sum spent by consumers, government, business (for investment and inventory accumulation), and net exports. Of this, consumer spending generally constitutes 60 to 65 percent of the total, business spending 15 percent, and government spending (that has risen in recent years) 20 to 25 percent. (Deficit spending has a particular effect on money supply and interest rates.)

Consumer spending has, to a large extent, been stabilized by government social welfare and government transfer payments, which now account for 18.5 percent of gross national product or about $2000 per capita. And government purchases now employs 15 percent of the labor force.

Business spending is influenced largely by consumer demand for goods and services, which entices expansion of production and thus investment in plant and inventory accumulation.

However, there are marginal factors that stimulate spending: created or new areas for consumer demand, or changes in marketing and pricing; and pump priming by the government, either by deficit spending or by other stimulations (loan guarantees, tax credits, or other means).

Keynes' economics ascribes no special weight, in the long run, to public or government spending as compared to privately financed spending by business for investment. All that is material in his view is total spending. There is no "crowding out," no Keynesian criteria for resource misallocation between public, private, or investment sectors.

However, some forms of spending have a much greater multiplier effect than others. A greater multiplier is accomplished by purchasing innovative products (e.g., by defense spending). Purchasing new arms requires not only an increase in product but usually an investment in new equipment, and often new plants to produce for a changed technology. It thus involves hiring more people, with a consequent ripple effect on a local retail level. It also has the basic effect of diffusion of innovation, for indeed new armaments open innovative industries. Moreover, public acceptance for defense spending is more readily attained than spending for most other programs, which are generally politically motivated pork barrel projects of questionable value beyond local satisfaction. Deficit spending for defense was a major factor stimulating the economy in 1812, 1820–21, 1824, 1861, 1916, 1933, 1937, 1949, 1963, 1982 and 1983.

Spending for social services has less stimulative effect. The funds enter the market and merely change the parties in the supply–demand balance, with only a ripple effect on the economy. A billion dollars spent for feeding the poor has a ripple effect on farm prices and retailing. Cleaning up toxic wastes could put 50,000 to work for a year. Building homes would have a greater multiplier effect but would compete with the market.

There are time differences in the relative effects and they change, depending on long-term cyclical circumstances. Keynes noted that during a prolonged downturn, such as might result after an excess of capitalization and speculation, public spending should accelerate.

INNOVATION

Kondratieff himself and all his protagonists have given to innovation the chief role as the force that moves a cycle from a trough toward the peak. Innovation in the economic-cycle sense refers to a change in any phase of the economic spectrum. It is more than merely invention or the diffusion or commercialization of a new development. It may be a war, a natural calamity, an epidemic, a change in the price structure, or even a change in taste, developed in the normal course of events or by an astute marketing program.

A pitfall continually noted by critics in the rationalization of long-wave regularity is the obvious fact that inventions or innovations follow no clock in their origins. Plants do not uniformly become depreciated or obsolete at a half-century mark. Why a 50 to 60 year cycle? Kondratieff accounts for increased diffusion of innovations during trough periods by the cheaper set-up cost and availability of capital in trough periods.

The pressure to find investments during trough periods was noted by Defoe in the seventeenth century:

Much greater were the number of those who felt a sensible ebb of their fortunes, and with difficulty bore up under the loss of a great part of their estates. These, prompted by necessity, rack their wits for new contrivances, new inventions, new trades, stocks, projects, anything to retrieve the desperate credit of their fortunes. ("Essay upon Projects," 1697).

Another response was that "inventions appear in swarms" (Schumpeter, Business Cycles). Inventions appear to arrive in groups because generally a basic invention leads to others that improve or extend it. A major breakthrough like the steam engine, the railroad, electricity, or the electronic chip is a seminal expansion of the economy. One machine leads to others, each with improvements, making possible greater specialization and division of labor. In addition there is a synergistic effect in a major technical breakthrough that inspires other cross-applications—the sewing machine suggested embroidery equipment, shoemaking equipment, and so on. Steam power showed the way to power-driven boats, trains, looms, and machines. The motorcar led to trucks, tractors, buses, even to motorized golf carts; it opened suburbia and distorted the whole pattern of shipping and transportation costs.

Recent events make more evident a limiting aspect of innovations and the seminal and cyclical nature of some of them. When the development of the basic innovation had run its course, the corollary industries declined, carrying with them associated industries that had also passed their peak. Expansion stopped. And a stagnant economy with a growing labor force quickly deteriorates.

Inventions by themselves do not change the economy. It is the exploitation of these innovations, their diffusion into the economy, that produces capital spending and ignites cyclical expansion. Inventions offer investment opportunities. And investment stimulates spending for new supplier ventures that have the necessary multiplier effect throughout the economy.

The time period involved for the transfer of technology for a new use in production is largely dependent on the economic climate at the time and the cost of the change, taking into account the inertia caused by reluctance to abandon old or obsolete equipment.

The clustering of innovations is described by Clemence and Doody:

> Once an innovation has been successfully introduced into the economy it tends to be followed by attempts at imitation and improvement. Some entrepreneurs enter the innovating area in the hope of making profits, and their success smooths the path for others to follow. The result of this sequence of events is the phenomenon known as the clustering of innovations.[11]

These investments, Kondratieff noted in his second paper, take place in spurts at a propitious (trough) time, which, reflecting the major economic cycles, become a basic cause of upswings.

Thus, he saw as preconditions to an upswing:

1. High propensity to save.
2. Relatively large supply of liquid loan capital at low rates.
3. Accumulation of these funds in the hands of powerful entrepreneurial and financial groups.*
4. A low price level, including savings and long-term capital investment.

He did not explain the immediate cause of the trough turning point. At the peak turning point, however, Kondratieff saw a shortage of funds inhibiting expansion.

---

*An element in the contemporary "trickle down" approach.

Kondratieff notes, in discussing the investment in cotton planting in the South during a recession,

> If we are to form an idea as to the quantitative adequacy of innovation, we must bear in mind that all it should, according to our schema, be adequate for, is ignition.

SMALL CHANGES ADD UP TO BIG CYCLES

An examination of change in a total economy indicates that a major change (or what appears to be a precipitous change) is really an explosion of an accumulation of many small influences and events, a procession of changes so small that pinpointing a date of a change in a trend is relatively meaningless. Charting a statistical series provides us with a numerical starting point, but each peak and each trough is the result of layering of a multiplicity of minor changes.

Schumpeter offers the analogy of "a vessel into which water flows at a perfectly steady rate but which is so constructed that it releases the water by a valve each time a certain weight has been accumulated." One such factor might be savings or debt, another, interest rates and capital availability.

In the economic sense innovations may be related or unrelated events: more efficient organizations of work or marketing, the opening of new lands, the discovery of new resources, and so on. Each development appears to enhance the climate for the next. And similarly, on the decline, little additional stimulus is needed to continue a spiral. The paucity of innovation and the weight of accumulated obligations and expectations may itself be one element.

Some innovations are principally cost-reducing for labor or capital. Some accent new products or new uses for old products. The difference between the two is not as material as it may appear. Lower costs tend to open new markets for a product or service that may be as investment-stimulating as an entirely new genre of consumer satisfaction. The story of aluminum, with decreasing costs and widening uses, is a matter of recent history.

Some cyclical element arises from market readiness. Kuznets points out, as an example, that

> electricity did not become available sooner because it had to wait until the potentialities of steam power were exhausted by the economic system and until the attention of inventors and engineers was ready to be diverted to the problems of electricity.[12]

One of the great spurs to the development of nuclear energy was the threat of removal of oil as a cheap source of power.

INVESTMENT

If innovation provides the ignition for cyclical stimulation, the fuel is supplied by capital investment. Innovation remains dormant until it is exploited by investment.

Mensch suggests some elements that are missing in Schumpeter's reasoning, but he objects to "the wave model [that] incorporates a determinable recurrence of phase transition." He holds that "the economy has evolved through a series of S-shaped cycles"—substantially what we term a sigmoid curve.[13]

All additions to spending (by consumers, government, or business) stimulate the economy. But spending for investment, especially those types of business investment that create new production facilities, have greater multiplier effects than others. This effect of the different components of investment should be noted. Inventory accumulation has a relatively static effect. Residential building has a large ripple effect (rugs, appliances, etc.). But investment in a new factory involves employment on several levels (construction, equipment, service facilities), the accumulation of producer inventory, and inventory in the marketing pipeline, all with ripple effects in the employment market and outward from there.

Railroads bring people, expand the use of land, and make distant marginal resources commercially viable. Cars open new areas, stimulate road building, and create new shopping patterns and new leisure time spending opportunities. Suburbia would be rural without them.

The development of steam power changed the nature of producing cotton textiles, iron, and steel, and produced the recession of 1801–1813, a depression in 1814–1827, the ultimate readjustment recovery of 1829–1842, and the prosperity of 1843–1857.

There are, as we see, negative elements in each adjustment. New developments make others obsolete. New industries mean not only new jobs but elimination of old jobs. Labor-saving devices make some laborers redundant.

Railroadization helped produce the panic of 1857, the recession of 1858–1869, the depression of 1870–1885, the recovery of 1886–1897, and the prosperity of 1898–1911.

Each step conditions other steps, creating bottlenecks and relieving them, finding new markets and exploiting them, then learning to supply an expanded demand.

Critics point out that theory assumes that all business reacts in the same way at the same time "to create a business cycle." Actually, rolling industry-by-industry cyclical adjustments are well recognized. But a cyclical adjustment initiated in some industries (e.g., construction,

14 percent of GNP; motor vehicles, 5 percent of GNP) is often so substantial and far-reaching in its effects that it tends to become contagious. An expansion or retrenchment in any major industry such as motor vehicle production can expand or destabilize business norms for a whole economy, even for the world.

WHY 54 YEARS?

The first criticism of the long wave dealt with the obvious failing that all plant and infrastructures did not wear out or become obsolete, requiring simultaneously replacement after 54 years.

Some cyclists defended the view that the average life span of durable investments is about 15 years, and their replacement is only one factor in generating new long waves. These cycles are seen as capital-hungry and capital-sated phases. Walter G. Hoffman made a study of British Industry from 1700 to 1950, and came to the conclusion that economic wave lengths were indeed determined to some extent by replacement of fixed capital.[14]

Kondratieff views the turn from prosperity to depression as merely the end of the line for a major innovation—the saturation of the major industries that provided growth. He sees stagnation as nothing but a lack of basic innovations, a technological stalemate. As innovations become integrated into an expanding economy, more dramatic innovations are required to motivate the spending necessary to expand or even to sustain the momentum.

Some analysts saw stagnation as a period of vanishing investment opportunities, a concept derived by Alvin Hansen from Marx's approach. This stagnation was seen as leading to a structural crisis and a change in the capitalist system. Keynes diagnosed this as a failing in the system: "The weakness of the inducement to invest has been at all times the key to the economic problems."

Contemporary experience seems to indicate that the long wave is created by a basic innovation (steam, electricity, the automobile) which becomes a marginal element in the economy. The life cycle of this element follows the life cycle of any product. When the period of expansion for this product reaches its saturation point, that industry and those industries which were created to support it cease expanding, face new competition, and begin to decline.

That the product cycle for steam, electricity, and automobiles should be in the range of 50 to 60 years may be a historical accident or may be due to other factors. Probably the cyclical forces that result from tired products create the new climate for innovation, reducing costs during trough periods to make practical the seeding of new ideas (often better or cheaper or substitute products), and providing a better reception in the marketplace.

Trough periods help overcome a mass of resistance to change which restrains the diffusion of inventions.

RESISTANCE TO INNOVATION

An aditional element flows from Mensch's idea of a series of normal S-shaped product curves, a cycle that follows the life of a major invention: speedy growth, a declining growth rate, a peak, a slow (plateau) decline, and a rapid decline (Fig. 9.1).

He believes, like others, that stagnation and depression result from a lack of basic innovations. Innovation turning points in the depressions of 1825, 1873, 1929, and 1973 were accomplished after these troughs were reached.

As Mensch sees it, inasmuch as firms will not innovate if equipment has not exhausted its profit potential, the way to get out of

Figure 9.1. The Metamorphosis Model Of Industrial Evolution

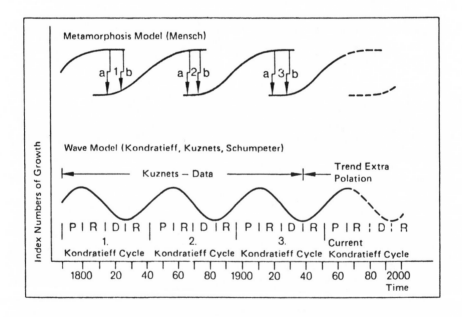

Source: Reprinted with permission from Gerhard Mensch, *Stalemate in Technology* (Cambridge, MA: Ballinger, 1979).

depressions is through stimulating innovations. He points to upper turning points where former growth industries are saturated, and lower turning points which occur when firms transform technological knowledge into basic innovations. Between these levels a technological stalemate exists.

Marketing experience makes it evident that industries parallel the S-shaped curve seen in the rise and decline of new products. In addition, the new industry, uninhibited by built-in self-satisfaction, ossified costs, union-contracted personnel inertia, and administrative overhead, offers inducements to the consumer that extend old markets, create new ones, or break price barriers.

Another inhibiting factor in the timing of adoption of innovations is an apparently inherent human resistance to change. As an economy becomes older and more stable, institutions develop for the purpose of maintaining the status quo, for retaining power in the entrenched establishment, or for fighting any change.

Old firms, organizations, and institutions with a strong hold on the market find little motivation to invest in new technology (Figs. 9.2 and 9.3). They resist changes that could endanger their own position in the market or their financial security on the theory that if it isn't broken, don't fix it. Established industries tend to accept change slowly, and then usually under extreme pressure. In the eighteenth century the wool industry resisted moving into cotton and fought changes through legislation. In the 1960s the U.S. auto industry resisted smaller cars, later demanding protective quotas on imports. The resistance of unions to labor-saving devices or methods in the printing industries was a major factor in the twentieth century decline of the daily newspaper press. In construction, resistance to new products raised the cost of building homes by as much as 50 percent in some areas. Featherbedding helped destroy American railroads and many other industries.

In the 1980s this resistance restrained Germany and England, nations long renowned for their advanced technology, from competing effectively. Strikes to keep open money-losing coal mines kept Britain in industrial suspense through 1984. In many industries in France, firing an employee was virtually impossible, even at the end of a probation period varying from two weeks for unskilled laborers to six months for senior managers.

The desire for union security and tenure eliminates efficiency as a gauge in employee selection or retention. Even in the United States in many industries it has become virtually impossible to fire employees. Even when there is a direct proper cause, the bother, cost, bad public relations, sympathy, resistance, and disruption inhibit firings. Every reduction in force becomes a prolonged matter of negotiation, which is often unsuccessful. Such resistance is particularly evident in

Figure 9.2. Recurring Renewal: U.S. Steelmaking Technologies, 1867–1977

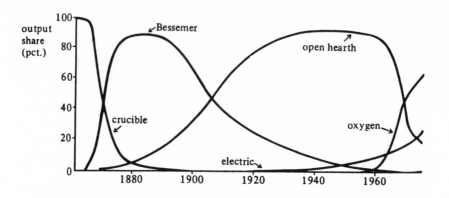

Source: J. J. van Duijn, *The Long Wave in Economic Life* (London: George Allen & Unwin, 1983).

Figure 9.3. Life Cycles For First-, Second-, And Third-Generation Computers (Market Shares In Great Britain: 1959–1967)

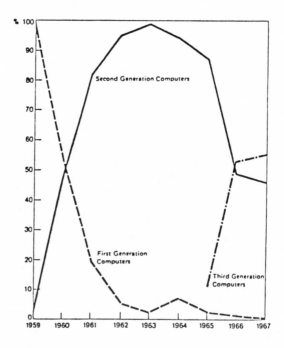

Source: Gerhard Mensch, *Stalemate in Technology* (Cambridge, MA: Ballinger, 1979), p. 73.

government, where teachers and other employees cannot be fired except for "cause," and almost always for "moral turpitude." Such procedural bottlenecks not only promote stagnation in a labor force and impair flexibility in the transfer and use of personnel, but foster a do-as-little-as-possible demotivation.

Another union-devised element creating a restraint on innovation and virtually any increase in productivity, is a policy of inflexible work rules. These may limit personnel to perform special, sometimes small tasks that could be handled incidentally by others. It is manifested in the right to select the specific job to be assigned, or by promotion simply by seniority. Still another factor is labor ossification, the gradual accumulation of higher wages, due to seniority alone, without increases in productivity.

Management was sometimes able to meet such contingencies by closing plants or moving, through wholesale layoffs and selective rehiring, by retraining programs, by making other decisive breaks with old patterns, or by renegotiation of contracts. Others were forced to wait until layoffs and imminent bankruptcy forced the issue.

All these resulted in a decreasing productivity that ultimately priced a product out of its extended market and invited competition from abroad or from other products. Contemporary examples flood the mind: steel, autos, chemicals, textiles, clothing.

Both labor and entrepreneurs often enlist government to sustain their position. Sometimes well-meaning groups achieve the same retardation. Delays and costs associated with government regulations discourage and often dissipate the influence of new developments, and help to consolidate the position of established companies and the previously approved methodology. Other roadblocks are erected by traditions and institutions.

In any community there is a strong tendency for inertia to dominate a system of living. Members soon take for granted everything they have and resist any diminution. They resist changes in policies, attitudes, location, and entitlements, even where these were established in relatively recent times and a continuance endangers the industry. In this way a social structure, an economy, a policy, even a way of doing things becomes entrenched.

Concomitant with this is greater regulation for public protection of goods. In the recent cycles these have included legislation increasing the power of labor unions, laws extending requirements for pollution control, consumer protection laws, anti-trust laws, product safety requirements, as well as import quotas, health regulations, and tariffs. All of these, each with its own justification, added to the cost of American products, making them increasingly noncompetitive.

Resistance to change increases with the age of a population as well as with the length of time a custom or an institution has been accepted. And the age of a population is cyclical, as we shall see.

OVERINVESTMENT AND IMBALANCE

A basically different view of causes of the long-wave cycles (based on "imbalance") is suggested by W. W. Rostow. He sees these as primarily the result "of under-shooting and over-shooting of the dynamic optimum levels of capacity" and output of food and raw materials in the world economy.

His "optimum levels" are "those levels which have been attained in a continuous dynamic equilibrium where capacity was smoothly adjusted to rates of increase in population and income, the income elasticity of demand, the rate and changing structure of industrial growth, and the pace and character of technological change."[15]

Similarly, Jay Forrester's System Dynamics Group explains Kondratieff's waves with a basic proposition: industrial economies tend to overinvest in existing technologies, especially in capital goods industries, and excessive investment leads to their decline when demand wanes (Fig. 9.4). It holds that the latest wave of overinvestment began in the 1960s, but is becoming obvious now. For evidence they point to worldwide overcapacity in steel, autos, diesel engines, chemicals, shipbuilding, machine tools, and even semiconductors.[16]

Other theories suggest underconsumption, lack of purchasing power, oversaving, various psychological factors, labor supply, government spending, money and credit supply, or all of these.

The inflation of 1965–1984 was a product of the concept that a cyclical depression could be avoided by government spending, financed through increases in money supply. In the era dominated by Keynesian views, the capital for expansion was provided in large measure by government, either through deficit spending, loan guarantees, monetary expansion, or all three.

The Keynesian formula for combating stagnation via inflation, together with a larger share of government in the national product, failed the test of reality in 1965–1974. Adequate funds did not avert the stagnation of 1974 and 1980, in conditions made more acute by the oil crisis. However, it may be that they were not sufficiently massed. But the billions of dollars appropriated for defense in the Reagan years did help to turn the corner in 1982.

Milton Friedman established the basic premise that the increase in the rate of rise in money supply was followed, a quarter later, by a rise

Figure 9.4. The Sigmoid Curve in Economic Indicators

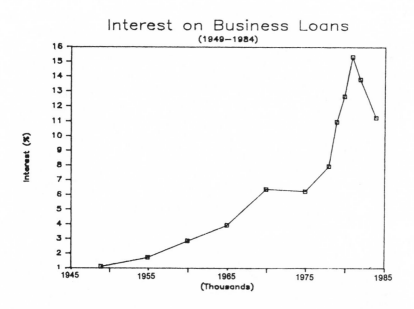

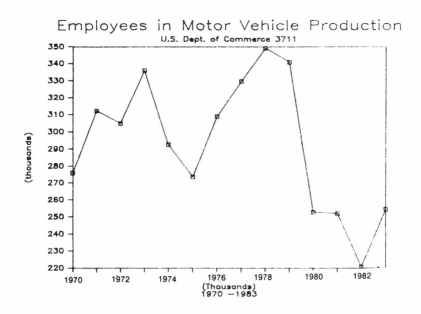

Figure 9.4. (continued)

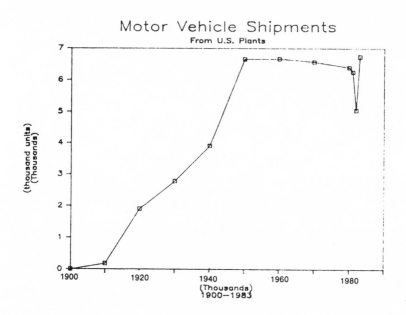

Motor Vehicle Shipments
From U.S. Plants

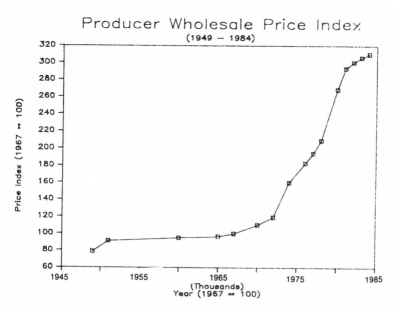

Producer Wholesale Price Index
(1949 – 1984)

Figure 9.4. (continued)

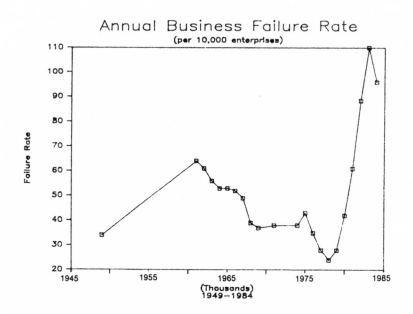

Annual Business Failure Rate
(per 10,000 enterprises)

(Thousands)
1949—1984

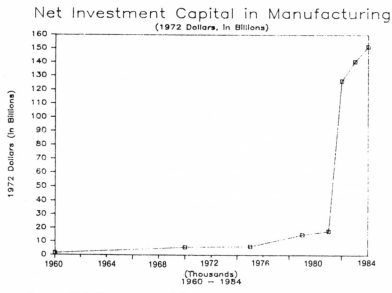

Net Investment Capital in Manufacturing
(1972 Dollars, In Billions)

(Thousands)
1960 — 1984

Source: U.S. Department of Commerce.

in gross national product. By his measure, the 12 to 13.4 percent rise from July 1982 to July 1983 sparked the 1983 boomlet. But experience shows that increasing money supply alone cannot stop a major downswing. A need and desire to use the funds must exist; and inflation must be held in check.

The deliberate regulation and/or manipulation of economic cycles by government spending and the loosening of the money supply is a technique relatively new to economics and widely accepted since Keynes, although it was practiced as early as the eighteenth century. The increased money supply made funds available for capital investment, funding government spending programs beyond government income, and thus increased consumer spending.

Causes And Consequences II: War, Demographics, And Social Change

OVERVIEW

The dynamics of the cyclical infrastructure of the Kondratieff waves follow the pressures that classical economists have readily recognized. The effect of deficit spending, interest rates and money supply, changes in productivity, and currency values and export surpluses are well known. These create economic cycles perceived over periods of months or periods of three to sixteen years. They are tools that serve for fine-tuning the economy.

Underlying causes of long waves lie in other directions, each identifiable as both a cause and a consequence of the dynamics that precede and follow it.

Authors have dealt at some length with the effect of "swarms of inventions" and their diffusion on investment spending in an expansive phase of the economy. But either as a cause or effect or both, other dynamics are seen in the cycle. Basic to these dynamics are wars, economic changes created by wars, demographic changes resulting from them, the psychological changes resulting from both of these, and changes in the social millieu.

THE CYCLE OF WARS

The cycle of wars and depressions has been widely perceived in United States history. The existence of 50- to 60-year cycles of wars, and the primary and secondary postwar depressions that follow them are evident. Kondratieff has identified their causes with economic pressures. The cyclical nature of wars was an integral part of his empirical data, not only as a part of the long wave but as both a product of it and as a force that kept the wave in motion. He insisted that wars were the result of natural tension in a capitalist economy. He put it this way:

> Wars and revolutions also influence the course of economic development very strongly. But wars and revolutions do not come out of a clear sky, and they are not caused by arbitrary acts of individual personalities. They originate from real, especially economic, circumstances. The assumption that wars and revolutions acting from the outside cause long waves evokes the question as to why they themselves follow each other with regularity and solely during the upswing of long waves. Much more probable is the assumption that wars originate in the acceleration of the pace and the increased tension of economic life, in the heightened economic struggle for markets and raw materials, and that social shocks happen most easily under the pressure of new economic forces.
>
> Wars and revolutions, therefore, can also be fitted into the rhythm of the long waves and do not prove to be the forces from which these movements originate, but rather to be one of their symptoms. But once they have occurred, they naturally exercise a potent influence on the pace and direction of economic dynamics.

Analysts distinguish two types of wars that occur at regular intervals. "peak wars," which are absolute wars, deeply involving the nation, and "trough wars," which are limited wars of less than universal commitment. Peak wars occur immediately preceding a peak (Fig. 10.1).

	War Began	Period between Peak Wars
War of 1812	1812	
Civil War	1861	49 years
World War I	1911	56 years
Vietnam War	1965	48 years

In economic terms, the peak war has a more disastrous impact, inasmuch as it falls on a society already overextended and strained to capacity. It results in a typical inflation blow-off, such as the years following 1814, 1864, and 1920. The Vietnam peak was similarly disastrous for the United States, as it imposed severe financial burdens on an economy already strained by two decades of unprecedented deficit spending and expansion.

As Kondratieff sees it, the peak war consumes whatever is left of liquidity. Thus it sets the stage for a postwar collapse and depression.

The recovery from the initial or "primary postwar depression," a plateau period of 5 to 10 years, is only temporary, as the government makes one final, desperate attempt to revive the boom. A devastating

Figure 10.1. Defense Outlays

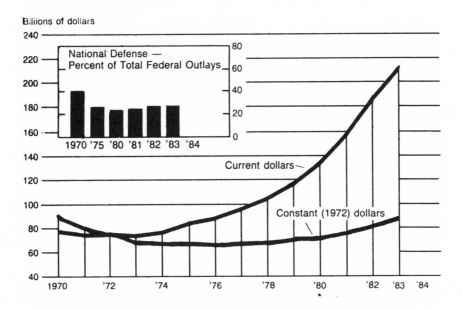

Source: Chart prepared by U.S. Bureau of the Census.

"secondary postwar depression," which arrives some seven to ten years later, initiates a final process of liquidation, which continues for approximately the remaining two decades of the down wave. The most acute financial stresses usually occur during the second or collapse decade of the 30-year period.

The peak wars thus have been associated with great tensions, substantial casualties, heavy costs, and rapid inflation. They are followed by a notable lack of public passion and eased tensions.

Unlike peak wars, trough wars fall early in an expansion period and on an economy with unused resources and idle manpower. As a result, the inflationary effects of trough wars are usually minimal. Sometimes they are not felt at all. The stimulation of the trough war is at least partly responsible for the beginning of a recovery.

Trough wars occur immediately after a cyclical trough:

	War Began	Period between Trough Wars
War of Independence	1776–1783	
Mexican War	1848	65 years
Spanish-American War	1898	50 years
Korean War	1950–1953	53 years

Obviously not all wars or economic crises are limited to the long waves nor do they originate in U.S. domestic policy. Each nation has unique, interrelated, often synchronous forces at work. The military activities of selected major nations have occurred as follows:

England	France	Germany	Russia
1789	1759	1815	1856
1846	1815	1870	1895
1896	1870	1914	1905
	1914		

The coincidences of the war cycles with the early and late phases of industrial expansion has led to much discussion among economists, particularly Marxists. It has been illuminated by studies of some Europeans who see a causal relationship between the approach of stagnation, increases in defense spending, and wars under the difficult to counter rationale of "national defense."

Gerhard Mensch suggests modern, logical, politically wise dynamics. After describing the economic pressures that lead to a weapons build-up, he sees declining economies resorting to defense spending as a stimulant because this form of government spending is most readily acceptable to the public, does not floor the marketplace with consumer goods, and has a high multiplier effect.

One cannot surmise that a period is particularly threatened by war simply because nations possess large defensive stockpiles; rather, when one or more nations actively begins to increase its arms supplies the danger of war arises. These sudden increases in armament levels have always occurred in our economic history at times when the era of prosperity in the most highly developed industrial nations has given way to an era of stagnation. Defense contracts had to substitute for sluggish private demands. According to the Kuznets model, these inflection points in the past growth trends occurred in 1801, 1858, and 1912. These dates provide us with a guess for the hindsight prediction of which years were particularly vulnerable to an outbreak of war, since the economy-boosting defense contracts that a state in a critical situation would suddenly promote would need to be justified domestically by the engagement in war-threatening behavior abroad. These tactics would soon create a *casus belli* whether or not it was desired.

The timetable of major wars fits into the stagnation scheme too well not to cause us some alarm. The economic preconditions for war include defense contracts used as therapy for a stagnating economy. This pattern was repeated before every large-scale belligerent encounter until World War I. World War II does not fit into the economic framework, but the contention that the United States became involved in Vietnam for primarily economic reasons has been discussed too thoroughly to require more elaboration. One can also use this progression with substantial justification to maintain that the years after 1967 also posed a high degree of danger that war would break out. The tragic protraction of the Vietnam War and the eagerness of the Great Powers to supply the Middle East combatants with arms also fit into the schema, as does the historical parade of great "architects of peace"—Metternich, Bismarck, Wilson, and *pro tanto*, Henry Kissinger. Analogous situations produce analogous men. One can also argue, however, that World War II and the balance of terror have made escalation toward large-scale war obsolete because nuclear weapons have made war unthinkable.

History teaches that a certain type of economic crisis follows war. After the armistice, people are still suffering from the horrors of war and governments will no longer be able to counteract the prevailing stagnation in private industry with defense spending. Therefore, the economic problem of stagnation will reappear in the postwar period, only in a more aggravated form. The so-called peace economy that was already stagnating before the war must now supply the returning soldiers with jobs. But why should these stagnating industries be more capable of creating jobs in the postwar poverty than they were in the prewar prosperity?

There is therefore an unhappy correlation between the years in which truces or armistices were signed and years in which signal crises occurred: The crisis years are 1815, 1866, 1920. The end of the war years are 1815, 1865, 1918. What these crises signal is the structural instability of a beginning technological stalemate.[1]

The cycle of conventional wars may well have changed since Hiroshima, but the tensions that produce them continue. For the present, the world has substituted other less self-destructive outlets, proxy wars (of which some 40 are continuously in progress), terrorism, assassinations, and cold wars.

World conflicts have produced a demographic cycle of mobilization of the labor force for fighting and wartime production; enlistment of more women into the labor force; postwar demobilization; a spurt in home formations; a new baby boom; and initiation of a new population bulge cycle. The balance of terror and mutual assured destruction has made large-scale wars (virtually) unthinkable, but does not preclude proxy wars or other stimuli to large defense expenditures.

POSTWAR PROSPERITIES

In terms of innovations, wartime periods provided a large reservoir of inventions that could be diffused into industry. The postwar period was thus stimulated by this peace-released exploitation. It is characterized by deflationary forces, including a decline in government expenses, demobilization of personnel, and a need for public revenues to aid in reconstruction, often an attempt to reduce the national debt. There is also stimulation to capital investment to replace equipment for which replacement has been restrained, often with new equipment made possible by innovations not exploited because of the war. The result is a short, precipitous postwar demobilization adjustment recession followed by equally sharp expansion.

Postwar economic miracles are part of this long-wave cycle. They arise with the need to replace production and consumer capital goods plus the elimination of legal and social barriers to their replication, which are found in a tired, mature economy.

Soon after peak wars end, deflationary forces begin to take effect. Governments retrench, deficits are replaced by surpluses as costs fall. This continues until a decline in revenues reverses the federal balance and deficits reappear. This postwar decline has followed each major war: in 1814, 1873, 1921, and 1972.

Second postwar depressions seem to catch the economy by surprise. They are more precipitous, more severe, and more stubborn than the first postwar depressions.

It is not uncommon among economists to believe that in a free market economy, economic crises are inevitable consequences of a long period of peace. It follows that the danger of war is closely related to sluggish economic conditions, particularly those existing in the nations most developed at any time. Kondratieff and others (Mensch 1973, Hansen 1932, Von Ciriacy-Wantrup 1948, Bernstein 1940) see wars as the culmination of an upswing leg of a long wave, a search for new markets, and an outlet for political tensions (Table 10.1). They echo the Marxist view that wars are a normal product of tensions, created by oversupply in the capitalist economies. Others saw conflicts as an outgrowth of increasing defense spending.

During the Reagan administration, approximately a trillion dollars was allocated for defense over a four-year period, adding almost 6 percent to the gross national product, providing a direct major spending stimulant, with a high multiplier effect, especially because of new technologies involved. These appropriations induced additional capital spending for production of high-technology weapons. They created a demand for a large variety of supplier goods, revived industries suffering from maturation, added life to communities becoming ghost towns, and

Table 10.1. Defense as Percentage of Outlays of GNP

	Total (billions of dollars)	Percent of Total Budget (billions of dollars)	Percent of GNP
1902	.111	29.1	2.35
1913	.155	26.1	3.89
1922	.270	24.0	8.48
1927	.249	18.1	8.99
1932	.244	17.9	.004
1936	.291	11.3	3.84
1945	81.585	17.3	34.5
1946	44.731	76.9	4.8
1950	13.119	29.1	10.5
1955	40.245	58.1	9.1
1960	45.908	48.1	8.9
1962	51.097	45.9	7.2
1965	49.578	38.9	8.1
1970	80.295	24.5	5.8
1975	87.071	26.4	5.0
1978	105.595	23.5	5.3
1980	136.067	21.5	6.1
1982	185.820	23.8	6.8
1983	211.860	27.0	9.0
1984	217.100	29.1	8.5
1985	253.800	23.9	5.98

Source: Council of Economic Advisors (updated).

provided jobs for the blue-collar workers who otherwise would have been cyclically and technologically obsolescent. In spite of the hue and cry about mounting public debt, the defense spending of the 1980s was a major factor in the turnaround growth of the economy in the United States in 1982, 1983, and 1984. By osmosis, this cycle of high federal deficits, high interest rates, high value of the dollar (attracted by this profit opportunity), and high imports salvaged the economies of most of the Western world, both by stimulating exports abroad and by restraining U.S. competition. It also restrained inflationary pressures in the United States.

The federal budget tripled in ten years from $118.4 billion in 1965 to $324.2 billion in 1975. Spending for defense rose from $56.3 billion in 1965 to $103 billion in 1975, and went on to reach $263.5 billion in 1984.

There are, of course, concomitant monetary effects. Deficits lead to increases in money supply and stimulate inflation and consumer spending in anticipation of price rises.

THE DEMOGRAPHIC CYCLE

Kondratieff made no direct mention of demographic changes affecting the long wave, but this force can be implied from his comments on wars and tensions that accompany the rises and falls in economic activity. If wars are cyclical, the concurrent decline in births and the following postwar population bulges are consequently also cyclical. The low birth rate during depressions and the higher birth rate during postwar expansions follow the long-wave cycle. And 22 years after the beginning of each baby boom, a new bulge in the births begins. These bulges provide a clue to the 50–60-year duration of each wave. It is thus clear that a nation's population changes follow a pattern very much affected by its economy and its military adventures, which are thus both a cause and consequence of long waves. Fewer are born during periods of depression; more are born during periods of expansion.

Although each deviation in the population mix is unique in its effect on the economy, the basic elements are described below.

The decline in the number in a productive age group by reason of a depression forces decline in a birth rate. On the other hand, mobilization, wartime casualties, or epidemics tend to raise wages and establish an aura of prosperity, increasing the birth rate.

A bulge in the age mix that increases the labor force at a rate faster than the expansion of the economy tends to increase unemployment, lower wages, and create the atmosphere of a recession. (This phenomenon occurs during postwar demobilization, creating a first postwar depression, and at the arrival of productive age of a postwar baby-boom bulge.)

Let us examine the recent phenomenon. By the mid-1960s the approaching peak of the Kondratieff cycle was already evident. Each year a million young people beyond the normal labor force absorption rate were ready to look for work. The basic industries were slowing, certainly not expanding, and were even laying off workers.

Job openings were increasing at the rate of about a million a year, 1.3 percent from 1955 to 1965. In 1966 the influx of baby boomers added two million, or 2.2 percent; the following years saw additional increases in the same or greater numbers.

The post–World War II baby boom added an additional one million a year to the labor force above the normal 1 percent annual increment. From 1966 through 1970, the average increase was over 2 percent, a total of 7.1 million bodies. In addition, 100,000 were leaving the farms for industry each year, and women were entering the labor market in increasing numbers.

Between 1946 and 1963 a total of 76,441,000 people were born in the United States, over four million for each year. The boom peaked in

1957 with 4.33 million births. The figure stayed near that level for five years. The group constituted one-third of the nation's population in 1965.

During the peak baby-boom years, the total fertility rate in the United States exceeded 3.7 births per woman in a lifetime. (By 1975, the rate had dropped to 1.8 births per woman.)

The economy could not create new jobs that rapidly; 5.6 million were added to payrolls. The unemployment rolls were to move up rapidly, at a pace not acceptable to a government committed to full employment.

Thus, a second postwar baby boom arrives in the labor market from 15 to 20 years after a war.

When the 1945–1949 baby-boom bulge became of age and began entering the labor force in 1963, there were 19 million young adults entering an economy in a single decade, an economy that had been absorbing about 1.1 million each year. At this rate, it appeared that 13.5 additional applicants for work might have been added to the 2.8 million unemployed in 1969, and to the 4.1 million unemployed in 1970, a large percentage of them teen-agers or 20 to 24 years old. In addition, the migration of workers from farms to cities was continuing.

In the decade that followed, the labor force grew from 72 million to 86 million, twice as fast as the population. The newcomers numbered 2.1 million in 1967, 2.3 million in 1968, 2.2 million in 1969, 2.5 million in 1970, 2.7 million in 1971, 3.6 million in 1972, 2.8 million in 1973, 2.9 million in 1974, and 3 million for each of the next five years. This amounted to a 32.5 percent growth in the ready-to-work force in 14 years. By 1975 7.9 million (8.5 percent of the labor force) were not working. In 1964 there were two million 18-year-olds, one million more than in 1963.

The teen-age group (16 to 19) constituted 10.8 percent of the United States population in 1975, 9.9 percent in 1980, and 8 percent in 1985. This bulge in the teen-age labor force has other implications. Some 15 percent were unemployed in 1981, when total unemployment was 7.6 percent. In 1983, when the unemployment total hovered around 10 percent, some 30 percent were unemployed. In 1985 teenage unemployment (during the last gasp of the baby boom) was 17 percent while total unemployment was 7.2 percent.

A close view of population trends and their ramifications makes difficult the effort to ignore the demographic determinism affecting the economy, national policy, and individual lives. There are good years in which to be born. The 1930s produced small cohorts, the smallest in 150 years. It grew up in a period of labor shortages. Baby boomers faced shortages in schooling and great competition in college placement, entrance job opportunities, and career promotion.

Historically, the baby booms appear to be followed 14 to 18 years later by major social explosions. Nazi Germany emerged between 10 and 20 years after World War I. The Chinese "Cultural Revolution" followed 1948 by 15 years. The "Sixties" was specifically baby-boom oriented.

Among the young in the 1960s and 1970s the percentage of unemployment ran at more than twice the overall average. Even when overall unemployment was at 3.5 percent levels, teenage unemployment ran at 16 percent. The number of 16- to 19-year-olds increased 46 percent in the period, the number of 20- to 24-year-olds, 60 percent.

A writer of the period, Landon Y. Jones, in a popular study of the generation, notes:

> Strictly in the sense of manpower alone, Lyndon Johnson has decided to go into Vietnam at the best of times. The nation's parent had just presented the military with the largest supply of potential soldiers ever. So massive was the generation that it looked as if he could train and field an army with a minimum of domestic dislocation. Fathers could be spared. So could graduate students and undergraduates.[2]

And the labor market was already surfeited. Vietnam was a sponge for the post–World War II baby boomers. Military draft and enlistments were able to absorb some of the 18- to 24-year-olds in its armed forces manpower.

The effect of the numbers in the armed forces on the labor market and unemployment may be gauged by the figures in Table 10.2.

An analyst could say that from the point of view of the economy the Vietnam War was "opportune." A national unease even exceeding the trauma of Vietnam might have occurred; a spiral paralleling 1930 might have been set in motion.

In 1964 there were two million 18-year-olds, one million more than in 1963. The economy could not create jobs that rapidly. The labor force was adding a million jobs a year, increasing 1.3 percent from 1955 to 1965. The baby-boomers required 2.2 percent economic growth. Even while total unemployment was at a low (3.5 percent) level, teen-age unemployment ran at 16 percent. After 1979 the growth rate dropped to 0.36 percent. The 16–19-year-olds increased the work force by 46 percent; the 20–24 year age group rose 60 percent. The Vietnam draft covered up the incipient unemployment problem.

The direct effect of the draft on unemployment was only one side of the picture. Defense spending increased 15 percent, adding 300,000 government-financed jobs on the home front plus an equal number in defense industries. Many more went to college or stayed there to avoid the draft. A few went to Canada. And, as the demobilized came back, many had a chance to get to college via the GI bill. The Peace Corps took some others.

Table 10.2. Civilian Labor Force, Military Forces, & Unemployment, 1950–1983

Year	Civilian Labor Force	Military Forces (in millions)	Percentage Unemployed
1950	65.9	1.460	5.3
1951	65.1	3.249	3.3
1952	65.7	3.636	3.0
1953	66.6	3.555	2.9
1954	67.0	3.302	5.5
1955	68.1	3.000	4.4
1956	69.4	2.806	4.1
1957	69.7	2.796	4.3
1958	70.3	2.601	6.8
1959	70.9	2.504	5.5
1960	72.1	2.476	5.5
1961	73.0	2.484	6.7
1962	73.4	2.808	5.5
1963	74.6	2.700	5.7
1964	75.8	2.687	5.2
1965	77.2	2.700	4.5
1966	75.017	3.094	3.7
1967	76.590	3.377	3.7
1968	78.2	3.548	3.5
1969	80.1	3.460	3.4
1970	82.7	3.2	4.9
1971	81.3	2.715	5.9
1972	84.0	2.823	5.6
1973	86.8	2.3	4.9
1974	91.0	2.161	5.6
1975	92.6	2.127	8.5
1980	104.7	2.1	7.1
1982	101.2	2.2	9.5
1983	102.454	2.127	9.8

As it ages, each bulge creates a cyclical force that tends to repeat itself. As a bulge reaches the age of household formation, it booms the economy and starts a baby bulge of its own. By 1974 the baby boomers were spawning their own baby boom, with birth rates up 60 percent in 8 years.

These bulges are accented by waves of immigration that follow similar patterns created by economic opportunities in boom times and pressures in bad times, both in the United States and abroad. The demographic problem for the economy is seen in the table of population changes.

Population Changes

Date	Total change (in thousands)
April 1, 1940	+ 285
July 1, 1940	+ 1,167
July 1, 1941	+ 799
July 1, 1942	+ 325
July 1, 1943	– 1,359
July 1, 1944	– 405
July 1, 1945	+ 7,574
July 1, 1946	+ 3,392
July 1, 1947	+ 2,646
July 1, 1948	+ 2,572
July 1, 1949	+ 2,033

In general, baby booms are promoted by economic prosperity and thus foresee the labor absorption problem (and a pressure for military adventure) 15 to 20 years after an expansion begins (1787–1812, 1843–1861, 1896–1917). Inasmuch as the cycle is not in exact synchrony in all nations, the rhythm becomes distorted.

In historical perspective, the effect of the baby boom on the labor force is indicated by the changes in the size of the 18- to 24-year age group during various periods.

The postwar baby booms occurred after 1918 and 1945, and created a labor-ready age bulge in the economy in the 1940s and the

18- to 24-Year Age Group

Year	Change (%)	Numbers (in thousands)
1900		10,307
1910	+ 23 (post 1898 war)	12,748
1920	+ 2	13,018
1930	+ 19 (post 1910 boom)	15,463
1940	+ 7 (post World War I)	16,616
1950	– 3 (Great Depression)	16,075
1960	+ .03	16,128
1970	+ 53 (post World War II)	24,687
1980	+ 19 (post Korean War)	29,462
1990 (est.)	– 15	25,148
2000 (est.)	– 2	24,653

1960s. Such bulges progressively affected school facilities, opportunities for high education, career opportunities, household formations, new birth rates (and a new bulge), the size of the labor force, and retirement costs. The effects of a large cohort of youths on spending, styles, and the body politic are too recent to require another description of "Flaming Youth" after World War I or the Woodstock generation after World War II.

As the baby-boom generation moves into middle age there will be major changes for the federal budget. Middle-age years are the most productive for wage earners. Thus more income is available to be taxed and becomes revenue for the federal government. By the year 2000, the median age of Americans will jump to 36.3, up from 31.2 in 1984, already the highest average in the nation's history.

Demographic changes and pressures are not unique to the United States. They are indeed well noted in recent history, especially in Japan.

The effect of population increases on ancient and medieval economies was more evident and inevitable. A farmer with five children could leave land for only some of his sons, and opportunities in trade and industry were extremely limited. It is no accident that wars were virtually continuous.* The crusades were a series of such outlets (spaced 50 to 60 years apart). In the twentieth century the pressure was evident in such slogans as "Drang nach Osten" and the Japanese "Greater East Asia Co-Prosperity Sphere."

During some periods service in the armed forces or "defense spending" absorbed some manpower. Theodore Ropp notes:

---

*Although Kondratieff makes only incidental reference to the rhythm of wars as a facet of economic cycles, later analysis and accumulated demographic evidence—principally related to the explosion of birth rates following wars and the perpetuation of these bulges in the cycle of household formations—illuminates at least one of the forces underlying cycles of belligerency. We can assume that *causus belli* are endemic in international relations and triggers are readily found ("Remember the Maine," Serajevo, Tonkin Bay). It would thus appear that in a climate of economic readiness, belligerency (B) is a function of the size of a cohort entering the labor force (c) and the ability of an expanding economy and emigration to absorb additional workers (a); thus $B = c/a$. B tends to reach a maximum point in cycles averaging 15 to 21 years following a prolonged war and in perpetuating cycles of 15 to 21 years. However, in a declining economy, when popular expectations are lowered, belligerency appears to be sublimated in efforts to achieve personal subsistence, notable as domestic xenophobia.

Moreover, if we give any credence to the thesis that "there are no accidents in history," we must take serious note of the coincidence of intervals of approximately 50 years between limited or optional wars (1776–83, 1848, 1898, 1950), and a similar interval between absolute wars during the height of an expansion period (1812, 1861–65, 1917, 1965–75). (World War II obviously does not fit into this chronological pattern in American history, but is obviously a result of pressures created by World War I.)

Fortifications which protect capital, surplus food, and occasionally a transportation network may have taken most of the social surplus which went to armaments. Such public works usually used the seasonally unemployed labor of a "backward" agricultural system.[3]

The population pressure on Japan was well known even in the nineteenth century. From the very earliest times Japan has been densely populated, compared to Western nations. A system of small farms and centuries of continuous warfare made this possible. During the seventeenth century lands were rehabilitated, leading to a rapid expansion of the nation's population, which was then kept stable through abortions and infanticides.

The Meiji Reformation in 1868 led to industrialization and "suppression of family restrictions." This absorbed the population increases until World War I, when industrial growth stopped. Ryochi Ishii, an analyst writing in 1937, noted the increasing problem, especially the predominance of minor age groups:

Thus, implying a large proportion of future potential mothers, is of great significance in the compilation of the future population figures. . . Beginning at an unusually low level, the birth rate has gradually risen since the reformation.[4]

The 1925 census already showed a population density of 993 per square kilometer, compared with 802 in Holland and 305 in Germany.

Without exception, all studies undertaken by experts in this field saw the fact that by 1960 the population of Japan will reach somewhere between 80 and 90 million. If we apply the present ratio of occupational figures to this population estimate it will be necessary for Japan to provide, annually, about one-half million new positions in her economic structure for this additional population. Such disparity, even temporary in nature, between a nation's economic possibilities and its population trends, may be considered a causal factor in the nation's problem of population.[5]

THE FISCAL ASPECTS

The fiscal response to imminent stagnation in the 1960s was what Kondratieff and Mensch might have anticipated.

Defense outlays rose $7.6 billion (in constant 1972 dollars) in 1966 (9.6 percent), another $14.3 billion in 1967 (13.4 percent), and $10.5 billion in 1968 (8.2 percent). The armed forces removed half a million additional young people from the civilian labor force; defense industry supplied a similar number of jobs. And the unemployment rate remained at 3.8 percent at least until 1970. In that year it rose to 4.9 percent.

The labor force expanded in part due to the needs of defense industries. By 1970 three million had been enlisted or drafted, a million more than the normal standing armed forces, in addition to civilian employees and those in defense industries.

The question obviously arises, what would have happened to the economy if Tonkin Bay and the Vietnam War had not happened?

The addition of 10 million to the domestic labor force in a single decade would probably have set in motion a downward cyclical spiral that could have matched that of the 1930s. Most of the basic industries had matured or were close to maturation, and there was little on the technical horizon that would have inspired the $400 billion in investment that could otherwise absorb the host of youths into the labor force.

The federal budget rose in 10 years from $118.4 billion in 1965 to $324.2 billion in 1975. Spending for defense rose from $56.3 billion in 1965 to $103 billion in 1975 and went on to $263.5 billion in 1984.

The unemployment rate record was:

Year	Percentage Unemployment
1969	3.5
1970	4.9
1971	5.0
1972	4.9
1973	4.4
1974	5.2
1975	7.9

When Vietnam was over, the new Department of Health and Human Services tried to provide a safety net with a budget of $170,303 billion in 1979 and $194,703 billion in 1980. However, spending to relieve the hungry and disabled does not have the same effect on the economy as defense spending. Social spending has a substantial ripple effect, but it stimulates only administrative spending and the purchase of food and other basics. It does little to raise the gross national product, and the ripple effect of spending for subsistence is minimal. Defense spending, on the other hand, absorbs the spending in new production with a high multiplier effect.

Ten years after Vietnam the problem for baby boomers remained.

A headline in the Herald Tribune in 1984: TIMES ARE HARD FOR SOME BOOM BABIES. HOMES AND JOBS CAN BE ELUSIVE FOR MOST 25 TO 34 AGE GROUP IN U.S.[6] The story goes on to point out "a hard reality: They are dramatically worse off economically than people their age were 20 years ago and are falling steadily further behind." George Sternlieb, director of the Rutgers Center for Urban Policy Research, pointed out that because there are so many people in this age group, "their bargaining position in the labor market is weak." The effect, noted by Michael Gardner, an economist for Chase Econometrics, is a decreased ability to qualify for home purchasing loans, and a consequent increase in housing costs as a proportion of income. As the baby-boom generation grows older—the over-30 population will grow by more than 21 million in the next decade—experience, not youth, is in fashion.

The aftermath of wars also changes the proportion of women to men in a population, the labor force pattern, and spending and attitude patterns, which involve two economic concepts: budget constraint and the indifference curve. These in turn affect personal income, relative prices, opportunity for leisure time, the shadow value of leisure time, and motivation goals.

Paul F. Secord of the University of Houston made extensive studies of societies where men outnumber women of marriageable age, a condition that existed in the 1950s. During such times women tend to be more highly valued, family life is more stable, and women tend to achieve fulfillment through traditional roles. They are economically upwardly mobile because they can marry men who are better off than themselves. During such periods, society (especially men) tends to promote sexual morality, especially for women.

When the numbers are reversed, with more women in the marriageable population than men, there is a strong motivation for women to enter the work force. The single population increases. This in turn stimulates feminist movements. In 1890 women constituted 14 percent of the labor force; in 1920, 20 percent; in 1984, 44 percent.

Investment of women into the labor force was a countering force to a declining population maturity in the 1970s, when the proportion of the force grew from 30 to 47 percent. Although the trend will continue in the sense that women will work more hours and with greater skills, the possibility of proportionate growth is obviously limited.

The demographic cycle continued to move the economy. The baby boom generation married later and less often, had fewer children, divorced more often, left more children in single-parent homes, and created a singles society and a baby bust for the next generation, from 1972 to 1985.

An increase in births in 1985 is the reflex of the baby boom of the period 1946–1964. Those who were requiring more schools two decades before were creating more households (2.7 percent a year versus 2 percent during 1980–1981), buying more houses, carpeting, appliances, and so on, creating the baby boom of the 1990s and the boom of entrepreneurship similar to the 1920s.

Between 1980 and 1990, baby boomers (from 1946–1964) reached the 25 to 45 age level, increasing the number in that age mix by 30 percent. This, in turn, increased the rate of creation of new households, and changed America's political leaning toward more conservative attitudes.

By 1990 this group will account for 54 percent of all workers. It was unique to the United States in its high education level (1 in 4 went to college versus 1 in 11 of those born before World War I), in its proportion of working women, in its spending priorities, and in its choice of leadership.

The effect of a small age group has similar economic implications. The Depression babies were the first generation in the country's history smaller than the one before it. This group was advantaged in their life cycle in schooling, job opportunities, home purchasing, and career promotions.

The labor force grew 11.5 percent (7.5 million) in the 1950s, 18 percent (12 million) in the 1960s, and 24.4 percent (20 million) in the 1970s.

THE RETIREMENT BULGE

The overall aging of Americans and its effect on the labor force, the retirement sector, and the economy have already been noted. It is reflected in a projection by the United States Census Bureau on the aging of the U.S. population. It reflects the bureau's "middle" series of assumptions about birth rates, death rates, immigration, and other factors.

Aging of the U.S. Population

Year	Median age	Under 18 years (%)	65 and older (%)
1983	30.9	26.7	11.7
1990	33.0	25.8	12.7
2000	36.3	25.1	13.0
2010	38.4	22.9	13.8
2030	40.8	21.6	21.2
2050	41.6	20.9	21.8
2080	42.8	20.3	23.5

These age bulges in the population have had and will continue to have substantial effects on productivity and distribution of income.

In the United States the bulges in age groups and the aging population thus place the burden of production on a decreasing portion of the economy. In 1940 there were 8.3 workers for each retiree. By 1980 the number had decreased to 5.4. By 1990 the figure will be 4.5; by 2020, 3.2; by 2030, 2.2.

Whereas six people supported one retiree in 1970, two of the working population will support one retiree in 1990. Earlier retirement, greater longevity, rapid changes in skills, and the massive increase in the number of working women all tend to speed disproportions in the effective labor force.

An aged population produces less, drains resources from the economy, and contributes less to the spending cycle. The average income of the elderly is, in general, lower than that of the average of the population. Before 1967 the contrast was even more acute. The 1965 reforms in social security reversed a 15-year decline.

A major cycle in population expansion—the largest in 1000 years—began around the world about 1790. At that time, 49 percent of the U.S. population was under 16.

In most developed nations, about 25 percent of the population is under 16. In less developed nations, the youth age group makes up 43 percent to 50 percent of the population. This has major consequences for the present and future world economy and its politics.

IMMIGRATION

The difference in economic opportunity provides a constant pressure for immigration to the United States.

Immigration helped to change the demographic picture of the American economy through 200 years (Table 10.3). In the past,

Table 10.3. Immigration Into The United States, 1820–1964

Year	Number Of Immigrants	Year	Number Of Immigrants
1820	8	1911–1915	4,460
1821–1830	143	1916–1920	1,276
1831–1840	599	1921–1925	2,639
1841–1850	1,713	1926–1930	1,468
1851–1860	2,598	1931–1935	220
1861–1870	2,315	1936–1940	308
1871–1880	2,812	1941–1945	171
1881–1890	5,247	1946–1950	864
1891–1900	3,688	1951–1955	1,088
1901–1905	3,833	1956–1960	1,428
1906–1910	4,962	1961–1964	1,154
Total		1820–1964	42,995

Figures are in thousands.

immigrants were substantially young males. They provided half the labor force in mines and mills in the nineteenth century and early twentieth century. They worked for relatively low wages and performed many necessary tasks that native Americans disliked doing.

Immigrants arrived in the United States principally because conditions in their native lands were intolerable. But they came also because conditions in the United States were better and laws permitted their entry. The rate of immigration follows closely the pattern of economic falls and rises. Whether the rise was a cause or consequence can be debated.

Immigration follows cycles of approximately 18.2 years. It changes the size, character, and productivity of the labor force as well as consumer spending patterns.

SOCIAL AND PSYCHOLOGICAL CHANGES

The effect of bulges in certain age groups goes beyond the obvious direct economic effect on supply and demand for resources, goods, services, and jobs. The changing age pattern affects changes in political and social attitudes as the bulges pass through various stages. And these attitudes are affected by and affect change in the economic climate.

Kondratieff noted at some length that major turns in the long wave were accompanied by major social changes. On the broad scale these are most evident in the 1820s, the 1830s, the 1870s, at the turn of the century, and in the 1960s and 1970s. Some of the changes, like the urbanization of society, the establishment of a factory-oriented society, the egalitarian movement, the emergence of women and their entry into the labor force, and the new polarization of education and opportunity are obviously of economic origin.

Intertwined as both cause and consequence of the economic and demographic cycles are the bulges in certain age groups, which arise from periodic wars, booms, and depressions. This sets up a series of identifiable waves which help to explain the 50- to 60-year periodicity.

Aside from the special effect that prosperity and depression have on different age segments in the population, the cycle of expansion and contraction in an economy creates recognizable moods. These accent, in a population, its ambition, politics, liberalism, moral attitudes, euphoria, speculative mania, panic, political conservatism, protectionism, xenophobia, or economic conservatism. When a cycle is expanding it creates both a special euphoria and a frustration among teen-agers, an effect different from that among those of middle age or retirement age. Similarly, a depression psychology during youth affects age segments differently.

The period of upswing immediately preceding a peak produces public tensions, a desire for restraints, and a pressure to restrain public spending (to "balance the budget"). At this point, immediately after a peak in the cycle, tax reductions are introduced. A reduction of taxes thus stimulates the economy and increases revenues. The economy sustains a small deflationary pressure. And usually the reduced level of receipts leads to a cutback in the cost of government operations.

On the other hand, an element noted by Paul Samuelson is the "weakening of the hungriness motive" which accompanies affluence, a phenomenon of peak periods, particularly important as secular increases resulting from improved technologies raise the common standard of living.

The mores during these swings and peak periods follow a widely recognized postwar pattern. Concern for financial security fades. Leisure time activities flourish. Interest in difficult careers (including demand for college education) declines. When security prices and wages are high, almost regardless of the changed value of the dollar, people perceive themselves as wealthy. This is true even if only nominal wages are rising, regardless of real wages. In such times people are subject to a peculiar element of group dynamics to suspend caution because their peers have done so. The feeling becomes general that debt is not such a bad thing because it is repaid with cheaper dollars. People assume that society is in a period of permanent prosperity. Debt is accumulated.

The pervasive confidence created by a generation of good times and uninterrupted growth fosters the belief that affluence is a normal, permanent condition. Attitudes toward work, risk-taking, money, social spending versus saving, and indeed all social values—individually and for the community—tend to be looser. During a downswing, expectations are lowered faster than incomes. Trough politics are tame.

Permanent affluence for some, a common product of 30 years of growth, tends to remove from the work force and the entrepreneur force some of the economy's best talent. This trend is exacerbated as a result of progressive income taxes, the failure to index income brackets, and the high return on invested capital.

In general terms, the period following the peak of a cycle is noted for the ebullience and euphoria previously noted—"The Era of Good Feeling," "The Gilded Age" of the Reconstruction period, The "Roaring Twenties"—and each such period occurs approximately 50 years after the previous similar period, and each is a phase of the long wave cycle. In such periods of economic euphoria, curious schemes succeed—"South Sea Bubble" in 1811, Crédit Mobilier in the 1860s, the Northern Pacific Corner in the 1890s, Florida land bubble, Goldman-Sachs and other investment trusts of the 1920s, probably similarly, leveraged buyouts in the early 1980s.

The rise in prices and seemingly universal prosperity give rise to steadily increasing expectations. Inflation makes people feel wealthier, for everything they own appears to be worth more, and what they owe appears to be less of a burden. Better incomes, rather than providing more contentment, stimulate greater demand. Relief from past economic pressures is replaced by dissatisfaction with the speed of greater individual prosperity. Labor, strengthened by fuller employment, increases its demands. Time lost due to strikes increases. The economy cannot and does not keep up with these expectations. During periods of inflation real wages actually decline for most workers.

This phase of the cycle can be measured in the contemporary economy in terms of the confidence level. In recent years this has been gauged monthly by the Conference Board.

The periods immediately surrounding a peak may be described simplistically as periods dominated successively by lethargy, ambition, "good feeling," speculation, euphoria, crisis, panic, and despair. Spending patterns reflect these changing attitudes and thus accentuate the spirals of inflation and deflation.

Radical politics tends to crop out during peak periods—not, as might be expected, during hard times. These outbreaks usually have an intellectual leadership which argues that some underprivileged are not sharing in the new affluence. They are a product of rising expectations for everyone by everyone. Peak politics are frenetic.

Kondratieff saw in these reactions part of the tensions that precipitated wars.

In each downward cycle there is first some psychological relief at the end of an intense rise in prices. It is only when income reductions begin to affect large numbers of people, and only for those directly affected, that a recession is meaningful.

The first decade of decline brings attitude changes without public announcement. Students become more serious about studies and less political. Hemlines go down. Music becomes less raucous. Massive layoffs make labor more receptive to changes in work rules and wage adjustments. And a nation becomes more isolationist.

The overall trend of the economy shapes perceptions as to its strength and direction. In a bull market, "experts" are almost uniformly optimistic; in a bear market the owlish analysts almost universally suggest caution.

It is during the upward swings, soon after a trough and just before a peak, that wars become more likely.

It should be noted that peak wars are the result of a different kind of socioeconomic psychological pressure and have quite different economic results than trough wars. Nations become socially and politically unsettled after a long period of boom and expansion, perhaps because in their final stages, peoples' expectations begin to outrun actual growth in the general level of prosperity. War then becomes the ultimate destination. Inasmuch as all nations are attempting to expand simultaneously, the intense competition for resources and markets leads eventually to military confrontations, which become contagious.

One explanation suggested is that during trough wars the public is still largely concerned with private considerations and their own well-being. They tend to be less interested in international disputes, world crusades, or campaigns involving large investment of cash, effort, and the nervous energy needed to pursue projects to a conclusion. Trough wars tend to be short. They are more a matter of choice and sudden decision by the stronger power.

Inasmuch as peak wars are the result of frustration of expectations (usually with economic elements), peak wars tend to be more desperate, more widespread, and more destructive.

THE YOUTH FACTOR IN SOCIAL CHANGE

Demographic changes have other effects beyond the traditional liberal-conservative viewpoints.

It is in the juvenile section that crime has flourished more than anywhere else, so that a bulge in the 15–24 age group is followed by a rise in crime. The 1981 figures for convictions and cautions for indictable offenses show that no less than 54 percent were offenses committed by those under 21, and almost one-third of all offenders were under 17. Whereas 70 youths per 1,000 commit crimes, only 12 adults per 1,000 do.

Revolutionary movements have erupted in periods after dramatic increases in the youth population, usually under young leaders. When the French Revolution began, 40 percent of the population was between ages 20 and 30, and only 20 percent over age 40. Similarly the Protestant Reformation and the American Revolution were manifestations of younger leadership. (The median age of the American colonies in 1775 was 17.)

The other side of the youthful society is its creativity—most major breakthroughs in the arts and sciences are conceived by those aged 30 or younger.

The bulge in older populations is associated with conservative, pacific policies. Geographically the largest elder-age group exists in northwest Europe, where more than 12 percent are over 65.

A practical facet in business management is seen by J.E.S. Parker:

> The ability of companies to perceive and respond to the challenge offered by innovations is likely to be influenced by the age, education and aspiration level of management.[7]

PROTECTIONISM

Another phenomenon characteristic of cyclical troughs is a pressure to raise tariffs to protect industry and a general xenophobia regarding trade, immigration, and foreigners and ethnic groups. Protectionism results from perception that tariffs are a means of preserving jobs. It follows the cyclical pattern of the economy. In periods of downswing, when marginal producers most feel the effect of lower-cost imports, the stridency of demand to protect jobs increases. Higher tariffs, quotas, and special barriers are promoted, and usually get substantial attention.

A protectionist era followed in the wake of the 1814 peak (higher tariffs in 1816 and 1824, a 41 percent Tariff of Abominations in 1828). The erratic 1880s stimulated the McKinley Tariff in 1890, the Wilson Tariff of 1894, and the Kingsley Tariff of 1897. Following the 1920 turn came the Fordney McCumber Tariff of 1922. The 1929 debacle gave birth to the Smoot-Hawley Tariff of 1930.

Each measure stifled imports, and subsequently exports. Both of course reduced living standards for all concerned. And all made payment of international debt more difficult. Schumpeter points out that:

> imposition of tariffs will thus act similarly to cheap money policy: it creates margins which will not otherwise exist and therefore calls for the enterprise and secondary expansion that may become a source of troubles.

The world agreed in 1948 to minimize restrictions on trade in an effort to improve living standards for all, by allowing the producers of lowest cost to produce for all. When the pressure to support exports (as by farmers in 1984) becomes too strong, substitutes for higher tariffs are created—quotas and procedural regulations, increasingly in the maturing industries (textiles, steel, autos, etc.).

Turning Points
And Triggers

Having hastened in telescopic fashion through 200 years of American history, what can we see in the Kondratieff waves beyond their configuration? What are the symptoms of their approach? Are they inevitable? Do the turns have to be triggered? And if a trigger is necessary, where does it occur? What is the relationship of the intervening short- and intermediate-term cycles? And what effects do the contemporary cyclical control measures have in the long term? What is the same about these waves and what is different?

The answers to these questions are more than academic. They point up the dangers to which the world economy is exposed, and they illuminate the contemporary scene.

From the record we can see what is common to each cyclical period. How much of each cycle is inevitable, how much accidental? Can we learn from history?

THE PATTERN

In purely chronological terms the Kondratieff cycle appears to follow a regular pattern, but it is indeed difficult to accept as a mechanical phenomenon. It leaves a trough with a rapid, irregular expansion of 20 to 25 years, increasing in momentum for the last 5 to 10 years. Each explosive expansion has, in the past, encompassed a period of a minor war (1848, 1898, 1950) and a major war (1812–1814, 1862–1864, 1917–1918, 1965–1975), followed by postwar adjustments. Each explosion in the past has been associated with vast (not merely large) investment in new industries, primarily based on latent new technology and new consumer products and services. Each peak has been followed by a short, sharp slowdown of expansion, a period of maturity in industry, and new major competition for the established industries, either from new development or a new competitive area, then a sudden panic and a long deep depression. Each expansion has involved the diffusion of major innovations surrounding a historic, expansionary revolution (the steam engine, canals, railroads, electricity, the automobile, radio and television) and a dramatic change in life style, economic and social.

The first wave beginning in the eighteenth century was a product of the industrial revolution that substituted mechanical power for manual labor. It saw an explosion of investments in the creation and use of machinery of many types, and a major change in the nature of the labor force, as well as ripple effects in the creation of new industries and new consumer demand. It ran its course as much human- and animal-powered equipment became obsolete, and the railroads replaced canals.

The second wave, beginning in 1843, was a product of the expansion of railroads and the utilization of farm machinery and fertilizers. Its diffusion came through the opening of new land in the West and through imperialism abroad. It ran its course as railroads ceased to expand, when they were replaced in large measure by motor vehicles.

The third wave, which came out of the 1893 trough, saw the expansion of investment in plants producing electric power (from $193 million in 1913 to $3.5 billion in 1920 and $8.822 billion in 1949). This power was applied to industry. There was also increased investment in communication and consumer goods and a new age of motor vehicles, with necessary construction of roads and bridges, the creation of suburbia, and the expansion of the associated steel, glass, and textile industries. There was a contributing diffusion of radio and other consumer durables. The wave peaked with a saturation in consumer durables in 1927 and a 20 percent drop in sales (from $2.6 billion in 1926 to $2.16 billion in 1927).

The expansion of the fourth wave that began in 1949 was the product of aeronautics, space exploration, television, communications, plastics and polymers, a massive building boom, and "defense" spending for wars in Korea and Vietnam. It was the first that was seeded and spurred largely by government actions, applying principles proposed by Keynes and Friedman. It was initiated by World War II and postwar reconstruction. It was stimulated by two limited wars, a huge building program, and social programs which brought large government deficits and consequent inflation.

Each peak period involved huge investments, large "defense" expenditures, and major changes in living standards and social changes, and each climaxed with extensive speculation. In each there was a cluster of new inventions and industries surrounding a basic technological change. And, coincidently, the industries created by these investments, largely during an expansion period, reached maturity at about the same time, usually caused by obsolescence or new competition. ⌋

As Kondratieff recalled and forecasted, each peak had its period of euphoria: the "Era of Good Feeling," the "Gilded Age," and the "Roaring Twenties" (the Jazz Age). On later graphs, these periods are visible as periods of slow decline of 5 to 7 years, but at a high plateau of prosperity.

At each peak there was a discernible maturation of the industries(which had contributed to the expansion phase of the wave)—a slowing or cessation of the investment, a saturation of demand, and a new competitive element. The canals and steamboats of the first wave were made obsolete by railroads by 1825. The railroads were made obsolete by the automobile and the truck by 1920. The frontiers closed about 1893. Steel, copper, textiles, and automobiles (as an expanding element) reached crises due to maturation of technology, synthetic substitutes, saturation of demand, and foreign competition by 1974. Each had in turn created a product or service sufficient to excite demand and ignite investment until demand was saturated or replaced. Each additionally spurred other expansions based on innovation, which Kondratieff saw as the "ignition" for a long wave. Schumpeter put it this way:

> Taken together, the innovations of the period and the adaptations they enforced explain primarily the turn of the Kondratieff. Again, as in earlier cases, it is not claimed that they explain the crises also, except in the sense that they make it understandable that speculative furor broke out and that error and misconduct accumulated. They thus furnish a reason why the situation became so sensitive as to be easily turned into a crisis by unfavorable events or by trouble arising out of weak spots. The actual picture of the crisis could never be understood from innovations alone.[1]

He goes on to elucidate

> that many things were done under the influence of artificial stimuli that would not have been undertaken without political and banking encouragement.

We see that each peak was followed by a sharp "post-peak" adjustment: a recession (1814–1816, 1864–1866, 1920–1921, 1973–1975) followed by a plateau lasting 5 to 7 years (1814–1819, 1866–1873, 1921–1929, 1975–1984) until 1974–1984. Each plateau was followed by panic with a following precipitous, devastating depression: 1819–1943 (the "Hungry Forties"), 1873–1893, 1929–1939 (the "Great Depression").

The economic depression of each trough was, at least to some extent, followed and mitigated by a "limited" trough war (Mexico in 1848, Spain in 1898, Korea in 1950), each about 50 years after the other. (This includes the Vietnam War.) And each recovery was stimulated by diffusion of a new cluster of innovations, which are usually related to each other.

Each economic decline came as basic industries matured, stopped expanding, and/or became obsolete. Such periods were marked by the absence of positive major investment or other spending stimuli. These are seen as periods of "paucity of innovations" following increasing costs of production. They are times of coasting and ossification of economic channels in entrepreneurship, labor adaptability, productivity growth, when costs of the elements of production moved into constantly higher levels.

It is apparent that when an economy was "ready" for a downturn or is undergoing a downturn, it became vulnerable to a precipitation trigger—sometimes an irrelevant trigger.

THE SIGMOID CURVE

The long wave in the form of an S-shaped (sigmoid) curve differs from shorter cycles because the oversupply or overdemand that provides dynamics for ordinary business cycles has fostered a seminal, basic development with tentacles in many other industries. Because it is obscured by the layers of time, it is not as clearly perceivable. To some extent, overinvestment may be a factor, but essentially the long wave is motivated by saturation of demand for a product or a family of products that seeded the expansion and make up a large, marginal portion of the economy.

Indeed, the long wave is closely related to the well-known product cycle—a marketing cycle—and the natural population expansion curve that is experienced as the life cycle of many and various elements introduced into economic life—well known to natural scientists as the sigmoid curve (Fig. 11.1).

As we have seen, the long wave is initiated by the introduction of a seminal element into the economy that in turn produces major changes, which together explode through an infusion of investment.

At a point in this development of the product life cycle, an exhaustion of further possibilities for technological improvements is reached. Improvements may exist that in some circumstances might be made, but possibilities for investment in other fields offer greater profit potential. This point is attained during the period of an industry's maturity, especially where the long-term outlook is cloudy or points to a market

Figure 11.1. The Sigmoid Curve Of Population And Economics

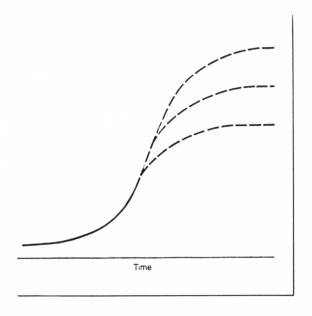

Source: Jonas Salk and Jonathon Salk, *World Population and Human Values* (New York: Harper & Row, 1973) p. 21, Fig.9.

saturation. The demand pull is thus not sufficient to warrant additional investment.

In an analogous situation, the launching of a new product or a new business starts with great enthusiasm, and if it is successful, sales (and production) zoom, then rise more slowly, reach a peak or maturation of the market, decline slowly, and then begin to drop, usually slowly at first, then precipitously.

Dewey and Dakin describe this cycle effectively with the curves of the rise and fall of horse-drawn vehicles and the steam railroads. It is seen in the charts of expansion in steel, canals, railroads, public utilities, cotton textiles and rayon, and virtually every consumer product, all of which contributed to Kondratieff expansion waves (Figure 11.2). The cycle for the automobile industry seems to be following this pattern.

Citing examples in the German economy, Gerhard Mensch implies that this S-shaped curve fits into the long-term trends as Kondratieff depicts them. He sees this curve clearly (in 1979) as having developed in the years after 1975 and predicts: "Only the new opportunities offered by basic innovations can prevent a depression, or if necessary, overcome

Figure 11.2. Industrial Expansion Curves

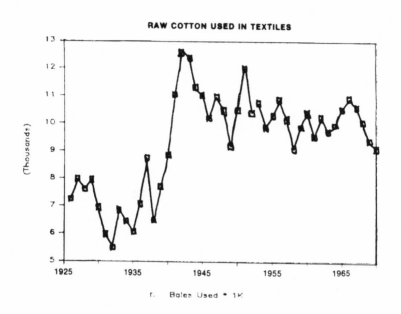

RAW COTTON USED IN TEXTILES

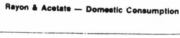

Rayon & Acetate — Domestic Consumption

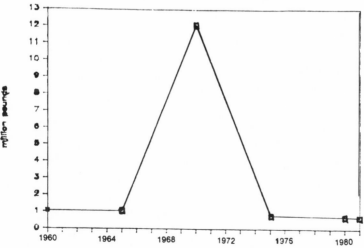

Figure 11.2. (continued)

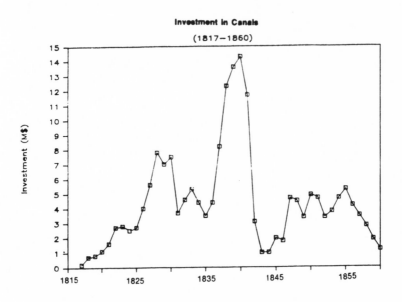

Investment in Canals

(1817—1860)

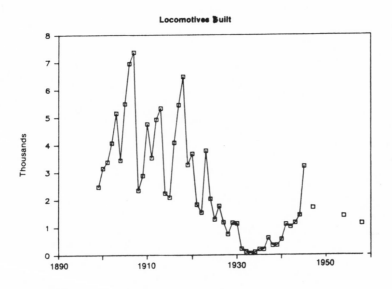

Locomotives Built

Figure 11.2. (continued)

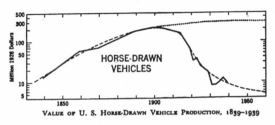

VALUE OF U. S. HORSE-DRAWN VEHICLE PRODUCTION, 1839–1939

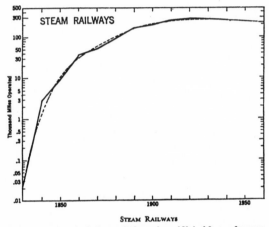

STEAM RAILWAYS
Miles of road operated (first track) in continental United States, 1830–1940.
Decennial data. A trend is shown, projected tentatively to 1960. *Ratio scale.*

Source: Jonas Salk and Jonathon Salk, *World Population and Human Values* (New York: Harper & Row, 1973). p. 21, Fig. 9. Dewey, Edward R. and Edwin F. Sakin, *The Science of Prediction* (Pittsburgh: Foundation for the Study of Cycles, 1947), p. 316.

its effects."[2] The form of the S-shaped trend derives from the diffusion of innovations throughout the leading industries.

THE GENESIS OF A WAVE

Both Kondratieff and Schumpeter's interpretation of the initiation saw the long waves created by major changes in technology or accompanying major events that changed the character of the economy. They cite specifically the introduction of steam power, electricity, railroads, and the automobile; the migrations from Europe to America and to the West; the influx of gold; and the dislocations caused by wars. Kondratieff saw these as endogenous factors. As he observed,

During the recession of the long waves, an especially large number of important discoveries and inventions in the technique of production and communication are made, which, however, are usually applied on a large scale only at the beginning of the next long upswing.

At the beginning of a long upswing, gold production increases as a rule, and the world market (for goods) is generally enlarged by the assimilation of new and especially of colonial countries.

It is during the period of the rise of the long waves, i.e., during the period of high tension in the expansion of economic forces, that, as a rule, the most disastrous and extensive wars and revolutions occur.

What becomes apparent is that the dynamics of an upswing in cycles are the result of increased spending induced by massive investment in new opportunities for profit.

As Mensch views this product cycle, it is set in motion by improvement innovations. Usually, life cycle following life cycle will be triggered by the seemingly continuous flow of improvement innovations that give momentum to the growth process "in the industrial branches." This is seen as stretching over one, two, or three decades.

Gabriel Tarde describes the product curve as an S-shaped curve with a slow advance, followed by a rapid, uniform progress which then slackens to a graphic plateau until it stops.[3] The duration of each stage varies, and somewhere each reaches a peak. Then the market becomes saturated; the product tastes change; values change and become obsolete; conditions change; competition for the market or for the consumer dollar appears. Sometimes new production methods reduce costs or produce a better product to bring a new birth to an old industry or to create a new subsidiary production.

Each change stimulates or sedates a long-wave cycle. Each market change stimulates or retards the cycle, increasing or decreasing its momentum. Underlying every phase of industry are the dynamics of a basic curve of growth, maturity, and decline.

Obviously some product cycles produce a different curve or shorter terms. The market for home video games, introduced in the 1980 period of recession, tripled in 1981 to $2 billion, matured in 1982, and toppled in 1983. The cycle of the auto industry reached maturity in 65 to 75 years.

A stage in the cycle may be renewed by improvements, new technology, new short-term uses, lower costs, new markets, or any of various marketing devices. (Steel expansion was renewed by the Bessemer process, open-hearth process, etc.)

THE PEAK

At some point (either market saturation, the arrival of a new product or technology, new competition, or merely a change of taste) the expansion of production for a product reaches a peak. Production remains steady for a period, for the short or long term, then drops quickly or precipitously, depending on the need for the production and substituted condition. The industry life cycle thus reaches a point where the exhaustion of further technological improvements stalls expansion, either because improvements are no longer worthwhile in a saturated market or because innovations are relatively too costly.

Kuznets in 1930 and Burns in 1934 studied 104 production series in the United States: 23 in agriculture, fisheries, and forestry, representing 65 percent of the total; 47 in manufacturing (representing 22 percent of output) and construction (22 in mining, representing 83 percent of the total output); and 12 in trade and transportation. They came to the conclusion that "when an industry tends to grow at a declining rate, its rise [is] eventually followed by a decline"[4]—now commonly known as the rule of retardation.

This rule must be adjusted for secular trends and the other pressures of the shorter business cycles, and it often does not hold in the initial stages or in the late life of a cycle. Thus the prediction value of the "rule" is limited. The rise and fall of the shoemaking industry is used by Schumpeter to illustrate the cycle in the second Kondratieff period.

WHY 50 TO 60 YEARS?

However, the question arises why does this occur for the entire economy at the same time and why in cycles of 50 to 60 years?

Kondratieff recognized the vulnerability of his hypothesis on this score:

Actually, we must recognize the fact that the various commodities and goods on hand in a capitalist society fulfill their economic functions during periods of time that vary greatly in length. Likewise, there is a great variation in the time and monetary outlay required for their creation. Some of them function without substantial transformations for a very short period of time. As a rule, they require a relatively short interval of time, and a relatively small, one-time investment for their production. In this category are considerable masses of consumer goods, many kinds of raw materials, and other means of production. Others function over a longer period of time, and require more time and a bigger investment for the production. A large part of the instruments of production comes under this head. Still others, basic capital goods, function for decades and require very long periods of time and tremendous investments for their production. These include such capital goods as big construction projects, the building of major railroads.

Actually, the training of skilled labor also belongs in this category.

He then points out:

> The replacement and expansion of the fund of these goods does not take place smoothly but in spurts, and the long waves in economic conditions are another expression of that.
>
> I stress once again that in the process of the cycle's development, the very equilibrium level, as it changes, shifts to another (usually higher) degree.

An empirical answer to simultaneous timing came in 1970–1978. Suddenly America's smokestack industries stopped growing; they began, in all their variety, almost simultaneously to decline. And the trend was contagious: auto sales declines caused declines in steelmaking, glassmaking, textiles, aluminum, and plastics, and eventually even petroleum. The whole nation hit a stone wall. It had stopped growing.

From the well-known and well-accepted acceleration principle quoted by J.R. Hicks, "it follows that investment affects changes in output—including the stimulation of more investment. The building of houses, for instance, reckons as investment activity; but an increase in the demand for new houses induces investment in brickworks, sawmills, and glassworks, . . ."[5] And subsequently for appliances, carpeting, drapes, furniture, and so on.

Although each product cycle follows its own course, each has an impact on other industries. Each industry follows a cycle affected substantially by the sum of the relevant product, which follows a well-recognized pattern of exponential expansion, then slower growth, maturation, and decline. This is essentially the sigmoid population pattern found in nature, the pattern of body growth, and the pattern of many other natural and economic situations.

However, once the surge of the parabola-like formation becomes functional, it may be renewed by other innovations at an accelerated rate.

Because of underlying interrelationships in industry and in basic technology there is a strong tendency for many key vectors to grow or to stagnate in proximate units. The effect is such that a decline in motor vehicle innovations (and consequent lack of expansion) results in a slowdown in the supplier and other associated industries, with multiplier effects in other directions spiraling alongside the slowdown in automobile sales expansion. This synergistic, almost contagious stagnation has affected key industries since the 1960s. The expansion slowdown phase of the long wave was increasingly obvious as the 1970s began, obscured but not eliminated by the press of increased money supply and the accompanying inflation.

One factor in the 50–60-year periodicity may exist in the integrated nature of capitalist production, which places several industries in a position marginally dependent on other industries. The motor vehicle industry in the 1970s accounted for five percent of the economy. But the production and use of motor vehicles accounted for more than 15 percent of the economy through its requirements for petroleum, roads, and lodging, in addition to its use of 15 percent of the nation's steel product, and much glass, textiles, aluminum, plastics, and so on. This synergism made the industry and the entire nation's economy most vulnerable to the 1972 OPEC price maneuver. Some 3000 automobile dealers went out of business between 1979 and 1983. Another 650,000 jobs were lost among suppliers. The layoffs (200,000 among automobile workers alone) destroyed neighborhood grocery stores, broke up households by increasing the divorce rate, and increased housing foreclosures in an endless chain of ripples.

The symbiotic relationship between the automobile and steel industries, both of which had a renaissance in the early twentieth century, is illustrative of the "cluster" effect that seemed so unreasonable when described in the 1920s.

The other major expansion that began at the turn of the century derived from the electric and telephone utilities.

Even the stability of electric utilities (that bedrock of securities insured by government-sanctioned monopoly) can be threatened in the 1980s by the changing political climate of nuclear development, by changing costs of fuels, by requirements of environmental protection, and even by the development of new products (e.g., the fuel cell that may decentralize the distribution of electric power).

On May 21, 1984, Business Week was motivated to ask in a leading article, "Are Utilities Obsolete?" Discussing the creation of new plants, Rosemary S. Pooler, a New York Public Service commissioner, is quoted as saying: "It's like building an awesome horseshoe plant after Henry Ford had insight into the automobile assembly line." As she sees the situation, "the large central power station is an idea whose time passed a decade ago. Existing plants will certainly continue to serve a useful function well into the next century, they concede, and many of the plants still under construction will come on line as well. Moreover, few electricity experts are prepared to predict that no United States utility will ever again build a large power complex. A surprising number see little need for anything more than isolated new orders in the intermediate future."

Cessation of expansion in auto market industries and steel have themselves substantial effects on the economy. These industries were customers of many others, and their employees were consumers.

Most of the smokestack industries had started early in the twentieth century. They were renewed by technological innovations that produced better and cheaper products within their industries. Eventually each reached maturation. Perhaps by coincidence, but more probably because of underlying interrelated economic forces, the maturation coincided between the countries of the Western world in the early 1970s.

In the 1980s, the structural problems of smokestack industries were evident in their failure to return to their earlier status in spite of recovery in the economy as a whole. When asked, "Do you think these industries will continue to be in trouble even in a time of economic recovery, or do you think they can be turned around?" 51 percent of business leaders thought in March 1983 that they could be turned around. Only 39 percent thought so in January 1984.

Each industry faced the gravitational pull of market saturation changes in public needs, new foreign competition, and other changed conditions.

DEFUELING THE ECONOMY—THE TRIGGERS

At some point in each cycle or long wave, after saturation has arrived, something happens to bring attention to the end of the expansion or to destroy the public confidence in its continuance. In most cases the stoppage appears as a block in the fuel line of money supply, bringing a loss of public confidence, a sudden realization that the expansion has stopped.

In 1792 it was the bankruptcy and arrest of William Duer and his Sciato Company, which had speculated in western lands.

In 1807 it was the cutoff of European markets and funds by British competition.

In 1837 it was President Jackson's pressure on Nicholas Biddle's Bank of United States, the issue of the Specie Circular, and the withdrawal of federal deposits from the banks.

In 1857 it was the failure of the Ohio Life & Trust Co.

In 1873 it was the attempt by Jay Gould and Jim Fisk to corner the gold market. (With help from bank failures in Europe).

In 1893 it was the problems associated with bimetallism.

In 1901 it was the stock market crash resulting from Hill and Harriman's fight to control the stock of the Northern Pacific Railroad.

In 1913 it was the foreign funds withdrawals—and American hoarding of gold—in anticipation of war.

In 1920 it was the bursting of an inventory bubble brought about by ordering banks to stop loans for inventory speculation.

In 1929 it was the stock market crash.

In 1931 it was the wave of European (later American) bank failures. In 1972 and 1978 it could have been OPEC's oil price rises.

THE CRASH

Crashes typically follow the Kondratieff peak, after a period of 3 to 7 years of slow decline. They come after a rapid contraction of perceived wealth, a contraction of credit and money supply, and a sharp change in money velocity. They come at a time of high vulnerability when consumers, business, and/or the government are deep in debt.

In each of the major declines (the 1840s, 1870s, and 1930s) little was available to change or buffer the extent of the credit contraction, so the decline fed on itself. Protective measures are provided in the modern economy, by the government's ability to inflate credit and thus buoy money velocity. In the early 1980s the economy experienced a mild contraction of the wealth base, evidenced by lower inflation figures. Should the rate of this contraction increase, the economy would become vulnerable to a period of severe deflation. In this environment falling prices of all goods would slow commerce, precipitating a sharp recession. In the 1960s monetarists played an important role in avoiding such triggers from pushing the economy into a traditional depression by increasing money supply. Their efforts led to a decade of stagflation. In the 1980s the effort was more successful because government defense spending and a burst of new investment in high technology were added to the Friedman-Keynes formula.

SPECULATION AND DEBT ACCUMULATION

It is seen that the trigger of monetary contraction has usually come to a mature economy from (1) an extraordinary and sudden need for and withdrawal of funds; (2) a sudden decrease in spending, as in a postwar situation when government pays off its debts; (3) a sudden loss of confidence created by a bank failure, etc.; or (4) an official decision that speculation has gone too far, and a consequent tightening of credit.

The last (and most common) situation usually arises after speculative excesses and the accumulation of excess debt.

At least one of these phenomena has been common to the prosperity phase of each cycle. It arrives in an economic euphoria that carries speculation beyond reasonable bounds. Each "investor," seeing yesterday's values increasing each day, seeks to own more equities and share in the profits. In each period there are glamor situations to draw out speculators. In 1825 it was in canals and in mining stocks in Mexico and South America. The railroads made canals obsolete.

In the 1860s it was Crédit Mobilier in railroads, following the fever that followed the Homestead Act of 1842 and later legislation, which granted 200 million acres to the railroads, which they in turn offered for sale. A steady drop in grain prices between 1866 and 1870 (50 percent) set the climate for a turn in 1873.

In the 1920s speculation ran to real estate and stocks bought on margin. During the height of the 1920s bull market, call money (funds borrowed to finance speculative margin accounts) rose from the $2 billion total at the end of 1926 to $3.885 billion at the end of 1928 and $6.640 billion on October 4, 1929. This diversion of credit from production to security trading tightened the money supply, helping to pull the trigger. Credit contraction has been part of every panic that triggered a depression (Figs. 11.3-11.5).

Ludwig von Mises, a great Austrian economist, put it this way:

The wavelike movement affecting the economic system, the recurrence of periods of depression, is the unavoidable outcome of the attempts, repeated again and again, to lower the gross market rate of interest by means of credit expansion. There is no means of avoiding the final collapse of a boom

Figure 11.3. Consumer Credit: 1965 To 1981

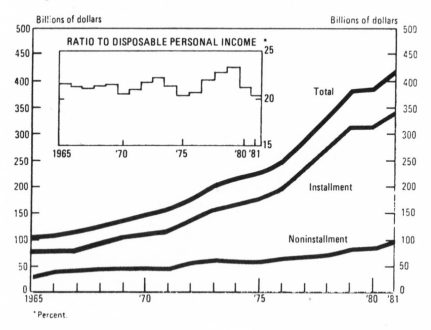

Source: Chart prepared by U.S. Bureau of the Census.

Figure 11.4. Federal Debt At 1967 Prices

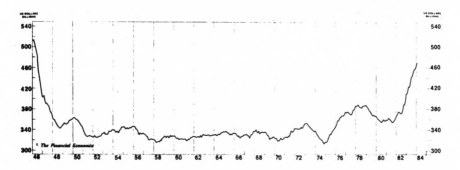

Source: *The Financial Economist* (April, 1983).

Figure 11.5. Interest Payments And Deficit As A Percent Of GNP

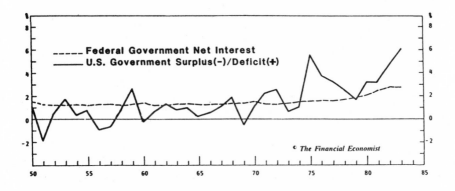

Source: *The Financial Economist* (April, 1983).

brought about by credit expansion. The alternative is only whether the crisis should come sooner as the result of a voluntary abandonment of further credit expansion or later as a final and total catastrophe of the currency involved.[6]

Extreme credit expansion has accompanied every expansion. By 1985 it had reached far beyond previous high levels for consumers and government, even in terms of percentage of disposable income and gross national product. In the business community it was accented by a rash of leveraged mergers and acquisitions.

W.T. Grimm, merger specialists, counted 1,337 corporate marriages and takeovers in the first half of this year. That was 17.8 percent above the same period last year. But the big difference was the amount of dollars involved. Total price of purchases rose to $80.6 billion, a leap of 157 percent.

Transactions for the first half of 1984 were only $2 billion short of the record for a full year—$82.6 billion, set in 1981. Twelve deals were valued at $1 billion or more, twice the number of billion-dollar deals a year earlier.

At the same time, consumers were accumulating debt at an ever increasing rate. By 1985 the ratio of installment debt was 18.3 percent, well beyond the 17.9 percent ratio in 1929 and 1979, and the government debt was close to 50 percent of annual GNP.

PARAMETERS

The Keynesian view that spending must be maintained to keep the economy in equilibrium is part of today's economic gospel. Kondratieff saw the cycles in spending moving in long waves, which he attributed to the investment in innovations, in part because spending for productive durables has a higher multiplier effect.

A principle accepted for a long period as Say's Law held that productive activity always generates demand to absorb the goods produced. John Kenneth Galbraith reverses the thesis to one more apt for the modern economy: "Such is the genius of capitalism that where a real demand exists it does not go long unfilled."

Experience indicates that given a normal increase in the population (1.86 percent) and the labor force (1.7 percent), gross national product must increase at a real rate of more than 3 percent to maintain an economy in equilibrium. But demographic changes (bulges in the population age mix or a high rate of immigration) may change these ratios. In the 1980's federal deficit spending accounted for 2 percent of GNP defense spending for 6.5 percent of GNP. Money supply was increased about 10 percent a year to provide the wherewithal.

The point at which the nation has not been able to grow was reached when 31 percent of the United States plant and 15 percent of its labor force were idle. The point at which the price structure goes out of hand and inflation takes a large leap forward appears to take place when 85 percent of the plant and 96 percent of the labor force are operative. The area most conducive to providing a stable economy lies in increasing productivity of plant and labor within these parameters. The tools to achieve this ratio lie in Keynes' concept of creating demand. And the means, at least in the short term, appear to be investment, creation of consumer demand, and/or government deficit spending.

Maintaining employment by providing adequate capital and maintaining demand remain the problems of the twentieth century. For a decade the monetarists led the way, easing the availability of funds with limited success.

Federal deficit spending and regulation of money supply have been useful tools in the past for diverting or fine-tuning the cycle, but the record of the side-effect of inflation, rampant from 1972 to 1980, is a warning that the cure could be worse than the disease. And, like a drug, it requires increasing doses to be effective. The triggers that break the pattern are usually the last straw—usually a dramatic business failure, at a home or abroad, but often only an event, even a rumor that sets in motion a "run" on some facet of the economy.

To maintain this balance between production and the expected secular growth and increasing population, productivity per capita must increase at a rate of 2.5 percent a year.

Historically the United States growth rate averaged 2 percent from 1843 to 1869. The rate was higher, 2.2 percent during the expansion phase of the third wave and declined to 1.7 percent from 1913 to 1939. The expansion from 1913 to 1929 saw an annual growth rate of 2 percent, the annual decline from 1929 to 1950 a drop to 1.8 percent.

The expansion from 1959 to 1969 saw growth at 2.3 percent including a slow decade at 1.4 percent from 1950 to 1960. The 1960 to 1969 expansion saw the economy grow at 3.2 percent a year. As the plateau is extended by federal deficit spending and monetary expansion, it becomes more fragile.

WARNINGS

Efforts to illuminate the signals of a cyclical turn are widely used not only by public agencies but by private organizations and indeed by company economists. The United States Department of Commerce publishes a monthly index of leading indicators made up of 12 moving series, including sensitive employment and unemployment indicators, new investment commitments, new business corporations, and business failures, profits and stock prices, an inventory investment and sensitive prices. Publications like *Business Week*, *Forbes*, and others provide weekly indices made up of other components.

It was long believed that the conjuncture of two or more short-term cycles would create an accent that could initiate a precipitous movement and possibly the turn in a long wave. However, the long-wave changes appear to be more directly related to more basic factors. The triggers which precipitate them are effective saturations in the market place, an accumulation of debt, a maturation of demand for a basic product, a slowdown or cessation of growth below the growth rate of the population and labor force. In this climate an event that destroys public confidence, even temporarily, precipitates a pattern of spending retrenchment by consumers, business, and usually by government that initiates the declining spiral.

Whether fiscal policy, money supply maneuvering, or other government measures can avert a major movement in the direction of the economy remains to be seen. During the 1970s and the 1980s, dramatic deficits and doubling of the money supply have affected the economy, but this was, relatively, only fine-tuning of what may have been relatively light pressures. Total debt of $6.6 trillion was triple the 1977 level.

The Fifth Wave:
Where We Stand

THE BEGINNING OF A NEW WAVE

Suddenly at the end of the 1970s America woke to a "new industrial revolution" that had been seeded during World War II and Vietnam—an electronics revolution that began with television and exploded with the transistor, the computer, the chip, and robotics; and a high-tech revolution in chemistry, biochemistry, and genetics (Fig. 12.1). This, perhaps, could renew a Kondratieff wave of expansion out of chronological context. Applied to old basic industries, new technologies might provide the means of renewal, as they did for steel during the fourth wave—the explosion that had been simmering for some years as government and industry continued to make breakthroughs in both basic science and technology, in chemistry, space research, microbiotics, electronics, and telecommunications. These innovations created new industries and sped the decline of the old, or perhaps provided technology to revive some industries just as new technologies had revived the steel industry through a century and a half.

Walt W. Rostow saw the new Kondratieff wave as the product of investment in new technology. He placed the beginnings of the new wave in 1972, after Vietnam, a protracted period of high commodity prices relative to industrial prices. Grain prices exploded at the end of that war.

One publication, *U.S. News and World Report*, put it this way:

With plastics, fiberglass, and high-performance composition providing high-strength and easily processed materials suitable for an infinite variety of applications; with energy provided by such simple and efficient devices as high-energy batteries, fuel cells, turbine engines, and the rotary piston engine; with computers providing a means of instantaneously retrieving, sorting, and aggregating vast bodies of information; and with other new

Figure 12.1. The Fifth Wave

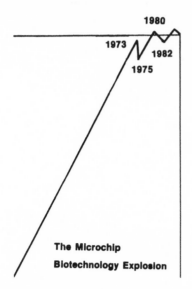

Source: *Statistical Abstract of the United States*, 1984.

electronic devices harnessing the flow of electrons for other uses, there appears to be aborning a second industrial revolution, which, among its other features, contains within itself the seeds of destruction for concentrated industrial structures.[1]

While the staple "smokestack" industries were struggling for markets in the 1970s, new industries and services burgeoned to stem the general economic drop and renew the business cycle (Fig. 12.2). During the first four years of the 1980s, computers and word processors became a $200 billion industry; in electronics, video cassette recorder sales went up from $800,000 to $27 billion; video disc players from $200,000 to $125 million; portable home telephone equipment from zero to $1.3 billion; telephone answering machines from zero to $250 million. Major breakthroughs were being made through new biotechnology in new enzymes, hormones, vaccines, and therapeutic drugs, new forms of life, and power generation; sight, tactile abilities, speech reception, and other identification in robotics; tougher new plastics; and laser technology in communications.

Personal computers, video records, decaffeinated soft drinks, and rubber roofing ranked among the 10 fastest-growing products in the United States. The rubber industry was revived by a new market in 1980. Rubber roofs, a product unheard of in the 1970s, was accounting for one-fifth of the nonresidential U.S. roofing market, with $1 billion in revenues.

Widespread diffusion of this new swarm of innovations began in 1982. The period through 1984 exhibited an increasing amount spent by business for plant and equipment, with a 13.3 percent increase in 1984 alone.

Expenditure for new plant and equipment (current dollars) was:

Year	Billions Of Dollars
1982	282.71
1983	269.22
1984	308.98

The salvation of the 1980s and the reversal from the stop-growth wall were largely the result of this major "revolution" in industry—possibly a revolution as substantial as the eighteenth century Industrial Revolution, which began with the substitution of steam power for human and animal power.

Although not all the conditions anticipated for a model climate for expansion existed, there was some compromise with the high cost level of the peak period. Interest rates were getting lower, and their effect was mitigated by an expanding money supply. Investment funds were available, although much came from abroad, from the surplus accumulated by Japan's favorable balance of trade and from petrodollars. The realization of the threat of foreign competition—and its implication of job losses—facilitated a dramatic shift to tougher employers and more disciplined wage and labor benefit policies, even "give backs" in labor contracts. Hourly earnings rose at an average rate of 8.5 percent in 1979 and 1980, but averaged 4.3 percent in the 1982–1984 period.

The 1970s saw long and hard resistance by unions to new technologies, electronic controls and computer typesetting in the printing industry, and robots in assembling durable goods. It required runaway shops, layoffs, and a 10 percent unemployment rate to bring unions reluctantly to a wage and work rule adjustment in industry.

Inasmuch as a high-technology revolution is, by its nature, a multiplier of spending, each technical advance created new processes and new products, making older products obsolete, inspiring more research. Each advance brought new products to market, from hand-held calculators, video games, and laser video records to home computers and space satellites. Each advance created new industries to manufacture new products and eventually robots to produce all of them and to lower costs in all industries. The spiral effect of this spending rippled into the whole economy, even adding vitality to the mature, declining industries with cost-effective automation.

Billions of dollars in research-and-development funds went into projects both exotic and mundane—artificial intelligence or "thinking"

Figure 12.2. Turning Points, 1970–1982

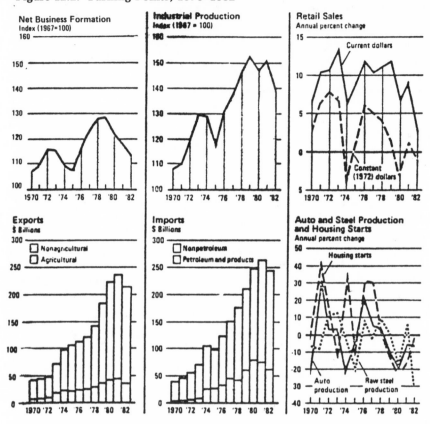

computers, meatier tomatoes through genetics, machines that could see and speak, fuel cells and cellular telephones, optical laser telecommunications, computer tomography, electronic imaging, gene probes, cogeneration, and extreme miniaturization—almost ad infinitum, it seemed. "The rise in capital spending since the end of the recession has been the fastest ever," observed Adrian Dillon, chief economist for the Eaton Corporation in Cleveland in 1984.

John Walter, chief economist for Dow Corning Corporation in Midland, Michigan, said that his firm's investment is not only growing, "but is accelerating" by more than 40 percent a year. Most of the capital-spending boom went to buy new technology that had a fast payback in terms of slashing production costs. A study by Dillon showed that nearly half of every business investment dollar was targeted for new electronic equipment, up from only 17 percent in 1965. Electronic equipment sales gained 17.7 percent in 1984 to reach $186 billion, with a $244 billion figure expected in 1985.

Figure 12.2. (Continued)

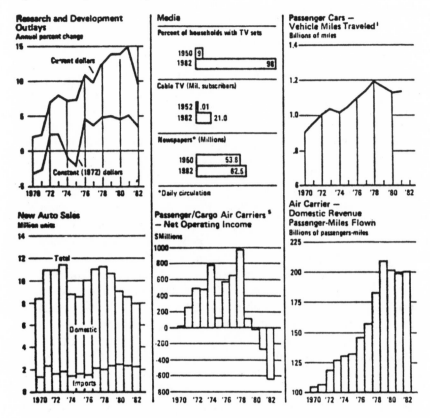

Source: *Statistical Abstract of the United States*, 1984.

In a decade the information-processing industry—word processors, copiers, computers—has moved from $60 billion in revenues to $268 billion in 1983. In a $3 trillion economy, electronics provided a new marginal 10 percent addition and a synergistic effect on new industries. But 1985 disclosed weaknesses in the new industries, under the pull of a declining industrial base.

WHERE WE STAND

In the past the expansion periods of long waves have been maintained for 20 to 24 years, sustained by expanding investment. As we have seen, each expansion has eventually led to a maturation of its seminal industries, a slowdown in expansion, a plateau of gradual decline, and an explosive crisis leading to a precipitous decline and a depression. Some industries were able to extend their life spans with additional innovations. Today, in the larger context of an increasingly competitive world, where does the United States stand?

During the period bridging the fourth and fifth waves, the plateau period leading to a depression in its historic context, the United States economy (and through it, the economies of the Western world) has been sustained by applications of Keynesian principles and the corollary expansion of money supply. Federal budgets and off-budget stimulation in the form of government guarantees to lenders and spenders have exploded. In 1975 the federal debt was $532.1 billion; in 1985 it was three times this amount. To make possible the necessary borrowing, and to provide stimulus to investment, money in circulation (M2) was increased from $1 trillion to $2.258 trillion. As was to be expected, the value of the dollar fell in about the same proportion, a 50 percent decline in a decade. In effect, government created a type of *seigneurage*, clipping a piece of every dollar each year out of each piece of currency and debt, including its own. Keynes had mentioned a fantastic plan originally proposed by Gesell. He would have required a monthly stamp attached to each piece of currency so as to speed its circulation and keep interest rates at a low level to spur investment. Inflation provided such an invisible stamp.

The pumping of money into the economy funnelled into financial assets in the mid-1980s while heavy imports and the break-up of OPEC helped restrain inflation.

Some of the mature industries have renewed themselves with new products or new technologies, just as steel renewed itself with each new development. Some new technologies in steel production are available, but competition for the investment dollar has directed investment in more promising directions. (The product of U.S. Steel was 73 percent oil, 23 percent steel.)

Three years into the plateau period of the fifth Kondratieff, the expansion wave appears to be continuing, albeit at a slow pace, hardly matching the expansion of the labor force. The crisis of 1974 (following a 1973 peak) seems to have been met: gross private domestic investment has kept a steadily increasing pace,

	Current Dollars (billions)	1972 Dollars (billions)
1982	414.5	194.5
1983	417.9	219.0
1984	604.6	277.4

spurring growth in gross national product:

	Current Dollars (billions)	1972 Dollars (billions)
1982	2,073	1,485.4
1983	3,310	1,535.3
1984	3,550	1,609.3

Led by the motor vehicle industry, the nation's 1000 largest manufacturers set a new record for capital appropriations in the second quarter of 1984. These giant firms appropriated $37.1 billion (seasonally adjusted) for new plant and equipment, a 38 percent jump over the first quarter. It marked the fifth quarterly increase in a row and foreshadowed a strong up trend in capital spending. If the motor vehicle industry is excluded, overall appropriations during the second quarter rose by a healthy 12 percent over the first quarter, the strongest of five increases.

A new demographic era began in 1985 when the last of the baby boomers were assimilated into the labor force. The numbers of those entering the labor force began to decline, to a more stable figure of 1.2 million additions annually foreseeable for the next decade. This would eventually reduce the unemployment figure and might, indeed, create labor shortages.

Although bankruptcies continued to grow in number in the 1970s and 1980s, the number of new entrepreneurships increased steadily. In 1984 600,000 new enterprises were started. During the same period, when new jobs were being created at the rate of more than a million a year, new claims for unemployment insurance continued to remain high, indicating a turnover in the labor force as the economy changed increasingly from smokestack to services.

Industrial production after the climax of the smokestack industries continued to decline at almost 1 percent a month in real terms. Factory employment dropped consistently; although this drop was offset by a greater growth in service employment and construction, the decline in manufacturing, following the Kondratieff pattern, was changing the nature of the U.S. economy.

Examined in a geo-economic perspective, the United States as a nation faces problems more difficult and more complex than any before in its history. The Kondratieff wave of tomorrow and its dynamics envelop the entire globe—West and East, first world and third.

COMPETITION

A primary concern is the U.S. competitive position in the world. The sigmoid curve shows maturation of basic American industries, and the increasing part played by services as the U.S. product. Can a nation long continue its position of world leadership when three of four workers are employed in service industries? Will the United States follow the pattern of Britain in world affairs? Can the nation's manufacturers compete in world markets or even at home in a free trade world? Must it be protected by tariffs, quotas, or other barriers and thus deprive its citizens of the best and the cheapest?

The United States enters the new wave with foreign competition already well established and growing, often with American capital and know-how. The problems are not limited to old products and old companies. The foreign share of the U.S. market in high-tech products jumped from 28.2 percent in 1982 to 43 percent in 1984. And the rate was increasing. The threat was basic. By 1984 electronics, with 2.5 million workers employed, had displaced motor vehicles as the nation's largest employer. And the market itself was growing at a rate of 18 percent a year. Was the nation losing its competitive productivity edge?

The high value of the dollar in 1985 made imports so competitive that a negative answer was not easy to give. A 1984 report of a presidential commission indicated that the nation had been slipping in comparative productivity for two decades. But other studies showed that capital and productivity offset the lower labor costs abroad, even in Japan. In current dollar terms, U.S. labor costs stood at $12.65 per hour, compared with $11.30 in Switzerland, $10.38 in Germany, $7.92 in Japan, and $6 in Britain. But productivity was 26 percent over Switzerland, 46 percent over Germany, 59 percent over Japan.

A team from the New York Stock Exchange studied the situation in 1984 and noted that

> The U.S. share of world manufacturing exports has not declined significantly over time. Compared with a peak of 14.2 percent of world exports in 1962, the United States still averaged 14.2 percent of world exports in 1979–1981. Only in 1982, 1 year of steep recession and high U.S. exchange rates, did a significant drop occur—to 12.3 percent.[2]

But realities showed a marked (30 percent) advantage by Japan and Germany.

Britain had a steady loss during the 20-year period studied, and the EEC countries saw a slow erosion. The big increase in share was achieved by Japan, which moved from 5.2 percent in 1962 to 11.6 percent in 1972 and 16.45 percent in 1982, all due to an increase in such durables as motor vehicles, electronics, and steel. The largest losers in these fields were the six EEC countries, whose share dropped from 52.5 percent in 1962 to 39.7 percent in 1982. In nondurables, both Japan and the United States lost ground to the EEC, which increased its share from 34 percent in 1960 to 42.6 percent in 1982. During the decade of 1975–1984, the United States added 10 million jobs; the Common Market lost 2 million.

Japan continues to present a similar and equal challenge to the United States in computers and high-technology items, as well as in the basic durables, but in a few of the new areas the United States appears to have a substantial advantage (Fig. 12.3). And Japan is only beginning to feel the pressures of an industrial society: labor demands, pollution control, foreign resistance to import restrictions, export quotas, and competition (from South Korea).

Nevertheless, the world marketplace is wide open and a nation dominated by five families can marshal great resources. A government appropriation of $65 billion for computer technology research and the establishment of myriad restrictions on foreign goods reminiscent of early mercantilism are difficult to overcome.

Some of the emerging nations (Taiwan, South Korea, Singapore, Brazil, Spain) and Japan present a new area of competition to the United States with low labor costs and more disciplined labor. In an era when skills are being replaced by electronic circuits, the competition is much more intense than it has ever been before. The trend has been slowed, hopefully reversed, by America's love affair with high

Figure 12.3. U.S. Share Of World Exports: High-Tech Versus Non-High-Tech Industries

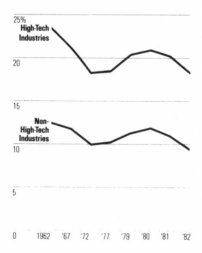

Note: World shares based on constant dollar data.
Sources: University of Maryland; NYSE.

technology. But American entrepreneurs are quick to export their knowledge and experience.

For some years, productivity grew much faster among other developed nations than it did in the United States.

Output Of Employees And Total Product Age

Country	1960–1969(%)	1950–1960(%)	1929–1969(%)	1984
U.S.	2.6	2.1	1.7	3.5
Japan	9.5	6.9		9.5
Germany	4.6	6.0	1.2	4.7
Britain	2.5	1.9	1.1	
France	5.0	5.4	0.3	
Italy	6.4	4.5	1.0	
Canada	2.2	2.1	2.0	
Total product:				
U.S.	4.5	3.2	2.9	
Japan	11.1	8.2	0.6	
Germany	4.7	8.6	1.9	
Britain	2.8	2.7	1.6	
France	5.8	4.9		
Italy	5.6	5.6	1.0	
Canada	5.2	4.0	3.2	

Overall, the United States has not lost its international competitiveness in 1984, in spite of an increasingly strong dollar.

THE DEBT BOMB

The United States faces major problems with its debtors and the debtors of other Western nations. Have-not nations owed $1 trillion to United States banks and institutions in 1985 (133 percent of their net equity), an additional $500 billion to other Western nations, the International Monetary Fund, and the World Bank. These loans fed the prosperity of the West during the 1960s when they stimulated exports. They are being extended, rescheduled, and supported with additional loans, but the volume of large exports these loans fostered in the 1970s can no longer be financed with new loans. The sums involved are three times the total monetary fund of this nation (M1)—more money than really exists. If the United States treasury was forced to guarantee the payments, a massive monetary inflation could follow. Much of the loans are recirculated petrodollars. Much represents proceeds of unfavorable trade, foreign debt callable on short notice. Much of the debt can be abrogated by sovereign nations faced with imposed austerity that threatens the political stability of their own governments, as Peru did in June 1985. Until now renegotiation and more loans have averted default. There is a distinct aura of Ponzi in this situation.

The shell game of foreign debt payments is hard to follow. When a nation makes payments to United States banks, they are made by the New York Federal Reserve Bank, which receives funds from the central banks of Mexico, Venezuela, Brazil, and Argentina, all of which receive the needed funds from the United States Treasury. Typically, the United States will be reimbursed from funds received by the debtors from IMF, which receives one-quarter of its funds from the United States.

Much of the huge debt that hangs over the world—government, foreign, business, and consumer—was accumulated with the promise, implied by recent history, that it would be repaid in cheaper currency. The anticipated inflation factor was built into the interest rates. An 11 percent loan paid 8 percent for inflation, 3 percent for interest. But the slowdown in inflation brought no relief in interest rates, and the expensive dollar has not made payment easier.

This cycle of lending and defaults has been repeated twice before in the twentieth century. Loans to China, Russia, and South America were defaulted in 1913, as were, of course, loans made to Germany, under the Dawes Plan, and those made to others in 1931. By 1932 every nation except Finland was in default to the United States. Here are two pessimistic views of the situation at that time: Harold Lever, interviewed for *London Washington Report*:

> It is indeed chilling to think that the major political figure who correctly foresaw and warned against the development of the world debt crisis, now believes that the political conditions do not exist to remedy it without a world shock. Lord Lever considers that the world shock is inevitable failing further measures of reform and that the shock itself is liable to create a dynamic of default. But after all, that is what happened in 1930.
>
> Whoever else might be surprised, it would not come as a surprise to the honored ghosts of Kondratieff, Irving Fisher, or Schumpeter. This would be more or less what they would have expected, 50 or even 60 years ago, to be the crisis of the late period of the 20th century.

Julian Snyder, at the Committee of the Monetary Reform Conference in 1984:

Inevitably, a great many foreign loans will have to be written off against bank capital. This will reduce profits and more important, cut down on the banks' capacity to lend. If the Fed simply bails out the banks through the purchase or other coverage of bad foreign loans, it will be the American taxpayer who pays. The most important external cause of the debt burden of the non-oil developing countries was the sharp increase in the price of oil in 1973–74 and in 1979–80. One of the more ironic aspects of the oil price rise is that it set off a borrowing spree by oil producers, particularly Mexico. The most commonly expressed reason for hope in this disastrous situation is for a world economic recovery that will increase demand for less-developed-country exports. I think that is dreaming. But when all these facts are considered, I think we can be sure of several things: One, there will be no real world economic recovery. Two, fiat money creation will take place on a worldwide basis that will boggle the imagination. Three, world inflation will come back with a vengeance and your dollars will either become worthless or embargoed. Four, gold will eventually rise with inflation. Five, faced with public outrage and possible financial collapse, the politicans and bankers will choose war of some kind rather than give up their power. But no one can guarantee a war of any kind can be limited. Thus, the world is moving into the most dangerous period in its history. So what is the solution? I talked with Otmar Emminger, the former head of the German Bundesbank, about that this summer, and he said there could not be a solution until there was a catastrophe. Currently, the debt crisis is a myth. Sooner or later, the bankers will inflate and depreciate all the LDC debt away. But at what cost to Western civilization? Worldwide hyperinflation? A new dark age? In the domestic and foreign policies of America, will the banking interests or the interests of the American people prevail? This is the question upon which the survival of the human race may very well depend.

Debt is the underlying gauge of the extent of speculation. The risk of high debt became so poignant in 1985 that *Business Week* devoted its cover to labeling the economy "The Casino Society" in its September 16 issue. The cover went on to note:

No, it's not Las Vegas or Atlantic City. It's the U.S. financial system. The volume of transactions has boomed far beyond anything needed to support the economy. Borrowing—politely called leverage—is getting out of hand. And futures enable people to play the market without owning a share of stock. The result: the system is tilting from investment to speculation.

Meanwhile, third world nations, whose imports helped fuel the boom of the early 1970s, are inhibited from borrowing to buy. New bank lending and credit guarantees were down for obvious reasons. Government pressures established new loans to pay interest and amortization on the oldest ones to avert default in a panic style charade.

Inasmuch as most loans bear interest at prime plus 1.5 percent, lower interest rates helped. But a lower rate of inflation makes the debts more difficult to liquidate, and the fall in petroleum prices forecast a catastrophe. Real interest has not fallen substantially.

As we have seen, the triggers that sparked the panics of past cycles were, in most cases, dramatic banking or business failures: the Mexican and South American loans in 1825, the Bank of United States in 1837, the Ohio Life and Trust Co. in 1857, the Northern Pacific Railroad in 1873, the Knickerbocker Trust Co. in 1907, the stock market in 1929, and the Kreditanstalt in Vienna in 1931. Private creditors have similar but more acute problems and fewer ways of handling them: of the $350 billion Latin American debt $75 billion is privately held.

Latin American Debt 1984

Country	Total Debt (billions of dollars)	Top lending Banks (billions of dollars)	
Brazil	93.1	Citicorp	4.7
		Chase	2.6
		Bankamerica	2.5
Mexico	89.8	Citicorp	2.9
		Bankamerica	2.7
		Manufacturers Hanover	1.9
Argentina	45.3	Manufacturers Hanover	1.3
		Citicorp	1.1
		Chase	0.8
Venezuela	35.5	Bankamerica	1.6
		Citicorp	1.5
		Chase	1.2

By April 1985 the five major Latin American debtors were Brazil (now $192 billion), Mexico ($96 billion), Argentina ($47 billion), Venezuela ($35 billion), and Chile ($21 billion). All were in difficulty in complying with demands for austerity in nations of questionable stability still new to democracy. All were asking for more advances.

THE BANKS

The nation's banks have been failing with little public panic, at an increasing rate. Failures have been salvaged by FDIC and other federal agencies. In the 1970s 10 failed each year. In 1984 75 failed. Depositors were protected by federal funds. But 54 percent of all banks were in trouble in 1984. The debts of foreign nations, energy companies, farmers, other banks, corporations, and institutions are dangerously less secure. In a lending spree of the 1960s, banks urged the loans on these nations, on many newly oil-rich nations, and on companies with prospective oil resources. The loans represented, for many institutions, sums greater than their total equity, and a total of 133 percent of all U.S. equity of all U.S. lending banks.

Federal insurance and consequent intervention avoided a domino effect after the failure of Penn Square Bank in Oklahoma, Drysdale Securities in New York, Continental Illinois, Equity Programs Investors Corporation, and Lockheed and Chrysler.

The typical tensions in the economy noted in past long waves are seen during such episodes. Even well-established financial institutions fail to earn at an expected return, then suffer a major loss and suffer a run on their assets. Individually these situations have been met by other institutions rushing to put a finger in the dyke, but the leaks have been getting larger, and each leak washes out into other problems. When E.M.S. Government Securities Corporation failed in Florida it dominoed 71 Ohio savings and loan banks into closing and sent the value of the dollar down 15 percent in two days. Continental Illinois ($41 billion in assets) was triggered by Penn Square Bank, which was affected by bankruptcies in Tennessee. Continental was itself a victim of $2.3 billion in "non-performing" loans.

THE DOMESTIC DEBT TENSION

The growth of domestic debt as a factor in the economy was seen as background in almost every crisis during the fourth Kondratieff wave. The picture is evident graphically.

Noting the implications of foreign transactions, the credit crescendo on the domestic scene cannot be ignored.

The four waves in United States history have often included prosperity aborted by a drop in prices (or a decline in the inflation rate) which made loans so onerous that an epidemic of bankruptcies resulted. This phenomenon appeared briefly in the 1970s but was halted by the 1982 recovery. It did, however, bring about the bankruptcies of some large and prestigious institutions and threatened many others.

By 1984 Americans were the world's most debt-burdened consumers. They owed $1520 per person. The figure in Britain was $369, in France $120. Consumers had borrowed 18.8 percent of a year's disposable income by 1986 and were still borrowing. The 1929 ratio was 17.9 percent. The ratio before the 1979 decline was 17.8 percent.

Farmers owed $212 billion against $22 billion in anticipated income. And their land was worth 23 percent less than in 1940. In the 1970s the total farm debt stayed around $50 billion.

The federal debt was increasing at the rate of $200 billion a year. Interest payments were growing at 11 percent a year compared with a 3.5 percent growth in GNP. About 60 percent of this borrowing was met by foreign lenders, thus forcing up the value of the dollar in terms of foreign currencies to new high levels each month. Although this helped to hold interest rates at moderate levels, it created a foreign debt for the nation that was reaching for a trillion dollars by 1990, placing a prospective burden of a hundred billion dollars a year for interest on the national economy.

And the federal debt was growing to 50 percent of gross national product. Jerome Smith, an investment analyst, puts it this way:

> It took 100 years (to 1976) for the federal debt to reach $600 billion, but only seven more years (to 1983) to reach $1,200 billion (it now stands at $1.5 trillion). Similarly, it took 200 years for federal spending to reach $300 billion plus per year, but only six years to reach $600 billion plus (1981). This year it is budgeted at $854 billion.

Business borrowing in 1984 was running at a rate of $462 billion a year in short-term funds and $245 billion long-term. A new form of debt arose from a spurt of leveraged mergers and acquisitions of companies principally by borrowing. (There were 2543 large company mergers in 1984.)

The effect on the value of the dollar was also significant. Demand for the dollar raised its price in terms of foreign currencies, stimulated imports, retarded exports (hurting farmers, drug producers, etc.), and provided intense competition for American manufacturers at home and abroad.

THE CONTINGENT DEBT

Even more dangerous than the direct federal debt is the mountain of contingent liabilities that will inevitably become due (FDIC, Ginnie Maes) or those non-guaranteed debts that will become due as a moral obligation in case of defaults by government agencies (Freddie Macs, Sallie Maes, etc.). These amount to some $7 trillion, more than twice the GNP and approximately five times the national debt. With farmers being foreclosed wholesale, the farm credit cooperatives were crying for a bailout.

One example of a contingent liability exists in the federal civil service retirement system, which is operated on a pay-as-you-go basis. The plan's unfunded liability in 1984 was $528 billion (equal to 60 percent of the year's entire federal budget) and growing at more than $725,000 a minute.

THE CREDIT BOMB

Just as hazardous as U.S. vulnerability to debtors is its vulnerability to creditors.

The recycling of petro-dollars, the adverse balance of payments almost everywhere, as well as continuing high interest rates in the United States and a swell of confidence in its growing economy have brought billions of dollars of foreign capital to America's shores. In 1984, for the first time since 1918, the United States became a debtor nation.

Much of this foreign money is in short-term obligations. A "run" on the dollar in this sensitive U.S. economy could trigger a major panic. It should be remembered that such withdrawals have occurred on seven previous occasions in the nation's history.

Foreign Investment In The United States (Billions of Dollars)

1950	3.391	1975	27.662
1955	5.076	1980	68.351
1960	6.910	1981	89.759
1965	8.797	1982	95.000
1970	13.270	1983	81.000

The U.S. entered 1986 with a net debt to foreigners of $160 billion. Its net investment had grown from a positive $6 billion in 1919 to $157 billion in 1982 when the balance turned dramatically.

THE POPULATION BOMB

Less obvious, more insidious, and probably in the long run more dangerous than the financial clouds over the economy is the explosion of expectations among the 81 percent of the world's people who live on incomes of $300 to $700 a year, whose gross growth rates run at less than 3 percent a year and per capita growth at zero to 1 percent.

The population of the world is growing twice as fast as that of the United States, while the polarization of income increases exponentially.

Of the world's $10 trillion product, the United States, with 5 percent of the world population, produces and consumes 30 percent. The rest of the "West" and Japan, with 8.5 percent of the people, consume 33 percent. Eastern Europe, with 7.4 percent of the people, consumes 24 percent. The 13 percent balance of goods is shared by 81 percent of the world's people.

Since 1960 the United States per capita income grew 59 percent. For the developing nations (excluding oil producers and a half-dozen emerging groups) per capita income has grown hardly at all.

Typical is the population problem of Mexico, where high fertility in the 1950s, 1960s, and 1970s created a baby boom paralleling the postwar baby boom in the United States. The postwar United States prosperity carried over into its southern neighbor. Mexico's working-age population is expected to double in the next 20 years and create an unprecedented demand for more than one million new jobs every year until the end of the century. From 1970 to 1980, Mexico created an average of 495,000 new jobs per year. Mexico will need to create an estimated 1.3 million jobs each year between 1995 and 2000. Its working-age population growth rate will be 24 percent greater than the nation's total population growth rate in the next decade.

Urban centers, particularly Mexico City, already have been experiencing an influx from rural areas. By the end of the century, Mexico City will have the world's largest urban population, exceeding the current population of California.

Faced with this pressure on its southern border, and similar pressure from in South and Central America and the islands around, can the United States fence itself in from massive immigration?

During four generations of the twentieth century, world product grew from $579 billion in 1900 to $6 trillion in 1975 to $10 trillion in 1984 (Table 12.1). But for some nations it did not grow at all. In spite of the billions of dollars of foreign aid provided in recent years, the average African's standard of living has declined by 10 percent since 1974. The tragedy of the 1984–85 drought accented the problem.

An element in capital and personal and national wealth that is often ignored in the computation of economists is human wealth—the values of time, effort, and money expended on education and skill development. This diversity in training and the family structure that creates it must be considered in evaluating a labor force and total assets, especially in appraising product in both high- and low-income families.

At the start of the twenty-first century, the United States will retain by far the world's largest economy, despite its moderate rate of growth.

Table 12.1. Rates Of Economic Growth: Estimates Of Annual Averages

	1980–85 (%)	1995–2000 (%)
North America	1.96	2.20
Western Europe (north)	1.80	2.00
Western Europe (south)	2.80	3.00
Eastern Europe	3.50	3.50
Japan	3.89	4.00
Middle East	4.80	7.00
North Africa	6.88	7.00
Indian subcontinent	6.30	7.00
South Korea, Taiwan, Singapore, Hong Kong	8.45	7.00

TRADE IMBALANCES

Monetary policies are creating huge new trade and current account imbalances. Consequently the trading system faces acute protectionist pressures, and serious fissures appear in the fabric of international economic cooperation, as they have during previous times of economic tension.

For the United States, substantially a trade-dependent nation for half of its history and capital-dependent until 1914, the cyclical turns and crises of Europe were particularly contagious. In spite of a greater self-sufficiency in the twentieth century, the military, economic, and financial fluctuations of Europe continue to be major elements in the United States economy.

Even the economic fluctuations behind the iron curtain, particularly in harvests and oil production, are now an element in U.S. economic well-being.

WAR IN A NUCLEAR AGE

International war as an outlet for tensions, surplus product, and exploding populations has probably lost its place as the expansion stimulus for Kondratieff cycles. The effects on humanity will probably eliminate this element in the long wave.

But wars as an instrument of world politics remain in other forms. Some 40 proxy wars or brush-fire wars continue. Terrorism as a war substitute opens other doors. A new element of "Green" activists, motivated by such causes as pollution control, conservation, animal liberation, banning nuclear energy and weapons, and feeding the world, provides another hopeful outlet and a form of less extreme pressure.

And the absence of outright war, as Gerhard Mensch points out, does not deter massive spending for defense. Each of the four years of Reagan defense spending substantially exceeded the Johnson spending for Vietnam not only in dollar amounts but as a percentage of GNP.

It should be noted that explosions (wars and revolutions) occur when a population is predominantly young. The average population age at the time of the American Revolution was 17. It is now 30. The average age of the population of the underdeveloped world hovers in the 14- to 15-year range.

THE CHANGING INDUSTRIAL–SERVICE PATTERN

The nature of U.S. product and employment has been changing, affecting not only the nation's trade but its attitudes, outlook, and morals. The durable goods products on which U.S. power and reputation and exports were based for a century have been changing to a product of high technology and associated services. The expansion of services sustaining the growth of gross national product obscures the continuing decline in the production of goods. It is the goods sector which bore the brunt of an import explosion when the dollar scaled new heights each month in 1984 and 1985. In addition, imports restrained the ability of American manufacturers to raise prices. Can a nation not dominant in manufacturing survive as a world leader?

This expansion of services as a portion of GNP has had something of an investment effect similar to technical innovations of the past.

The changing pattern in American product has been a continuing evolution during the fourth wave (Table 12.2).

In the United States, the twenty-first century is a race between the rise and diffusion of new industries and the decline of the old. Or it may be a time when the applications of new technologies are used to revive the old industries, just as the steel industry revived itself with new manufacturing techniques decade after decade, and computers were rejuvenated through their generations from vacuum tubes to laser chips.

Just as it has been in the past, the initiation of a new Kondratieff expansion must be a product of such new technologies. Walt W. Rostow predicted this in 1982 and considers the changeover year to be 1972.[3]

The most certain path for U.S. expansion lies in increased productivity, and the most certain approach to this is a sustained and increasing investment in productive capital. The rate of capital spending has been

Table 12.2. Share Of U.S. GNP, By Industry

Industry	1930	1940	1950	1960	1970	1980	1984
Agriculture	8.3	7.6	7.4	4.1	3.1	3.0	3.4
Mining	2.1	2.3	2.1	1.4	0.9	3.5	1.4
Construction	4.3	3.2	4.9	5.0	5.3	4.5	4.3
Manufacturing	24.3	27.4	30.9	30.5	27.6	22.5	22.5
Trade	16.3	17.6	17.8	15.6	15.4	16.6	14.5
Finance, insurance, and real estate	14.1	10.1	9.0	11.2	11.0	15.0	15.3
Transportation, communication, and public utilities	11.2	9.9	8.5	8.5	7.6	12.6	8.6
Services	12.3	11.0	9.6	10.8	13.1	13.0	15.7
Government	7.1	10.9	9.8	12.9	16.0	11.4	14.2

Figures are percentages.
Source: *Statistical Abstract of the United States*, 1985.

increasing steadily since 1980: 13 percent in 1984, 18 percent in 1985.

For fine-tuning the direction of the economy, the paradigms of Keynes, Friedman, Feldstein, and Kaufman remain as guidelines, in spite of their failure to predict the course of the economy for two decades. History acknowledges that the Keynesian philosophy leads to tremendous debt and the Friedman philosophy can lead to unmanageable inflation. But the trillion-dollar deficit of 1980–1984 helped pull the economy out of a downswing that might have led to the ski slope remembered from 50 years before. Given the alternatives of a huge national debt and a huge national depression, the choice was not in doubt. Given the choice between runaway inflation and depression, there remains a more difficult choice.

However, the hazard of living on a mountain top remains. The world is supremely sensitive to financial signals, as if it is waiting for a major financial crisis. Such a crisis was narrowly averted in 1974, again in 1978 and 1980, and in 1983 and in 1984. But each year the debts continue to escalate: 30 percent in 1983, 33 percent in 1984.

Each of the Kondratieff waves has culminated in a peak of production, prices, and interest rates followed by a gradual, almost unnoticeable euphoric period of decline, and a sudden panic that destroyed the climate of economic confidence. In each case, the panics were precipitated by monetary forces that appear, in a historic view, as minor transitory phenomena—a corporate bankruptcy, a contraction of the money supply, a withdrawal of gold deposits, or a bank failure. But the triggers were pulled on a matured economy already overextended in production, debt, and low productivity.⌡

Viewed objectively, the 1980s show no paucity of possible crises. Production is in an interstitial phase, with basic industries well past the stage of expansion. Gross national product continued to expand marginally, as it must to absorb an average of 100,000 monthly additions to the labor force, but at an annual rate of 1.2% in the fourth quarter of 1985. The expansion is maintained by new high-technology and service industries, which provide opportunity for most new workers and a quarter of a trillion dollars annually in defense spending, much of which maintains old industries.

In 1985 the U.S. economy was in a struggle between declining (certainly not expanding) smokestack industries and burgeoning new high-tech industries and expanding services. The balance of growth was being provided by the Keynesian formula of government defense spending channeled into non-consumer products—analogous to Keynes' facetious suggestion that product be buried into a deep hole. This policy entailed annual deficits in the range of $200 billion and defense spending in the same range.

Nevertheless, basic industries could hardly be sustained otherwise at old levels. Steel reached its production peak in 1974. Mining, metals, textiles, glass, petroleum products, and energy industries showed level or negative growth. New technologies held some small promise, as in the past, for steel, motor vehicles, and utilities.

But the hope for a new wave of expansion—new products and new industries—lay with new, technological breakthroughs, following the transistor and the microchip, in biogenetics, lasers, and so on.

Meanwhile, time is running out. Large federal deficits kept interest rates high, attracting foreign investment, sustaining a high dollar, stimulating imports, creating difficult competition for American industry, creating a huge negative balance of payments (much reinvested in the United States and providing half the cost of the federal deficit), and mortgaging the U.S. economy. Japan was buying $20 billion of U.S. industry each year from the proceeds of a $37 billion favorable trade balance. By 1990 the United States could expect to be paying $20 billion a year in net outgoing interest.

The political pressure of these trends, most poignantly expressed in unemployment figures, was mitigated by a turn in the demographic cycle. The growth rate of the labor force dropped from 2.7 percent in 1980 to 1.8 percent in 1984, to an anticipated 1 percent in 1990.

However, with the added straws of increasing debits by consumers, business, the federal government, and foreign debtors—the imbalances created in a free, increasingly deregulated market that make for an extremely fragile situation—we are apparently waiting for the dramatic crisis that will start the banking and speculative dominoes falling.

References

This study is based on three papers on the long wave in economic life published by Nikolai D. Kondratieff for the Conjuncture Institute in Moscow during the period 1920 to 1928.

The primary essay was called "Long Economic Cycles" and was published in *Voprosy konyunktury* (*Problem of Economic Conditions*) in its first issue in 1925. The following February it was read at the Economics Institute of the Russian Association of Social Science Research Institute. A book, *Long Economic Cycles* by N. D. Kondratieff and D. I. Oparin (who contributed a criticism), was published in 1928.

Kondratieff's publications include: *Agrarnyy copros* (The Agrarian Question); *Mirovoye khozyaystvo i yego konyunktury vo vremya i posle voyny* (The World Economy and Its Situation before and after the War); *Sotsializatsiya zemli* (Socialization of the Land; 1918); *Proizvodstvo i sbyt maslichnykh semyan v svyazi s interesami krest'yanskogo khozyaystva* (The Production and Marketing of Oil-Producing Seeds in Relation to the Interests of the Peasant Economy; 1919); *Mikhail Ivanovich Tugan-Baranobskiy* (1923); *Perspektivnyy plan razvitiya sel'skogo khozyaystva 1923–28 godov* (The 1923–28 Long-Term Agricultural Development Plan); *Sovremennoye sostoyaniye narodnogo khozyaystva v svete vzaimootnosheniya industrii i sel'skogo khozyaystva* (The Present State of the National Economy in Light of the Interrelationship of Industry and Agriculture) (1925); *Zadachi v oblasti sel'skogo khozyaystva v svyazi s obshchim razvitiyem narodnogo khozyaystva i yego industrializatsii* (The Tasks of Agriculture in Relation to the General Development of the National Economy and Its Industrialization) (1927); *Bol'shiye tsikly kon'yunktury* (The Great Economic Cycles; 1928).

The primary paper was translated into German under the title, "Die langen Wellen der Konjunktur" and appeared in *Archiv für Sozialwissenschaft und Sozialpoliln* in 1926 (vol. 56, no. 3, p. 573). And in a critical review by George Garvy it appeared as "Kondratieff Theory of Long Cycles," and "The Long Wave in Economics" in the *Review of Economic Statistics* in November 1943, pp. 203–20.

A complete translation of the 1928 papers by Guy Daniels was published in 1984 by Richardson & Snyder of New York. Julian M. Snyder, who wrote a lengthy introduction, is the editor of several newsletters, including *Moneyline*, which gives much credence to the Kondratieff approach.

Except as noted, statistical material is from United States Department of Commerce publications, including the historical series, the statistical abstracts, and current releases.

The author is indebted for much material to George Garvy, who made the first translation of Nikolai Kondratieff's papers in 1935; to Guy Daniels and Julien Snyder, who provided translations; to J. J. vanDuijn, whose 1983 study "The Long Wave in Economic Life" organized many of the viewpoints on the subject; to Dr. Gerhard Mensch, whose *Stalemate in Technology* (Cambridge, MA: Ballinger, 1975) brought up to date some of the original concepts; and of course, to Joseph Alois Schumpeter, whose massive 1939 study, *Business Cycles*, provided the major early acceptance of Kondratieff paradigms in the West.

Notes

CHAPTER 1: ABOUT ECONOMICS, CYCLES, AND ECONOMIC CYCLES

1. Dewey, Edward R. and Edwin F. Dakin. *Cycles: The Science of Prediction* (Pittsburgh, PA: Foundation for the Study of Cycles, 1947).

2. Burns, Arthur F. and Wesley C. Mitchell. *Measuring Business Cycles*, Studies in Business Cycles, no. 2 (New York: National Bureau of Economic Research, 1946).

3. Marshall, Alfred. *Principles of Economics* (New York: Macmillan, 1940).

4. Arrow, N. J. and G. Debrieus. "Existence of Equilibria in a Competitive Economy." *Econometrics* 17:6 (1954).

5. Keynes, John Maynard. *A General Theory of Employment Interest and Money* (London: Macmillan, 1936).

6. Thurow, Lester. *Dangerous Currents* (New York: Random House, 1983).

7. Ibid.

8. von Mises, Ludwig. *Human Action* 1949 (New York: Penguin, 1970).

9. *Business Week*, December 23, 1983.

10. Schumpeter, Joseph A. *Business Cycles* (New York: McGraw-Hill, 1939).

CHAPTER 2: THE LONG WAVE

1. Trotsky, Leon. "On the Curve of the Capitalist Revolution." *Sotsia-Vestriv-listcheskoi Akademii* 4 (1923): 3–12.

2. van Gelderen, J. (J. Fedder). "Springvloed beschouwingen over industrielle ontwikeling en prijsbeweging." *De Nievwe Tijd* 18 (1913): 253–57, 445–64.

3. DeWolff, Samuel. "Het economisch getif" (The Economic Tide) and "*Prosperitaks und Depressionsperioden.*" In *Der lebendige Marxiums*, edited by Otto Jensen (Festgavezum, 70 Geburstage von Karl Kautsky, 1924).

4. Spiethoff, Arthur. *Die Wirtschaftlichen Wechesellogen, der stand und die nächte sukunff der konjunktur forschung* (Munchen: Dunckner & Humblot, 1938).

5. Beveridge, Lord William Henry. *Prices and Wages in England from the Twelfth to the Nineteenth Century* (New York: Longmans Green, 1937).

6. Nove, Alec. *An Economic History of the U.S.S.R.* (London: Pelican, 1972).

CHAPTER 3: COMMENT AND CRITICISM

1. Bazaroff, W. A. "The Lines of Development of the Capitalist and the Soviet Economies." *Planovol Khoiziaistvo*, no. 5 (1926): 88; Studensky, G.A. "The agricultural Depression and the Technical Revolution in Farming." *Journal of Farm Economics* 11 (1930): 552–72.

2. Trotzky, "On the Curve."

3. *Malaia Sovestskaia Enziklopedia*, vol. IV, p. 133 (Moscow, 1929). Translated and published by Scribner, New York.

4. Garvy, George. "Kondratieff Theory of Long Cycles." *Review of Economic Statistics* 25, no. 4 (November 1943): 203–20.

5. Schumpeter, Joseph A. *Socialism and Democracy* (Cambridge, MA: Harvard University Press, 1942).

6. Dewey and Dakin, *Cycles.*

7. Frickey, Edwin. *Economic Fluctuation in the United States* (New York: Russell and Russell, 1942).

8. Forrester, Jay W. *Business Structure, Economic Cycles and National Policy* (New York: Simon and Schuster, 1973).

9. Rostow, W. W. *Getting There From here* (New York: McGraw-Hill, 1978).

10. Mensch, Gerhard. *Stalemate in Technology* (Cambridge, MA: Ballinger, 1975).

11. Valentine, Lloyd M., and Carl A. Dauten. *Business Cycles and Forecasting.* (Cincinnati, OH: Southwestern Publishing, 1983).

12. Burns, Arthur F. and Wesley C. Mitchell, *Measuring Business Cycles.*

13. Burns, Arthur F. *The Business Cycle in a Changing World* (New York: National Bureau of Economic Research, Columbia University Press, 1929).

14. Kuznets, Simon. *Economic Change* (New York: W. W. Norton, 1953), p. 109.

15. Rothbart, E. *Economic Journal* (June–September 1942): 226.

16. Hansen, Alvin E. *Fiscal Policy and Business Cycles* (New York: W. W. Norton, 1964), p. 358.

17. Stoken, Dick A. *Cycles: What They Are, What They Mean, How to Profit by Them* (New York: McGraw-Hill, 1978).

18. Samuelson, Paul. *Economics* (New York: McGraw-Hill, 1982).

19. Clemence, Richard V. and Francis S. Doody. *The Schumpeterian System*. (New York: Kelley, 1950).

20. Forrester, N. B., *The Life Cycle of Economic Development* (Cambridge, MA: Wright Allen Press, 1973).

21. Schuman, James B. and David Rosenau. *The Kondratieff Wave* (New York: World Publishing, 1972).

22. Daniels, Guy (trans). *The Long Wave Cycle* (New York: Richardson & Snyder, 1984).

23. Frost, A.J. and Robert R. Prechter, Jr. *Elliot Wave Principle*, (Gainesville, GA: New Classics Library, 1978).

CHAPTER 5: THE FIRST WAVE: 1789–1814–1843

1. Frank, Andre Gunter. *World Accumulation 1491–1789* (New York: Monthly Review Press, 1978).

2. McGrane, Reginald Charles. *The Panic of 1837* (New York: Russell & Russell, 1965).

CHAPTER 6: THE SECOND WAVE: 1843–1864–1896

1. Van Vleck, George W. *Panic of 1857* (AMS Press, 1957).

2. Hoffman, Charles, *The Depression of the Nineties* (Westport, CT: Greenwood Press, 1970).

3. Ibid.

4. Ibid.

CHAPTER 7: THE THIRD WAVE: 1896–1920–1949

1. Schumpeter, *Business Cycles*.

2. Hoffman, *The Depression of the Nineties*.

3. Gordon, Robert Aaron. *Economic Instability and Growth* (New York: Harper & Row, 1974).

4. Ortega y Gasset. *Revolt of the Masses* (New York: Norton, 1927).

5. Kindelberger, Charles P. *The World in Depression 1929–1931* (Berkeley, CA: University of California Press, 1973).

6. Kenwood, A.G. and A.L. Longhead, *The Growth of the International Economy* (London: George Allen-Unwin, 1971).

7. Friedman, Milton. "The Lessons of U.S. Monetary History and Their Bearing on Current Policy." Memorandum to Board of Governors, Federal Reserve System, October 7, 1965, p. 141.

8. Allen, Frederick L. *Only Yesterday: An Informal History of the Nineteen Twenties* (New York: Harper and Brothers, 1931).

9. Friedman, Milton and Anna Schwartz. *Monetary History of the United States, 1867–1960* (Princeton NJ: Princeton University Press, 1963).

10. Schumpeter, *Business Cycles*, p. 907.

11. Kindelberger, *The World in Depression*.

12. Schumpeter, *Business Cycles*.

13. Fisher, Irving. *Booms and Depressions* (New York: Adelphi, 1932).

14. Friedman and Schwartz, *Monetary History*.

15. Schumpeter, *Business Cycles*, p. 94l.

CHAPTER 8: THE FOURTH WAVE: 1949–1973–2003

1. *New York Times*, March 3, 1984.

CHAPTER 9: CAUSES AND CONSEQUENCES I: INNOVATION, INVESTMENT, AND MATURATION

1. Van Gelderen, "Springvloed," pp. 253–77, 369–84, 445–46.

2. Lescure, J. *Des crises generales et periodigner de surproduction,* 3d ed (Recueil Sirey).

3. DeWolff, "Het economich getif."

4. Clark, C. C. and L. Freeman. "Long Waves, Inventions and Innovations," *Futures* (1981) 13:308–22.

5. Kitchin, Joseph, "Cycles and Trends in Economic Factors. *Review of Economic Statistics* 5 (April 1923): 10–16.

6. Woytinski, Lorenz W. "Das Ratsel der langen Wellen." *Schmoller's Jarbuch* 55, no. 4 (1931): 1–42.

7. Cassel, *Theoretische Sozialokonomie, Deichertsche Veragschuchhandlung,* 5th ed (Oxford: Clarendon Press, 1932).

8. *Warren, G. F. and F. Pierson. Gold and Prices* (New York: John Wiley, 1935).

9. Friedman, "The Lessons."

10. Sirol, Jean *Le rôle de l'agriculture dans les fluctuations économiques* (Paris: Recveil Sirey, 1942).

11. Clemence, Richard V. and Francis S. Doody. *The Schumpeterian System* (New York: Kelley, 1954).

12. Kuznets, *Economic Change*, p. 113.

13. Mensch, *Stalemate in Technology*, p. 72–73.

14. Hoffman, Walter G. *Study of British History, 1700–1940* (London: Basil Blackwell, 1965).

15. Rostow, Walter W. *Getting from Here to There* (New York: McGraw-Hill, 1978).

16. Forrester, Jay W. "Growth Cycles." *The Economist* 125:4, (1977) pp. 525–43.

CHAPTER 10: CAUSES AND CONSEQUENCES II: WAR, DEMOGRAPHICS, AND SOCIAL CHANGE

1. Mensch, *Stalemate in Technology.*

2. Jones, Landon. *Great Expectations* (New York: Ballentine, 1980), p. 107.

3. Ropp, Theodore. *Dictionary of the History of Ideas* (New York: Scribner, 1973).

4. Ishi, Ryochi. *Population and Economics in Japan* (London: King & Son, 1937).

5. Ibid.

6. *Herald Tribune*, Paris, September 13, 1984.

7. Parker, J.E.S. *The Economics of Innovation* (New York: Longman, 1974).

CHAPTER 11: TURNING POINTS AND TRIGGERS

1. Schumpeter, *Business Cycles.*

2. Mensch, *Stalemate in Technology.*

3. Tarde, Gabriel. *Les lois de l'imitation* (New York: Holt, 1890, 1903).

4. Burns and Mitchell, *Measuring Business Cycles.*

5. Hicks, J.R. *A Contribution to the Theory of Trade Cycles* (Oxford: Clarendon, 1941).

6. Von Mises, *Human Action.*

CHAPTER 12: THE FIFTH WAVE: WHERE WE STAND

1. *U.S. News & World Report*, October 8, 1983.

2. New York Stock Exchange. *U.S. International Competitiveness; Perception and Reality*, Special Report, New York Stock Exchange Study of Trade, Industrial Change and Jobs, August, 1984.

Rostow, W.W. *The World Economy, History and Prospect*, (Austin TX: University of Texas Press, 1978).